The Consumer Experience of Higher Education

The Rise of Capsule Education

Also available from Continuum

Rethinking Universities	Sally Baker and B. J. Brown
Philosophies of Research into Higher Education	Brian J. Brown and Sally Baker
Pedagogy and the University	Monica McLean
Internationalizing the University	Yvonne Turner and Sue Robson

The Consumer Experience of Higher Education

The Rise of Capsule Education

DEIRDRE McARDLE-CLINTON

continuum

Continuum International Publishing Group

The Tower Building   80 Maiden Lane
11 York Road   Suite 704
London   New York
SE1 7NX   NY 10038

www.continuumbooks.com

British Library Cataloguing-in-Publication Data
A catalogue record for this book is available from the British Library.

ISBN: 978-1-4411-7919-7

Library of Congress Cataloging-in-Publication Data
The Publisher has applied for CIP data

Typeset by Aptara
Printed in the United Kingdom by Biddles, Norfolk

For Pat

Contents

Preface

This study challenges the nature of Education at its very fundamentals. In particular, it explores the experience of schooling – albeit at third level – and concludes that there is much that is disabling and oppressive in this experience for all involved. It also shows how unproductive, if not even counterproductive, much of the experience is at both a personal and social level.

Schooling evolved historically out of the recognition that there were societal requirements for knowledge and expertise which could not be met by other systems such as the family and community. The beginnings of universal primary education in the first half of the nineteenth century in England and Ireland reflected the requirements of an industrial society for mass literacy. In addition, schooling introduced or further developed other key disciplines necessary for the effective functioning of an industrial society. These included punctuality, following instructions and an appreciation of the concepts of specialisms and standards.

Today, we expect different things of schooling. A child entering primary school this year is likely to remain in full-time education until the year 2022. If education is about envisaging and preparing for the future, we know little enough about the world these children will emerge into. How should the education system respond to such an uncertain context? Dealing with the challenges of the present is difficult enough. Anticipating and planning for future ones is even more daunting. It is self-evident that if we do not know what the future holds, the education project should be one of preparing children to respond to the unknown. This is a profound challenge to the education system, accustomed as it is to operating from a position of superior knowledge and certitude.

However, what we can be sure about is that the education system must now move from a focus for preparing children for a life of work to one which is concerned with preparing them for a life of learning. This changed focus transforms the purpose of early life education.

As the focus of education shifts from one of lifelong work to one of lifelong learning, each of the education sectors must move somewhat for a focus on what is learned to one which is more concerned with the learner's capability for learning, disposition and motivation for learning and readiness to move to the next learning stage.

The psychologist, Howard Gardner, talks about the five minds of the future. These are the disciplined mind, i.e. subject mastery; the synthesising mind, i.e. the capacity to abstract and organize information; the creative mind, i.e. the capacity to see new solutions; the respectful mind, i.e. the capacity to work with difference, and finally the ethical mind, i.e. the motive towards goodness.

The Irish Experience

The foundational importance of the pre-school years for readiness to learn through life, though well established in the literature is only slowly being realized in the institutional provision of pre-school education in Ireland. This is despite the emergence of the overwhelming body of research showing the pivotal significance of effective early intervention in the educational development of the pre-school child, particularly for children from disadvantaged backgrounds.

At primary level, curriculum changes introduced incrementally over recent decades, and enabled by the abolition of the Primary Certificate in the late 1960s, has allowed for the development of a child-centred curriculum which appears to be highly effective in engaging the children in multifaceted ways in their own learning. The sector however is not without strain. While pupil–teacher ratios have consistently improved over the years, many of the additional staff have been deployed in much needed, but specialist, one to one services. Class sizes, therefore, have remained worryingly high. There is a strong educational case for tackling this issue. Furthermore, there is some anecdotal evidence that as post-primary looms from fourth class onwards, the focus of the primary syllabus begins to shift to the more traditional 3Rs where concern for the child's ability to handle the predominantly cognitive agenda of second level begins to take precedence.

Second level education in Ireland has functioned within a clearly defined policy framework, i.e. a transparent points system which rewards students on the basis of performance in the Leaving Certificate. The sector operates, therefore, within clearly defined parameters where the purpose is clear and unambiguous – to maximise points gained. Career choice, mediated through the third level applications system, is determined by achievements here and, theoretically at any rate, the student's life course is now laid down.

At a time of rapid changes where old certainties no longer hold true, assumptions such as these are poorly grounded. In a context where insecurity is the norm, such long-term determinism can straitjacket students and limit their ability to adapt and respond to new situations and unanticipated threats and to find new solutions to problems we cannot yet even envisage. For such situations attributes of creativity, imagination and lateral capabilities are the essential attributes.

The challenge which this presents to second level education arises from the fact that this sector has traditionally been seen as the end of education. Compulsory education ends at 16 years. The terminal examination at the end of post-primary is referred as the 'Leaving' certificate. The characteristic urgency of second level then arises from a historical commitment to make sure that the students get everything needed to sustain them for the rest of their working lives.

This of course, patently no longer applies. More than 60 per cent of the cohorts now go on to post-school education and this figure continues to rise. Many more will return to education on and off throughout their lives. There is now no reason why their futures should be pre-destined by achievements at second level. For this reason, addressing their current developmental needs is likely to be the best way of preparing them for their future lives.

This book shows that at third level, the Education project is fragmented, reductionist and instrumental. It draws attention to the barriers and constraints to providing and developing a third level experience that is liberating, energising and enriching. In short, it challenges all involved in Education, at whatever level, to revisit the experience from a perspective of critical, emancipatory learning and to move the project on in radically new ways.

Professor Tom Collins,
National University of Ireland, Maynooth.

Part 1

Introduction

All the best stories start with the words: 'Once upon a time ... ' So it is with this story too. Once upon a time – five years ago, to be exact – the author had a supermarket experience which presented a startling eureka moment. She observed that food items were being presented for sale in capsule form. For example, a small tray contained several tiny, evenly sized potatoes complete with a knob of butter and a scattering of chives, covered with cling film and ready to be inserted into a microwave oven. Rather nonplussed, the author mused whether anyone prepared meals in the traditional fashion any more and whether purchasers of prepared foods would be able to recognise the originals. Immediately, and shockingly, came the realization that this was the same process which was being followed in the academic field. Formed by the kinds of life and educational experience which they have undergone, students bring a new perspective to education. They exhibit an increasing reluctance to purchase or consult texts and because of their 'shopping' approach, many lecturers prepare notes for easy academic consumption and tend to examine these notes rather than examine a subject. The input of students is decreasing on a continuing basis and they are becoming increasingly disengaged from their studies. This realization was the beginning of a journey from potatoes to postmodernism.

This book deals with the philosophy underpinning current educational provisions. Anecdotal information would suggest that students, their perception shaped by the educational experience they have undergone, view education as a *consumer experience* and require that information be packaged for easy consumption. This book provides support for this perception and examines the current situation in education against the backdrop of an emerging trend that sees education as a product and students as consumers or customers.

The subtitle of this book is *the Rise of Capsule Education*. The word 'capsule' is derived from the Latin diminutive, 'capsula' from 'capsa', *a box*, and 'capere' meaning *to hold*. Dictionary explanations involve the concepts of small size, abridged form and separateness. A capsule is often understood as a tiny packet which, because of its membrane, an individual may absorb without the distress or effort of chewing or tasting. The contents are sealed; there is, therefore, no sense of touch or involvement. What is significant about a capsule is that someone else shapes and probably prescribes it. The recipient need only swallow the capsule whole. It is clear that consumers are, more and more, purchasing 'capsule' products, that is, items such as food, holidays and decor, where the product is shaped by the provider and the input of the consumer – if it exists at all – is very limited. To the dismay of educators, students are adopting a similar approach to education.

Traditionally, higher education was the preserve of the elite and there was a strong link between qualification and education. That is, the signifier represented the signified. The growth in democratisation during the middle of the last century exposed the inequities in the education system and made a claim for the provision of higher education for all. The link between higher education and high status, high paying careers is a seductive one. Bound together with those who *want* such an outcome are those members of society who feel that they *ought* to want it. These two groups provide the population willing to undergo the higher education treatment. Such mass provision places a considerable strain on funding. The outcome of this constraint is that educational institutions should operate on a business footing in the belief that such a model can deliver maximum efficiency. Applying the business paradigm ushers in a new framework as the education field becomes a market with its outputs measured against external criteria. The budget becomes the overarching tool of management in a constrained resource environment. Funding is driven by enrolment and issues of quality acquire new interpretations such as organization size and numbers qualified. Education becomes an industry with students as customers/consumers and staff as processing units. As education shifts from elite to mass, there occurs a rupture between the signifier and the signified with a qualification no longer representing either education or competency.

In this education field the aims of students and administrators coalesce but are opposite to the views of lecturers. The goals of many students, to obtain a qualification with the least possible effort, commitment and input, are in line with the goals of administrators who need to have as many qualified 'outputs' as possible in order to garner maximum funding. Lecturers, the traditional gatekeepers of quality, see the concept in terms of learning on the part of students and are dismayed to see that their understanding of quality no longer provides foundations for practice in education. They recognise that many students are reluctant to purchase or read texts and they acknowledge that their own response is to supply students with sets of notes. There is an understanding and expectation on the part of students that there will be no surprises in examinations. This chasm between the lecturers' ideal and the students' approach may cause the kind of disenchantment first noted by Marx, as lecturers now need to produce an alien, petrified product – *education as a consumer experience*. Additionally, semesterisation seems to have the effect of increasing the pressure to deliver an examinable module in a time span of 12 or 13 weeks. There appears to be a relentless drive towards the 'encapsulation' of education and towards the perception of education as a market commodity.

The difficulty for lecturers is that there is a gap between what they want to give, in terms of education, and what students wish to receive. It is possible that this may be because students may be attuned to the *postmodern* whereas lecturers may be firmly rooted in *modernism*. The postmodern approach is one based on consumption where there is attachment to the fleeting and the ephemeral, where image is more important than reality. Postmodernism and its perspectives and terms have infiltrated society over the past number of decades. The most striking aspect of this perspective is its overturning of modernism which has traditionally provided the underpinnings for our institutions and our thinking. Modernism offers clear meaning and defined terms. Postmodernism, on the other hand, plays with indeterminacy of language and refuses to fix meaning. One of the most significant revelations of postmodernism is the concept of the *simulacrum*. This occurs when the boundary between a simulation and reality implodes so that the basis for determining the real is gone; the signifier bears no relationship whatsoever to the signified. The zeitgeist of the post-modern is the consumption, not just of goods and services, but of their symbols as well. Advertising and public relations engage in what is called the 'theft and re-appropriation of meaning'. In the education field the symbol of qualification has subsumed the reality of education. A postmodern perspective sees the shift in society from production to consumption. The concepts of education as product and students as consumers impact on education, on students and on educational practitioners. Education, conceived as a product, makes for a pedagogy of confinement which limits the creativity of students and inhibits any achievement by them beyond the limits which have been set for them. Such an education has, at its roots, society's desire to control and to ensure that everyone fits into allotted places in its plan. This ideological intent shapes education as an industry – the largest single industry in the world – where students are processed as inputs and awarded a qualification, the educational value of which is in serious doubt.

Chapter 1

Modernism, Postmodernism and Higher Education

The terms *traditional, modern* and *postmodern* indicate specific conceptual structures, not to be confused with the common usage that merely designates temporal reference. In common use *modern* is defined as contemporary, current or new, whereas *traditional* is synonymous with old or past. Within the current postmodern paradigm the word modern, according to Moncayo (2003), refers to modernism as 'the secular scientific paradigm with all its accompanying aesthetic and ethic values, whereas tradition refers to cultural traditions existing before and outside the western scientific paradigm ... ' (p. 6). He continues: 'postmodernism points in the direction of a new cross-cultural paradigm that permutes and combines without necessarily integrating or synthesising traditional and modern western and eastern European and American conceptual structures' (p. 6).

Viewed through its own prism, modernism represents a model of reason, rationality, cause and effect and a faith that there are universals, which act as conduits for arriving at *truth* and *reality*. Modernism, for western society, has for so long represented an ontological and epistemological compass that little attention has been paid to the philosophical reasoning. It, further, does not query the concept that language can be used as a known and reliable means of accessing and communicating that truth. So steeped did western society become in the morass of these 'truths' that it is shocking to have postmodernism query their provenance and ask from which natural law might they have sprung. Modernism, according to Bloland (1995),

> has long been considered the basis for the emancipation of men and women from the bonds of ignorance associated with stagnant tradition, narrow religions and meagre educations. Championing

democracy, modernism promises freedom, equality, justice, the good life and prosperity.

(p. 522)

The reader may find cause in his/her own life or in biography to support this view of modernism as an escape hatch to a 'better' life, without querying that it is modernism itself, which both manufactures the straitjacket and provides the means for escape. The individual acquiesces, locked as s/he is into modernism's understanding of *better*, *prosperity*, *justice* and *equality*. Modernism's fascination with binary oppositions dexterously provides a lexicon from which an individual can draw understanding in order to live a *successful* life under the banner of modernism. Citizen is better than slave, middle class better than working class, white better than black, man better than woman, teacher better than student, boss better than worker, master's better than primary degree, university better than institute of technology. It falls to postmodernism to demolish these binarisms with the challenge that there are no natural hierarchies, only those which are socially constructed.

Modernism promises a *better* life to all who understand and obey its rules; it promises – through science – better health, the eradication of crime, hunger, disease and poverty. It claims ongoing development towards the knowledge of the universe and equates change with progress – progress which is defined as increasing control over nature and society. Control is the crucial leitmotif of modernism, a leitmotif, which Freire (1972) chillingly describes as necrophilic. This descriptor challenges us to raise an eyebrow at the claims of modernism and to listen to its sceptics.

Modernism carries within itself the seeds of its own destruction. According to Max Weber (1958 translation) an over-organized economic order has imprisoned people in

an iron cage of work incentives. This order is now bound to the technical and economic conditions of machine production which today determine the lives of all the individuals who are born into this mechanism ... with irresistible force.

(in Bloland, p. 523)

Moncayo reminds us that the Frankfurt School presented a critique linking modernism with masked forms of oppression and domination. This school, itself a modernist construct, sought to articulate a critical reason which would free modern rationality from the bonds of instrumental scientific rationality. By contrast, the postmodern paradigm questions the superiority of reason itself. According to Bloland, 'instrumental rationality, in its current postmodern reading, is seen as having forged the consumer society in which commodification, the definition of persons and activities solely in terms of their market value, has become dominant' (p. 524) – an ironic observation, given that the brickbat most frequently hurled at postmodernism is the latter's fetish with the *product*. Even science, traditionally one of modernism's foundation stones, has given modernism a bad press, becoming the purveyor of death through annihilation and illness and environmental problems through pollution and uncontrollable technology.

The beginnings of the postmodern debate can be traced to the United States in the 1960s. The debate gained currency in the arts and social theory in the 1970s and by the early 1980s, became, according to Huyssen (1990), one of the most challenged areas of intellectual discourse in the west. Following its sweep through the humanities and social sciences, the debate has receded, the current period being referred to largely as *post-theory*. Postmodernism, as a worldview, represents a fearful shifting sands scenario to a viewer steeped in modernism. It dismantles the underpinnings of modernism on which western civilisation and western social thinking is, not simply posited, but riveted. Modernism is characterised by its offer of the comfort of certainty, with social rules set out in language which is determinate and absolute. Postmodernism questions the determinacy of the very language we use to express our views, or to enter debate. Anderson (1996a) describes four contemporary worldviews. People who share one of these worldviews understand each other fairly well but do not well understand those of a different worldview. The four worldviews encompass the postmodern-ironist view, which sees truth as a social construct, the scientific-rational which discovers truth through systematic logical enquiry, the social-traditional in which truth is found in heritage, and the neo-romantic which finds truth through harmony with nature and/or harmony with the spiritual inner self.

Neo-romantics are strongly linked to the past. Rejecting the postmodern and the modern, they long for a romanticised, imagined golden age before the Industrial Revolution and the Enlightenment. The *postmodern* represents a worldview in which truth is not found but made. In Anderson's opinion it has three subgroups. (The irony of Anderson's categorisation and labelling of postmodern groups will not be lost on the reader.) The first group comprises those who actively think and live a *constructivist* worldview. While they may be outwardly conventional, their inner attitude questions acceptance of the value of one set of ideas or rules over another, but not enough to engage in revolutionary change. The second group, described as *ironist*, plays mix and match with cultural heritage, fashion and religious rituals, is comfortable with virtual reality and at home in theme parks. People in the third group, labelled *nihilists*, are so bewildered with so many conflicting beliefs that they conclude that they are all bogus. These are not nihilist in the same sense as Nietzsche. He was nihilist, not in terms of throwing out all moral standards, but in asserting that moral standards have no inherent morality. He maintains that, at the dawn of time, the strong simply selected those standards that would best serve them and imposed them on the weak, a notion which is supported by Becker's *Birth and Death of Meaning* (1980). Anderson's nihilists represent the face of postmodernism that induces fear in conservatives – fear that it will lead to alienation, hedonism and contempt for mainstream society. Moncayo, aware of this perspective, suggests that, in order to combat the possible anarchy of ego-autonomy, it is important to regenerate a non-authoritarian or non-moralistic heteronomy.

Anderson claims that scientific-rationalistic culture is most strongly entrenched in academia and the sciences. 'For a good scientific-rationalist', he says, 'the main sources of evil in the world are sloppy thinking and lack of respect for hard facts' (p. 109).

The scientific-rational and social-traditional cultures occupy an occasionally uneasy coalition as the power structure within countries. 'The official realities of our time are to be found there' (p. 109). If you want to be the President of the United States, warns Anderson, you must eschew all signs of postmodernism. He further suggests that the spectacular growth of neo-romantic culture represents, not alone, a disaffinity with modernism, but a distrust of the uncertainties of postmodernism.

A synthesis of the main responses to postmodernism ranges from *social conservatism* (underpinned by nostalgia and religious fundamentalism), to *chaos theory* which, like postmodernism, presents us with the core concepts of disorder and indeterminacy but which emphasises the possibility of creating order from disorder.

At the heart of the confrontation between modernism and postmodernism is the question of whether or not there are basic standards underlying human behaviour – standards like reason and justice. Postmodernists question if reason is simply the name the powerful offer in support of their rationale for holding power and if justice is no more than an excuse for the majority to impose its ideas on the minority.

Rorty (1989) is emphatic that there is no objective truth, no *skyhook*, no *God's Eye* perspective. He replaces objective truth with solidarity and describes the ideal situation for society as one which achieves maximum voluntary agreement in addition to some tolerated disagreement. Less dismissive of modernism, Shweder (in Anderson 1996a), recognises that in a postmodern world it is more and more difficult to take a stand on issues of fact and value without appearing to be dogmatic, hegemonic or prejudiced. He suggests that prejudice is not always a bad thing; it fixes a starting point from which we may examine other viewpoints. Becker (1980) summarises the postmodern condition and lifts the veil on the symbolic environment which, from prehistoric times, has facilitated human action and interaction in a psychological world of human aspiration which is largely fictitious. Man is free to inhabit this world, from which lower animals are excluded – a world which is free from the enslavement of the present moment, from the immediate stimuli which bind all lower organisms. Man's freedom, says Becker, is a manufactured one and it carries a price tag – the imperative that he must at all times protect this fragile construct and at all times deny it's fiction. Man must understand, he says, that this is how *this* animal must function if he is to function as *this* animal. Man's fictitious fabrications are not superfluous creations which he can set aside in order to get on with the real business of life.

They are at least as important a part of the business of life. Becker describes these fictions as a 'flimsy canopy' (p. 142) flung over the social world from the dawn of time. He expresses awe, not that these fictions exist, but that man should be sufficiently willing to subject himself to self-scrutiny that he is able to see through them. History, he says, will marvel at this discovery and see it as one of the most liberating of all times, a discovery that was made in Becker's time – during the third quarter of the twentieth century. Hayakawa et al. (1990) also draw attention to the symbolic in the lives of humans. The difference between man and animal is, they say, is that while animals struggle with each other for food or for leadership, man, in addition to those struggles, will also battle with his fellow man for things that *stand* for food and leadership – such as paper symbols of wealth, badges of rank or January registration plates. For animals, the relationship in which one thing stands for another, in so far as it exists, does so only in the most rudimentary form. The human, with his highly developed nervous system, understands that there is no *necessary* connection between the symbol and that for which the symbol stands. Our current human environment is shaped by hitherto unparalleled semantic influences; we need, therefore, to be aware of the powers and limitations of symbols. A naïve attitude towards symbols can result in attributing a 'mystical power' to what are mere words (p. 98).

Habermas (in Bloland), a member of the second wave Frankfurt School, often finds himself pitted against Foucault, Gadamer and Lyotard in theoretical debates surrounding postmodernism – essentially a recasting of the debate between Kant and Hegel. Habermas is clearly a follower of Kant in his dedication to reason, ethics and moral philosophy. The defender of modernism, he sees much of value in postmodernism's critique and, taking some of it on board, seeks to develop a renewed modernism, improving democracy, freedom, equality and progress through open communication. He is a staunch advocate of the principles of reason and justice and believes in a humanism or universalism, that is, 'in our everyday knowledge of how language is properly used we find a common ground among all creatures with a human face' (in Stephens, 1994), a theme reflected in Hayakawa (1965) and Hayakawa et al. (1990). While postmodernists reject such beliefs out of hand, Habermas (1987) clings resolutely to the view that through communicative action humans can, over time, overcome their biases and prejudices in order to achieve social emancipation.

> I think that a certain form of unrestrained communication brings to the fore the deepest form of reason, which enables us to overcome egocentric or ethnocentric perspectives and reach an expanded . . . view.
>
> (in Stephens)

The transformation of societies into radical democracies through the process of communicative action is a leit-motif of Habermas' (1989) philosophy as he expresses concern at the erosion of demographic freedom by the growth of technocratic bureaucracies. He believes that the structures of these institutions – which emanate from natural scientific methodologies – are insensitive to the true nature of human social interaction and often have the effect of reducing human beings to mere functional objects. He places crucial emphasis on the political responsibility of the intellectual and regrets the diminution of twentieth-century democracy to a mere plebiscite. Considerations of instrumental efficiency, he claims, serve to block out the more profound questions about the nature of society and its purpose. In *Public Sphere* (1989) he explains how the instrumental rationality of the system can colonise the lifeworld – the accepted social skills and stocks of knowledge of its members – so that social agents can no longer question, or even understand, the rules that govern their actions. He refers to this systemic integration as 'structural violence' that attacks communicative action and induces losses of meaning and legitimacy plus the reduction of stability of collective identities. Bureaucracies and the market are paradigmatic examples of such systems.

Former U. S. President Bill Clinton, in his (2005) autobiography, supports this view. He reflects on the propensity of the system to become institutionalised, so that 'vested interests become more committed to preserving their own prerogatives than to meeting the needs for which they were created' (p. 78). Illich's (1972) assertion that school prepares people from an early age for the alienating institutionalisation of life also supports the stance of Habermas (1989). Through school, Illich claims, people learn, unwittingly, to 'put themselves into their assigned plots, squeeze into the niche ... put their fellows in their places too, until everybody and everything fits' (p. 40). Greer's (1998) reading of Habermas asserts that the difficulties connected with postmodernist interpretations are due 'in no small part to the means of mass communication including education' (p. 106).

There is criticism of modernism from Feminists, Marxists and Post-colonialists. Feminists have much to criticise in modernism, especially its binary oppositions, but realize that postmodernism's refusal to recognise such oppositions leaves them without a stable ground on which to fight their post-feminism gender battles. The Marxist response to postmodernism is the recognition of cultural fragmentation and a reification of social and political life. Based as it is on its own metanarrative, Marxism, like feminism, has no firm ground on which to stake its claim. The postcolonial perspective, articulated by Spivak (1985), sees all binarisms as emanating from colonialism, and, like postmodernism, seeks to demolish metanarratives, especially those which defined their histories, took over their culture and presented them with images of themselves and their political lives.

Giroux (1992) attempts to negotiate liminal space in his effort to combine postmodernism, feminism, culture studies and postcolonialism. He invites students, teachers and cultural workers to critique and challenge the institutions, which define the relationships currently dominating society. This process he calls 'border crossing'. Its purpose is to establish alternative public spaces where the changing structure of agreed and constructed realities allows others 'to rewrite their own histories, identities and learning possibilities' (in Bloland, p. 539). Lest this sound like a description of the tower of Babel, Giroux confirms that the principles underpinning this approach are firmly rooted in the modernist values of freedom, equality, liberty and justice – each of which is a metanarrative.

The *liberal pragmatist* approach, like Giroux's border crossings, attempts to include the marginalised, but clings more strongly to modernist principles on which higher education is founded, not on the grounds that such principles are superior but that enough people in academe espouse them, making it pragmatic to retain them and thus enable them to cling to power.

As lenses through which to view higher education, modernism and postmoderism (with its particular emphasis on the commodity) present polarised views. Higher education is seen as both a face and a function of modernism. It espouses the binary opposites of modernism, believing that high culture is of a higher order than popular culture, that middle class values are better than working class values. It believes that education is the road to upward mobility, towards which, it believes, all individuals are drawn. It assumes that success in higher education can be measured through higher status jobs, prospects for promotion and greater prestige. Higher education values differentiation of discourse, distinguishing between what it calls 'hard' and 'soft' subjects. Clearly placing a higher value on 'hard' subjects, rooted as they are in the rational contexts of science and engineering, it perceives differences between academic institutions and recognises differentiation of discourse inside and outside the academic institution. It values research over teaching. According to Bloland, higher education

> assumes that progress is possible and good and that the way to move in that direction is through education ... that some fundamental set of values, some basic accepted rules of conduct, and some sense of limits are good.
>
> (p. 523)

It sees knowledge as superior to skill. This distinction between mental knowledge and manual skills has its roots in the division of labour established during the Industrial Revolution and in the Greco-Roman disdain for slave labour and the Christo-feudal elevation of spiritual contemplation (Zuboff, 1988). Modernism has long provided the underpinnings for the traditional perspective on education, a perspective which, for a long time, saw the function of education as the preservation and maintenance of cultural norms. Casazza (1996) reminds us that these norms were imported into

America from Europe. Brubacher and Rudy (1976) describe the commencement address which lauded the foundation of Harvard university by Puritan settlers. Otherwise, the address concluded,

> the ruling class would have been subjected to mechanics, cobblers and tailors, the gentry would have been overwhelmed by lewd fellows of the baser sort, the sewage of Rome, the dregs of an illiterate plebs which judgeth more from emotion, little from truth.
>
> (1976, p. 10)

– a, perhaps, intemperate address which may itself owe more to emotion and to the logic of binarisms than it does to education. The authors refer too, to the dismay which greeted the arrival at Amherst and Williams of poorer students who were described as 'rough, brown featured, schoolmaster-looking, half bumpkin, half scholar, in black, ill-cut broadcloth' (p. 40).

Donnelly (2004) draws on the Garavan et al. (1995) Report which testifies to the bias both in Ireland and the United Kingdom towards academic achievement rather than towards vocational training. Both countries lag behind their European counterparts in the provision of vocational training.

What a comfort to the follower of modernism to have his/her world so clearly described and prescribed. How unassailable is his/her position and how certain is his/her judgement of comparative situations as s/he combs the encyclopaedia of binarisms for validation. It is no wonder that modernism, with its attendant characteristics of control, oppression and necrophilia, attracts the backlash of postmodernism. Even Habermas (1987), the defender of modernism, admits that it has lost its way, resulting in a high level of institutional dysfunction. While modernism claims to be democratic it may, in its effort to fit humans into systems, have moved too far along the continuum thus depriving humans of their autonomy. Bloland issues a salutary reminder that modernism's attempts to unify and totalise are as often associated with Nazism, Fascism and Communism as they are with democracy.

Postmodernism's appraisal of higher education, borrowing from the vocabulary of post-structuralism, focuses on the indeterminacy of language, the abandonment of the metanarrative and a deep distrust of reason as a means of problem solving. A post-structuralist, Jacques Derrida (1976), attacks the basic modernist assumption that thoughts and realities precede language and that language is the vehicle for expressing them. He claims that language comes *before* knowledge and that the meanings of words are constantly re-interpreted in different social settings. He claims that final meaning is difficult to achieve in the concepts we use and he challenges us, instead of reading the central arguments of a text, to search the margins and to deconstruct in order to unearth hidden meanings, oppositions, contradictions and the underlying pattern that informs the language. He asserts that the binary oppositions which inform western philosophy and culture construct a set of 'far from innocent' hierarchies which attempt not only to guarantee truth but also to exclude or devalue allegedly inferior terms. 'This binary metaphysics, thus works to positively position reality over appearance, speech over writing, men over women, or reason over nature, thus positioning negatively the supposedly inferior term' (in Bloland, p. 525).

O'Donohoe (1997) also warns against too much thoroughness in fixing meaning. When we do this, she says, we do it by silencing or negating different or opposite meanings. The goal of deconstruction is, not alone to unmask the arbitrariness of hierarchies, but to do so without replacing them by polar opposites, or any opposites. Higher education exhibits a rigid hierarchical structure: physical sciences are valued over social sciences while research is valued more than teaching. Doctoral studies are valued more than master's degrees and master's more than bachelor degrees. Private education is valued over public, lecturers over students, administrators over lecturers and tenured over non-tenured lecturers. Deconstruction of these binarisms subverts the pretence that they are founded on any universal logic. This subversion exposes the fault lines in the dominant culture of the academic system and calls into question our belief in the assumptions embedded in higher education.

The postmodern critique of hierarchies erodes the foundations of higher educational institutions, which see themselves as the prime creators and distributors of knowledge, civic values and meaning. These institutions act as mechanisms of social placement with the middle class as the significant datum and students arranged along a

continuum according to the coordinates of examination results. Institutions are producers of large numbers of professionals whose stock-
in-trade is expertise – itself a suspect criterion when viewed through
the lens of postmodernism because it places clients and lay people in
inferior positions. Derrida deftly deconstructs the language and hierarchies of the history of the west, a history which has always tended to
silence differences by categorising as inferior the dissenter, the exile,
the outsider and the marginalised. Those who queried the received
wisdom were derided as not knowing their (modernist) place, not
knowing the culture, that language where 'once you are a member of
the group, once your behaviours count as meaningful within the social
practice, you get the meanings free' (Gee, 1992, p. 10). Bloland neatly
sums up Derrida's deconstructionist approach. 'Deconstruction celebrates differences but refers, not to the difference of heterogeneity,
which is intrinsic to modernism, but to the difference of disruption,
tension and the withholding of closure' (Bloland, p. 527).

Young (1990), in a reference to community, suggests that a politics
of difference should be organized which would have as its chief characteristic 'inexhaustible heterogeneity' and an openness to 'assimi-
lated otherness' (Bloland, p. 527).

In his perspective on the world Foucault (1979) also uses deconstruction techniques underpinned by what he terms archaeology
and genealogy approaches. The archaeological approach encourages a dig to discover '. . . what rules permit certain statements to be
made . . . what rules order these statements . . . what rules permit us to
identify some statements as true and some false . . . what rules allow
the construction of a map, model or classificatory system' (p. 69).

Foucault aims to attack great systems, great theories and great
truths and to give free play to difference. With the genealogical
approach he draws attention to the power/ knowledge relationship
within institutions, suggesting that there is no knowledge without
power and no power without knowledge. He does not see power
solely in terms of prohibition, nor solely as a force for repression. He
suggests that we cannot study power without studying the strategies of
power, that is, the networks, the mechanisms and the techniques by
which a decision is reached and accepted and by which that decision
could not but be taken in the way it was. We cannot, he says, resolve

the question of *who exercises power?* without, at the same time, answering the question *how does it happen?*. Despite knowing who is in charge and who the decision-makers are we still do not know why the decision was made, how it was made, how it came to be universally accepted and how it is that it helps one and hurts another. Taking examples of garrisons, prisons, workhouses and boarding schools Foucault refers to a technique of what he calls 'human dressage' (Anderson, 1996b, p. 39) which controls people by location, confinement, surveillance and continuous supervision of people and tasks. These methods of conditioning human behaviour have a rationale, a logic usually expressed in economic, political or social imperatives. Reflecting Nietzsche's stance he questions why we are so in thrall to the truth. Why are we not, instead, attached to lies, to illusion, to myth? This view is in sharp contrast to that of modernism, which holds that there is objective value in each discipline over and above politics, economics, culture and other external differences. For Foucault, therefore, there is little interest in the substance of a discipline or in whether legitimate rules exist for distinguishing between good and mediocre work. The only interest lies in an understanding of the power relations that are permitted and assumed. The power/knowledge relationship is embedded in discourses, and discourses are the fields where groups and individuals battle for supremacy. For Foucault the knowledge/power nexus means that knowledge ceases to be liberation (as the modernists would claim) and becomes a mode of surveillance, regulation and discipline – an opinion also held by Freire (1972), and a counter view to the position espoused by the institutions of higher education which promise freedom and liberation through knowledge.

For Lyotard (1984) the postmodern is defined as incredulity towards metanarratives – metanarratives, which focus on God, nature, progress and emancipation. These metanarratives – stories of how the world works – provide unifying images and analyse ideas by breaking them down into simpler parts. Any attempt to define postmodernism runs the risk of destruction by postmodernists who view such efforts as flawed attempts to totalise, confine and systematise. This is a charge laid at Lyotard's door, an accusation he refutes. His rejection of metanarratives and hierarchies mirrors the outlook of Derrida and Foucault that language is not a path to the discovery of truth or a means of adequately describing reality. Recognising that metanarratives are the foundation of university and college life, Lyotard forecasts a bleak future for higher education. His assertion that performativity – the use of targets and performance indicators to drive, evaluate and compare educational products – is the only criterion in a postmodern environment, means that higher education's sole raison d'être is its ability to contribute directly to the economic system. Lyotard (1984) also describes performativity as the 'soft and hard terrors' (p. xxiv) of performance and efficiency, the pragmatic that an institution be operational or be gone. The task of higher education is to

> create skills and no longer ideas. The transmission of knowledge is no longer designed to train an elite capable of guiding the nation towards its emancipation but to supply the players capable of acceptably fulfilling their roles at the pragmatic post required by its institutions.
>
> (p. 48)

– a theme later reflected in Ainley (2000) and others. Lyotard sounds the death knell for the professor whose teaching will still be necessary but who is now reduced to instructing students in the use of terminals. If there are no legitimate grand narratives there is no need for lecturers to teach them. Ball (1999) asserts that the teacher is reconstructed as a technician rather than as a professional capable of critical judgement and reflection. Machines can teach students what they need to know in a performativity-driven society. Sambataro (2000) takes a positive view on this theme. She suggests that learning at computer terminals is now big business, particularly in the IT sector. Knowledge gained from classroom teaching, she says, quickly becomes obsolete, and, indeed is often obsolete before it is taught. Self-guided tutorials and databases allow users to 'fill specific knowledge and skills gaps with nuggets of information they need' (p. 50). This approach saves travel and education costs and confers the benefit of working at one's own pace. Sambataro reminds us that one day of electronic learning costs $100 to $500 compared with $500 to $1,200 per day for classroom learning. This just-in-time system is also superior for keeping up with rapid changes in technology, although, she says, agreeing with Lyotard, there is no suggestion that this kind of learning can fully replace classroom teaching. Ives and Jarvenpaa (1996), however, suggest that this is precisely what will happen – publishers and software houses, they claim, are developing multimedia products which will substitute rather than complement traditional education. Forecasting the imminent arrival of education on demand to homes, schools and workplaces, they believe that it will be a vastly bigger business than entertainment on demand. They see many advantages in such a futuristic technology-centred system. Students in a virtual learning environment will be grouped on the basis of homogeneity of interests and intellect while benefiting from heterogeneity of cultural background and life experiences. Schools, instead of providing a discrete, career-spanning set of concepts and tools, will now help build the skills and motivation needed for lifelong learning. Students learn, not by memorising, but by doing, albeit in a simulated environment. Because humans are better equipped to deal with images than with either text or audio – language having emerged relatively recently in our evolution – the visual presentation will allow us once again to leverage our ability to process images. Preliminary studies, they claim, show that employees assigned to virtual reality training make fewer mistakes than those assigned to traditional training, at a much reduced cost, although they recognise that it is not yet clear what kinds of innovations in learning can have the greatest impression on the greatest number of learners. Their proposed revolution in higher education – which has still not come to pass, more than ten years after writing (although much of what they say is repeated by Wood et al. (2005)) – faces some obstacles, they admit. Chief among these obstacles are the linking of tenure and promotion to research so that lecturers, to maintain their career, must engage in research which is out of date by the time it is published. Other obstacles are the estimation of research into learning or pedagogy as third rate and the need for lecturers, still wedded to the traditional paradigm, to re-skill. Ives and Jarvenpaa (1996) consider that, in the long run, nothing will protect the business school from being drawn into the current of technologically driven change. The soil around higher education institutions is crumbling fast and only the elite universities will be able to withstand the onslaught of the virtual campus. According to Bartlett (1997), however, many elite universities which have long equated quality of education with ivy-clad walls and personal time spent with professors, when faced with competition from online programmes from private educational providers, could also be forced to rethink how they teach. The University of Phoenix claims to be the biggest online education provider in the world. It is America's largest accredited university with over 17,000 qualified instructors, 170 campuses and worldwide internet delivery. All teaching is provided online and it is location loose, enabling a student to study from anywhere in the world. The university's website claims that degree holders in America earn 75 per cent more than high school leavers and that this can represent one million dollars over a career lifetime.

Kerr (2002), like Sambataro, does not foresee that e-learning will be a low cost total replacement for traditional teaching and learning although he holds the door open on this view, asserting that, if e-learning should turn out to be a total replacement rather than primarily an add-on, it would become the great theme of this century, dwarfing all the changes effected so far by the multiversity. Lanham (2002) and Tomlinson-Keasey (2002) make a strong case for e-learning with Lanham, in an amusing aside, cautioning against wiring traditional classrooms in a well-intentioned effort to embrace the advantages of technology since classrooms are where students have just escaped from.

Lyotard criticises the dominance of science and scientific method in the modernist world. He removes its underpinnings by suggesting that it is just one more metanarrative. Science is not objective and value free, he says, but a discourse like any other discourse, a political landscape where power engages in combat for the control of meaning. A reading of Kaku's (2005) *Parallel Worlds* – describing the centuries long, and ongoing, battle among physicists for an understanding of how the universe was formed – supports this assertion. Performativity, according to Lyotard, is the most powerful criterion for judging worth in a postmodern world and it replaces truth as the measure of knowledge. The questions 'is it true?', 'is it moral?', 'is it just?' have been replaced by the performativity driven values –'is it efficient?', 'is it marketable?', 'does it work?'.

Baudrillard (1998) reflects Lyotard's central placing of economic performativity as a core driver of higher education provision – its type, the modes of delivery, the independence of educational institutions and their positioning in an increasingly market driven, competitive environment. In a world where service jobs have overtaken industrial jobs the consumption of goods takes primacy of place over work as a focus for our lives, a point also made by Riesman as far back as 1961. The production of information, says Baudrillard, is more important than the production of goods, an assertion which may evoke a dusty echo from the myriad reports and surveys which clutter the shelves of institutions, including academic institutions, and which, in many cases, are never read. Their production, however, justifies the existence of some bureaucratic system.

One of higher education's chief functions is to decide what is merit because merit separates and places in a hierarchy those who meet merit standards from those who do not. In its pursuit of scholarly merit, higher education is constantly creating and justifying exclusions. Derrida would not eliminate merit but sees it as capricious and arbitrarily exclusive in its consequences. He sees no fundamental justification for claiming that one standard for merit is better than another. This issue is faced, and answered, by Gibbs and Iacovidou (2004) who question the value of examination-based grading. They suggest that students' effort, commitment and engagement should be taken into account in awarding grades. Grading, they say, should encompass a recognition for a 'growing moral maturity' (p. 117). They further distinguish between two interpretations of merit – a formal one and a morally rich one. This distinction allows that a good education be judged by the worth of its accomplishments and not simply by the achievement of its criteria-based outcomes.

Despite the assumption endemic in higher education that it prepares large numbers of professionals for high status careers the outcome may, in fact, be quite different. Given that so many second-level students (approximately 54 per cent in the case of Ireland) progress to third level (OECD 2004) the assertion may be made that, either there are many performing work roles for which they are over-qualified or else, that the qualification they have achieved is of a questionable standard. Many service jobs simply provide non-career, low-paying positions (Edwards, 1993). He refers to the continuous re-arrangement of apparently simple operations into ones involving technical and social skills. This is a form of horizontal job loading which apparently satisfies the worker who undertakes this job in exchange for his/her qualification, but is, in fact, not much more demanding than the jobs performed by early school leavers in the past, or even, according to Ainley (2000), by those special school leavers with moderate learning difficulties. Drawing on an earlier study with Corbett (1994), Ainley (2000) takes shelf-filling in super-markets as an example: the requirements for this task have been much changed in recent years. In the mid-1970s the task was ade-quately performed by those with moderate learning difficulties. By 1986, continues Ainley (2000), 'the National Council for Vocational Qualifications was calling shelf-filling "stock replenishment" and set-ting it at NVQ Level 2 as "stock control"'.

Competence in stock replenishment was then a component part of the NVQs demanded of Youth Trainees in the retail sector. It has now been placed at NVQ Level 2 as 'stock control' and has become significantly more complicated through the inclusion of ICT. Such a process has meant that recent graduates may be employed as trainee managers to do this task among a range of others. The re-badging of the job with its attendant acceptable social signifier allows the worker, in good faith, to trade his/her educational qualification in decent exchange. Ainley (2000) emphasises that this newly designated *career* is not necessarily demanding of new knowledge and skill, however. The horizontal connection of modular competencies is an indicator of the stamp of Further Education rather than Higher Education, but not immediately obvious to the onlooker. As Baudrillard (1998) him-self might paraphrase it, an evanescence of education in the epiphany of the sign.

A graduate destination report prepared by an Irish third-level insti-tution (Dundalk Institute of Technology Graduate Careers Service 2005) reveals the real world findings of some Business Studies grad-uates that a degree is not enough for a good career and that many companies will pay as much to a school leaver as to a graduate with a certificate or a degree. 'Bachelors degrees have become a commodity; good enough for getting a job but not good enough for a "real" job or career' (Appendix G, Graduate Survey).

For this reason many claim to have undertaken further study at Master's level in an effort to progress their careers. This raises serious questions about the standard of qualifications and credential inflation in the current educational environment.

A further assumption of higher education is that it can provide economic 'diplomats' for multinational organizations in far flung global sites – educated, socially aware, multilingual executives who can operate with ease in diverse cultures. This, again, has not proven to be the case. Not alone have multinationals chosen the advantages of local labour, familiar with local culture and language, willing to work for lower wages and with no desire to globe trot, but indeed, many western workers in these, sometimes footloose, global enterprises have found their jobs transferred to low-cost economies.

In his reading of Baudrillard, Bloland discusses the impact of post-modernism on consumer culture and its potentially disruptive effect on higher education curricula. Bloland asserts that the conventional understanding of consumer culture education is that such an education prepares workers to manufacture and supply consumer goods and services to a population surrounded by displays of conspicuous consumption. The postmodern interpretation suggests that since consumer activity is now a central drive of peoples' lives, a consolidating bond of society and the foundation of the economic system, the orientation of higher education should be, not alone to prepare students to be manufacturers and suppliers of consumer goods, but to be 'intellectually and philosophically skilful and knowing consumers'.

The traditional model of higher education, steeped as it is in the *truths* of modernism would be unlikely to pursue such a low-brow syllabus. Secondly, it is unlikely that it would have any success, given that its competitors – television, advertising, the mass media – fully embracing postmodernism, have already taught students about choice and comparative shopping and how they can access much of what they want outside the walls of the academic institution.

Perhaps the work of Illich (1972) may throw some light on the education/consumer culture nexus. He argues that the consumption patterns of college graduates become the standards for all others: 'If they would be civilised people on or off the job, they will aspire to the style of life of the college graduate' (p. 35). This gives educational institutions the power to define the expectations of society and to hold unparalleled power in the world's economic system. The hidden curriculum serves as an initiating rite into the consumer society for rich and poor alike, a rite which engenders a style of life which is 'merely a way station on the road to the depletion and pollution of the environment' (p. 52). American students, he says, if they learn nothing else, learn the value of escalation – the American way of life.

Students, Bloland acknowledges, are approaching a point where they are looking for a different education than the one provided by the grand narratives of modernism and they are prepared to look elsewhere to get it. This reflects Zemsky's (1993) understanding of student as consumer. 'Students today want technical knowledge, useful knowledge, labour related knowledge, in convenient digestible packages' (p. 17) – the capsule education approach which forms the major question in this book. Bloland recognises that higher education still has a tenuous grip on its claim to legitimacy in providing qualifications, which give a launch pad to graduates towards a middle class career although Edwards, Ainley (2000) and others dispute this claim. Changes in consumer culture and emphasis on performativity also render the future of this claim very questionable. With the advance of consumer creep in education, a consumer culture challenges the notion that a higher educational institution has a monopoly of knowledge. Knowledge, previously seen as the preserve of the academic institution, is now available outside of it through talk shows, documentary, fact on film (a simulacrum surely!), advertising and entertainment. Handy (1996), his finger on the pulse of change, asserts that 500 years ago, technology, through the printing press, allowed individuals to have their own bible at home, eroding the power of a licensed minister to interpret it for them. In contemporary times 'CD Roms and the internet make the knowledge of the world available to all, depriving teachers everywhere of their competitive advantage over their students, authority eroded there as well' (p. 7).

This is the new competition for higher education. Illich challenges the educational closed shop and the right of only certified teachers to teach. He argues that most learning occurs outside the ritualised educational setting but is either not taken seriously or is viewed with suspicion if it is not accompanied by a certificate from a licensed institution. Ball (1999) calls attention to the blurring of the divide between the public and private sectors and between public and private goods, evidenced in the shift in education systems. Education, one of the former objectives of which was the development of citizenship, is now becoming commodified and, in many ways 'the fragile and labile insulations between the economic and education systems are being thoroughly breached'. Another boundary collapse in higher education is the erosion of difference between high culture and low culture. In a process of cross-colonisation, academics enter the world of popular culture and interpret it, their interest and interpretations offering respectability to low culture. The sacrificial lamb in this instance is the expert status of the academics. Students, who in most cases have a part-time job, inhabit the liminal space between the academic institution and the world of work, deriving from the latter a power commensurate in force, if not in direction, with a third-level education – a power which delivers them a slice of pseudo-democracy as they exercise their spending power in a commodity driven environment.

Postmodernism presents us with a viewfinder through which we can see the disappearing *reversed front* (Foster 1985) of modernist higher education. In a performativity-driven world, Bloland reminds us that higher education can no longer act as though it has a franchise on truth. It can argue only that what it does is useful but not that it is true. Handy also argues that certainty is out and experimentation is in. He paraphrases George Bernard Shaw, asserting that the future belongs to 'the unreasonable ones, the ones who can look forward and not backward, who are certain only of uncertainty and who have the ability to think completely differently' (Handy, p. 16).

He says that what school taught him was that every problem in life had already been solved; the solution was in the head of the teacher or some other *expert*. This crippling and erroneous assumption caused him later in his work life to run for an expert when confronted with a problem. He contends that 'the world is not an unsolved puzzle waiting for the occasional genius to unlock its secrets ... it is an empty space waiting to be filled' (p. 17).

The modernist approach is to resolve problems and inconsistencies; the postmodern revels in preserving the contradictions in discourses. Should higher education, Bloland asks, accommodate an increasing agglomeration of incommensurate values, ethics and standards or should it seek to better understand these values and their meanings and provenance in an effort to determine new values which fit the world of higher education and support its mission? In a world of simulacra and the power of signs, higher education may have to seek a new kind of authenticity of information and knowledge. With the pressure of the market dissolving boundaries between the academic world and the world outside, Bloland believes it is essential to provide for some sanctuary, oasis or enclave which is not measured by market driven outputs but reflects the age old ivory tower concept of the pursuit of knowledge for its own sake. He suggests that as business becomes more globalised 'more boundaries may blur ... a kind of in-between moral relativism may result' (p. 545) – the kind of liminal space now occupied by higher education practitioners who are torn between delivering the accepted modernist package, with its concomitant oppression, or entering a postmodern field which is democratic in theory but may have uncertain foundations in merit. This kind of liminal space is occupied too, by educational institutions which seek to trade education as a commodity with a country such as China whose record of human rights is at odds with western values (Amnesty International, 2004).

Chapter 2

The Packaging of Education – Education as Oppression

Modernists tend to have a mechanistic view of reality and may not realize that their consciousness of reality colours their attitudes and their approach to dealing with reality. Becker (1980) offers an explanation for the ferocity with which mankind clings to its convictions. He claims that the ceremonial attached to social life must be such that it does not unravel. This flawlessness is the only method by which man can disguise his fictions and provide justification for them. He cannot admit to himself that his life-ways are arbitrary because to do so would expose their possible meaninglessness. If the fictional nature of culture is revealed it deprives life of its heroic meaning 'because the only way one can function as a hero is within the symbolic fiction' (p. 143). In this context the word hero is used to distinguish man from animals which live at the level of basic physical existence. It is what makes him different from the animal. What distinguishes man is that, not alone is he aware of himself as a unique individual, but he is also the only animal with an awareness that he will die. This leads to what Becker (1980) calls the despair and death of meaning which man carries by virtue of his basic human condition. The possibility that billions of years of evolution and several thousand of history, added to the unique circumstances of individual life, might count for nothing is, in Becker's view, an affront to reason. Man's only defence against such annihilation is to assign meaning through cultural contribution, through an attempt to make his fictitious world real. For this reason he must desperately defend his 'cultural-hero system' (p. 144) against opposing ones, because to allocate equality to competing views is to acknowledge that his own do not uniquely explain or validate his position in the story of creation. Postmodernism, in this situation, is conducive to despair. The attempted resolution of man's fundamental contradictions of existence – the miraculous nature of his emergence and the hopelessness of his mortality – lie in all human strivings, strivings to deny eternity. Humans use different coping strategies to avoid despair. Man's obsession with the meaning of life and with his own significance as a creature gives to his life a drive which is under-pinned by desperation. This means that every person, from the most primitive to the most civilised, creates a prison out of freedom. Some become embedded in others and never risk individuality and others 'bury themselves in the form of things, by so carefully, correctly and dedicatedly playing the hero-game of their society that they never risk uniqueness' (p. 147). Man closes himself off from situations which would query his standardised reactions. 'He will', says Becker, 'have it his way if he has to strangle the segment of reality that he has equipped himself to cope with' (p. 152). He will manipulate the world in such a way as to make it match his fantasies, fears and desires. He will unconsciously fail to notice things which are obvious because they are a threat to his system of belief. He will happily settle down under some kind of authority which provides him with a mandate for his life and nurtures his equanimity.

The most cursory glance at the works of Paulo Freire shakes to its foundations the modernist's hold on his/her world. All but the most intransigent of modernists could not fail to be induced to take a serious personal inventory of their perceptions. While the words 'modernism' and 'postmodernism' make no appearance in Freire's works, his major writings – *Pedagogy of the Oppressed* (1972), *Educating for Critical Consciousness* (1974) and *Pedagogy of Hope* (1995) – present serious criticisms of the influence of modernism in education.

Notwithstanding the fact that Freire's ideas sprang from the social struggles in Latin America in the 1950s and 1960s, Freire can now, through his writings, claim the whole world as his classroom. What began as an attempt to perfect a method for teaching disinher-ited adult illiterates in Latin America now points the microscope at current education practice to reveal it as a potentially oppressive force – a shock to modernists who believe that education represents liberation. Who can peel away the unconscious layers of acceptance of the modernist *truths* about education and reveal current educational practice as, not an agent of freedom, but an instrument of oppression? Freire (1972) can, with a deft, devastating hand. He draws our attention to the fetish of current education with 'banking', that is, the creation of deposits of information to be given to students. It is a natural consequence of the banking concept that the function of the educator is to control the way the world *enters into* the student. Mace's (1974) admonition to 'ask not what is inside your head, but what your head is inside of' (in Ainley, 2000), strikes a chord with Freire's writings, confirming, as it does, that paradoxically, learning does not primarily occur within the head of the individual but is to be found in shared consciousness and practice. Freire (1972) points out that the practice of education as 'the exercise of domination, stimulates the credulity of students, with the ideological intent (often not perceived by educators) of indoctrinating them to adapt to the world of oppression' (p. 52).

Education in the Freire (1974) mould, on the other hand, is the practice of liberty because it emancipates both lecturer and student from the binary spell of silence and monologue whereas education for domination breeds passivity.

> The educated man is the adapted man because he can fit or mould himself to the world ... this concept is well suited to the purposes of the oppressors, whose tranquility rests on how well men fit the world the oppressors have created, and how little they question it.
>
> (1972, p. 50)

It is interesting to note in this context the public scepticism in relation to college education for women in America in the early twentieth century. Such an education would raise a woman's aspirations above her station.

> A man would not love a learned wife. Better far to teach young ladies to be correct in their manners, respectable in their families, and agreeable in society ... They were such delicate creatures, so different in mental as well as in physical make-up from men, that they would never be able to survive the prolonged intellectual effort.
>
> (Brubacher & Rudy, 1976, p. 65)

In the context of banking education the lecturer is both oppressor and oppressed. An *oppressor* in delivering a system of education which kills creativity and questioning – Gibb (in Carroll, 1998) asserts that lectures are constructed to inhibit students from asking questions – and *oppressed* in being straitjacketed in the role of educator as one who *knows* despite his foundational intuition that his own education can only progress through mediation with the world, including students. Gibbs and Iacovidou (2004) reflect Freire's (1972) sentiments concerning the potential of education to be an oppressive force. They suggest that the use of external measurement as an indicator of quality creates a 'pedagogy of confinement' (p. 113). It restricts students to the technicalities of the workplace rather than emancipating them to develop their potential as human beings. Dunne (1995) advocates what he calls 'instructional conversation' (p. 79), which, he admits, seems something of a paradox with instruction implying planning and authority and conversation implying equality and responsiveness. It is the teacher's task, he says, to resolve the paradox. Students should have the courage to undertake risks in attempting to achieve an understanding rather than relying on 'correct answer compromise' (p. 79). Corry (2005) also echoes Freire's theme: 'The education experience is not neutral. It has the capacity for domestication or freedom. It can dampen down the spirit, will and creativity of a child through testing, labeling, outdated curricula, in a constant atmosphere of judgement and comparison'.

Freire's *concientisation* (1974) has many resonances with Habermas' (1989) key political emphasis on radical democracy. Both demonstrate an unswerving belief in the achievement, over time, of emancipatory social thought through the medium of dialogue. Neither Freire nor Corry attend to the postmodern rejection of emancipation as a grand narrative.

Freire's use of vocabulary appears to be modernist rather than postmodern. There appears little sign of indeterminacy of language in the starkness of the descriptors 'sadistic' and 'necrophilic'. He borrows from Fromm (1966) to explain that the aim of sadism is to transform a man into a thing, since total control causes the living to lose one essential quality of life – freedom. 'Sadism', says Freire (1972), is perverted love, a love of death, not of life. Thus one of the characteristics of the oppressor consciousness and its necrophilic view of the world is sadism. As the oppressor consciousness, in order to dominate, tries to thwart the seeking, restless impulse, and the creative power that characterises life, it kills life

(p. 36)

– a wake up call for educators who deliver easily digestible packets of information to students and examine, just their memory in most cases, for formulaic answers. This is lifeless education, thwarting any impulse on the part of the student to learn creatively. Such an education, in James' (2004) view is simply geared to grade students for the job market as 'subservient worker bees' (p. 77). Claiming that education encourages subordination and conformity, James reflects Foucault's view that knowledge, instead of being a conduit for liberation, may be used to confine and discipline.

Bloland's fairly positive assertion that, currently, institutions of higher education are still able to offer legitimacy and credentials that promise to give graduates an initial start on middle class careers can be countered by Freire's (1972) view that 'those who are invaded, whatever their level, rarely go beyond the models which the invaders prescribe for them' (p. 48) – a natural firewall for the oppressors who continue the cycle and a reinforcement of Marx's view that 'it is not the consciousness of men that determines their existence, but their social exclusion that determines their consciousness' (in Lee 1993). This also supports Mace's stance that behaviour is determined more by external context and the behaviour of the group than on what is going on inside our heads (in Ainley, 2000).

Applying the metaphor of necrophilia to education may provoke a feeling of revulsion in the reader, but a compelling revulsion which holds the reader in thrall and encourages further reading of Freire (1972).

Oppression – overwhelming control – is necrophilic; it is nourished by love of death, not life. The banking concept of education, which serves the interests of oppression, is also necrophilic. Based on a mechanistic, static, naturalistic, spatialised view of consciousness; it transforms students into receiving objects.

(p. 51)

In his poem, *The Leaden Eyed*, Vachel Lindsay, supports the theme 'it is the world's sore crime its babes grow dull'.

Freire (1972) reveals the educator–student relationship as fundamentally *narrative* in character. He paints a vignette of a narrating subject (educator) and patient, listening objects (students).

> The contents, whether volumes or empirical dimensions of reality, tend in the process of being narrated to become lifeless and petrified ... The teacher talks about reality as if it were motionless, static, compartmentalised and predictable ... his task is to fill students with the contents of his narration, contents which are detached from reality. ... Words are emptied of their concreteness and become a hollow, alienated and alienating verbosity.
>
> (p. 45)

Should an educator, reading Freire, seek to salve his/her guilt-stricken conscience and attempt to make amends to the oppressed, Freire (1972) deconstructs this sentiment and warns against 'false generosity' (p. 36). The generosity of oppressors is copper-fastened by an unjust order, which must be maintained in order to justify that generosity. Even oppressors who join the oppressed in their struggle do not come alone but with the baggage of their prejudice and a lack of confidence in the ability of the oppressed to want, to know, to think, to create. The generosity of such a 'convert' is just as false, founded as it is on the will of the convert to be the executor of the transformation. 'A real humanist can be identified more by his trust in the people, which engages him in their struggle, than by a thousand actions in their favour without that trust' (p. 36).

Freire (1972) reminds us that those who support the cause of liberation are themselves informed by the environment which generates the banking concept and often do not perceive its impact or its dehumanising power. One cannot, he says, emancipate by creating another deposit. For the oppressors *to be* is *to have* and to be of the having class even at the expense of those oppressed who must, therefore, have less. The oppressors see themselves as worthy of having because they themselves have made an effort and therefore deserve. Situated on this moral high ground they feel justified in their view that the oppressed are idle and incompetent. They condemn their envy and their lack of gratitude – these traits show them to be enemies who must be watched. It is functional to hold these opinions in order to preserve the hegemony which status differences bestow. 'The inarticulate always has the last word' (Polanyi, 1958, p. 71).

A reader who may be faced with students who have access to very high disposable incomes may be puzzled that they can be described as oppressed. Baudrillard (1998) reminds us that the fact that economic inequality is no longer a problem is itself a real problem. The illusion of choice and sovereignty, exercised in consumption, blinds us to the shifting of inequality to a more general social field where, 'functioning more subtly, it makes itself all the more irreversible' (p. 55). Bloom (1987) supports this view. What students lack is what is most necessary, he says, that is 'a real basis for discontent with the present and awareness that there are alternatives to it' (p. 61). Baudrillard also finds allies in Habermas (1987, 1989) and Illich, both of whom express concern that in modern society human beings lack freedom. Rich and poor alike depend on education to form their worldview. This education exercises a monopoly over the social imagination. Such dependence means that people abdicate responsibility for their own growth leading, for many, to 'a kind of spiritual suicide' (Illich, p. 60). Illich further reminds us that as long as we remain unaware of the rite through which we are shaped into progressive consumers – society's major resource – we cannot break the hex of this economy and develop a new one. Modern man, he says, exists in a vortex of his own creation. The spectre of rising expectations is merely the institutionalisation of permanent disappointment and existentialist angst – the denial of the exercise of what Marx calls man's *species being*. Institutions, including educational institutions, both create needs and control their satisfaction, thereby annihilating man's creativity. Marcuse (1986) also offers support for Baudrillard's (1998) view. He argues that the affluence of the working class is not the manifestation of a new social utopia but, instead, represents the stronger grip of capitalism in the exercise of control over extended areas of working class life.

Freire (1972, 1974, 1998) acknowledges that his ideas are for radicals. Radicalism is always creative, underpinned, as it is, by a critical spirit. There are many who would brand as innocents, dreamers, revolutionaries, reactionaries, or *lefties* those who would challenge the status quo of educational practice. The unitarist perspective on conflict, supported by modernism and the teachings of the great western churches, sees difference as an aberration, threatening rather than creative, and therefore, something to be silenced. Differences are not accommodated and dissenters are viewed with suspicion. Suppression of conflict is functional – it protects the status quo and the petrified system beloved of modernists whose own position can only be maintained by the excluding nature of sectarianism. Sectarianism, according to Freire (1972), is in all cases castrating, it makes myths and thereby alienates, whereas radicalism is critical and emancipates. 'Sectarianism because it is myth making and irrational turns reality into a false (and therefore unchangeable) reality', he warns (1972, p. 17).

Habermas' (1987) writings reflect Freire's (1974) approach to education, asserting that *communicative action* is the foundation for emancipatory thinking. He differentiates between instrumental reason, which has achieved hegemony in today's world, and dialogue which has the power to transform societies into genuine democracies.

Freire's (1974) optimism that *education for critical consciousness* can emancipate the individual is not reflected in the views of Caillois (1960), Bataille or Lacan (in Barglow, 2001). Caillois and his circle of French intellectuals deliberately distance their position from those of the left, insisting, for example, that there exists in some individuals a measure of intrinsic willed, and even enjoyed, experience of domination and powerlessness. The social etiology of their views is relevant. Benjamin (in Barglow) criticises Caillois' notion of voluntary servitude, recognising that Caillois and his coterie were in the business of legitimating current authoritarian movements, thus carving out a path which would be followed by their intellectual descendants in the French New Right of the 1960s. Caillois exhibits a sceptical approach to democratic aspirations and supports social stratification which he views as necessary. He shares the Lacanian perspective that the individual wishes to blend in – '... inevitably drawn towards the annihilation of his own separateness. Camouflage is protection, a way of staying alive, but only by simulating death' (in Barglow).

Caillois draws a parallel between the behaviour of the individual who chooses powerlessness and that of the cricket faced with the preying mantis. Barglow identifies a third response in this situation over and above the fight or flight dynamic with which we are all familiar – a response which, instead, incapacitates the person. This incapacitation may be the lot of the student oppressed by a system of banking education.

Freire (1998) would not agree that individuals choose oppression. He disagrees with the notion of docility as a character trait and asserts that it is the result of formation through a historical or sociological situation. His *model of education for critical consciousness* (1974) presents this type of education as a subversive anarchic force. The word subversive has negative connotations, particularly for the modernist mind. But surely it can only be negative to those whose position in the current (unjust) system might be at risk? 'Oppressors care neither to have the world revealed nor to have it translated as empowering. The sectarian oppressor sees the oppressed as the pathology of a healthy society – marginals who need to be integrated' (1972, p. 48).

The method of integration chosen is the banking education system, the humanist approach of which masks its objective to turn students into robots who fit the society structured for them by the oppressing class. Education as the *practice of freedom*, according to Freire (1972), is

> not the transfer or transmission of knowledge or cultures, ... nor the extension of technical knowledge, ... nor the act of depositing reports or facts in the educatee, ... not an attempt to adapt the educated to the milieu, ... Education as the practice of freedom is a truly gnosiological[1] situation.
>
> (1974, p. 149)

To *know* is to intervene in one's reality, according to Freire (1974). Developing critical consciousness is contingent upon the educators'

---

[1] Gnosiological – from *Gnosis* a special knowledge of spiritual things.

willingness to shift away from their current position, which is opposite
the position of students, in order to seek a reconciliation – 'a solution
of the teacher-student contradiction so that both are simultaneously
teachers and students' (1972, p. 46).

Writing almost 40 years ago, Postman and Weingartner (1969) also
criticise the traditional system of education which, they say, focuses on
the product (predetermined curriculum and test scores) and diverts
our attention from the complex processes at work in learning. They
promote the notion of teaching as a subversive activity, that is, a
conscious act of teaching based on the 'inquiry method' (p. 27). This
method is not designed to improve what older, traditional methods
do. It works in a completely different fashion – in fact a subversive
fashion.

> It activates different senses, attitudes, and perceptions; it generates
> a different, bolder, and more potent kind of intelligence. Thus it will
> cause teachers and their tests, and their grading systems, and their
> curriculum to change. It will cause college admissions requirements
> to change. It will cause everything to change.
>
> (p. 27)

In challenging the traditional approaches to education Postman and
Weingartner describe school as a place where real issues are not dealt
with. Education, they suggest in a stinging criticism, is a game called
'Let's Pretend' and if that name were chiselled into the front of every
educational institution in America there would be, at least, an honest
acknowledgement of what takes place there. This game, they say, is
based on a set of pretences which include:

> Let's pretend that you are not as you are and that this sort of work
> makes a difference to your lives; let's pretend that what bores you
> is important and that the more you are bored, the more important
> it is; let's pretend that there are certain things that everyone must
> know, and that both questions and answers about them have been
> fixed for all time; let's pretend that your intellectual competence
> can be judged on the basis of how well you can play Let's Pretend.
>
> (p. 49)

Postman and Weingartner suggest that when learning environments are no longer based on the teaching of trivia the entire psychological context of education is transformed. Learning is no longer a battle between the student and something outside him/her. 'This is the basis of the process of learning how to learn, how to deal with the otherwise meaningless, how to cope with change that requires new meanings to be made' (p. 97).

While Freire's (1974) ideas on education for critical consciousness have tremendous appeal it has to be questioned if reaching critical consciousness comes at the expense of dialogue. Mejia (2004) describes the irreconcilable tension between the two pillars of Freire's philosophy. He suggests that, in order to stimulate enquiry, a neo-Marxist reading is imposed. Without this imposition the students may remain passive and may not enquire but, with it, the conscientisation achieved results in a convergence of knowledge – the kind of knowledge that is underpinned by a neo-Marxist perspective.

Taylor (1993) suggests that, not alone the questions posed by the educator, but their sequence, carry with them implicitly the answer required. Buckingham (1998) and Mejia point to the prisoner's dilemma with which the student is faced. If students resist a traditional or banking approach this is hailed as a struggle for freedom. If, on the other hand, they resist a form of critical pedagogy they are described as having done so because they are oppressed – they have internalised the dominant ideology. In all cases the judgement call is made by the educator. Even if the students discover generative themes for themselves it is the educator who can assess whether or not they have been perceived in a proper, undistorted way. Mejia cites Buckingham, Taylor and Burbules (1993) in support of his view, that in the struggle for the reconciliation of dialogue and critical consciousness, dialogue has been the victim. Mejia suggests that Freire himself recognised some of these difficulties and modified some aspects of his philosophy throughout the years – in later times he conceded that the teacher is not in exactly the same position as the students. Writing in 1998 about the being and becoming of a teacher Freire suggests that when we live our lives with the authenticity demanded by the dual role of teachers as learners and teachers we participate in a total experience 'that is simultaneously directive, political, ideological, gnostic, pedagogical, aesthetic and ethical' (1998, pp. 31–32).

The boundary crossing and necessary exploration of new terrain advocated by Freire (1974) and Habermas (1987) finds voice also in the work of David Whyte, corporate poet and seminarist. He encourages what he calls 'courageous conversation', that is, a diligent effort to explore our understandings and to convey them to others. Once something honest is said the relationship is emancipated to a new level; there is no going back. In an echo of Freire's (1972) dictum that to know is to intervene in one's reality, Whyte (2004) quotes Robert Frost 'my object in living is to unite my avocation with my vocation' – a recognition that, in Freire's opinion man's ontological vocation is to act upon and transform his world. As Whyte (2004) puts it, 'there are questions in our life and in society that have no right to go away . . . we must engage in conversation to negotiate the frontier'.

The frontier, he says, drawing on his experience as a marine zoologist, is where most life is created. Where water meets land, where currents and temperature collide, that is where natural life is most interesting, adaptive and creative. It is the same in the human world, provided that the edges are negotiated with openness. Should Freire's educator register discomfort in the shift from teaching the student to learning from what the student brings to the situation, Whyte (2004) reassures us that this dissonance is to be expected. One of the measures of the success of courageous conversation, he says, is that we wish we hadn't had the conversation. We never emerge intact because we have had to let go of some protocols. The world is a place of revelation, not one we can manipulate for ourselves. This is a direct contradiction of the world as it is perceived by Freire's oppressor, for whom prescription is the chosen method of communication *to* the oppressed, a prescription, which is the imposition of one person's choice upon the other, a colonisation of the mind of the oppressed by the consciousness of the oppressor. If we refuse to have the conversation, refuse to listen, we become bullies, manipulators, Whyte (2004) warns us; if we do not use our own voice, we become victims. Good poetry, according to Whyte (2004) can provide explosive insight, grant needed courage and stir the dormant imagination of individuals to respond to the call for increased creativity and adaptability in the complexity of the postmodern world.

In an amusing cameo, (that can be seen as a criticism of the banking system of education), Whyte (2004) describes his experience as a naturalist guide in the Galapagos Islands. None of the wildlife had studied the same zoology books as he had done! Stop trying to fit life into quadrants, he warns, and just pay attention: listen and observe and negotiate the edges and frontiers by having the courageous conversation. What is the conversation we are *not* having, he challenges us, with our bosses/customers/students/ patients/partners and, most importantly, with ourselves? For any of us who are troubled by the authenticity of our work, he admonishes that too many people *haunt* their life instead of living it, they are sold to the system. In Wordsworth's words, 'bonds unknown to me were given . . .'. Wordsworth was vowed to the priesthood in childhood, the rest of us vowed by parents, teachers, ancestors, to the system. In Whyte's (2004) own words: 'we shape the way we face the world and by the world are shaped again'. A major part of our lives is predicated on defence of the status quo. He draws on Robert Blythe's translation of Rilke. 'All of you undisturbed cities, have you ever yearned for the enemy, because the enemy here is light itself?' – an affirmation of Jung's assertion that in adversity we meet ourselves; an affirmation, too, of the emancipative consequences of Freire's education for teacher and student alike and the potentially emancipative consequences of unsought change. Whyte (2004) reminds us of the contrasting philosophies of east and west. In the west, he says, we look for one individual idea and all support. In the east an idea is sculpted from the background and then given individual voice. Courageous conversation must necessarily be fierce at times, sometimes confrontational. But if we do not have the courage to engage in conversation all is not lost in terms of employment opportunities, Whyte (2004) reassures us with great irony 'there are plenty of dinosaur companies out there who would be delighted to have us'.

Writing almost 40 years earlier, Hayakawa (1965) makes even greater claims for poetry and education. An understanding of language, literature and history constitutes an agent for world peace, he says. He emphasises the civilising nature of literature and its importance in widening consciousness and understanding. Like Becker (1980), he recognises the importance of the symbolic in human life. The production and enjoyment of literature are symbolic devices which equip us for day to day living. Poetry and the arts, he says, fulfil a necessary biological function for a symbol using class in helping us to maintain psychological health and equilibrium. Asserting that poetry is the most efficient use of language because it condenses the affective elements of language into patterns of infinite subtlety, he draws on Graves who suggests that a well-chosen collection of poetry is a complete dispensary of medicine for preventing and curing common mental disorders. Using an analogy with processed food, which has the semblance of nourishment but contains little, he warns against certain kinds of literature and entertainment which will not assist one's spiritual nourishment. Fantasy living, he says, can be exacerbated by the consumption of what he calls 'narcotic literature' (p. 150). Acknowledging that the relationship between literature and life is by no means fully understood, he, nevertheless, cautions us to be aware that some kinds of literature keep us permanently infantile and immature in our evaluations – a warning he extends in his later (Hayakawa et al., 1990) work to television and other media. Hutton (2007) agrees with Hayakawa. Poetry, he says, understands and celebrates the frailty of the human condition with a humanity and insight that is breathtaking. In a swipe at low educational standards in the United Kingdom he finds it astounding that, while people understand that knowing the biology of their forebears is important to the understanding of their own health, 'there is no such readiness to want to get to grips with our past when it comes to culture, politics and values' (p. 23).

Chapter 3

Education Systems – Education as an Industry

The theme of the ironclad nature of the system and our unwitting part in it is expressed also in the work of Chaharbaghi and Newman (1998). They provide a Popper-like falsification scenario in an effort to explore our understanding of organized education. The model they use is conspiracy theory, the central assumption of which is that the government makes an implicit deal with the providers of education to compete for a diminishing supply of natural resources in the form of the unemployed through a system of artificial values that the providers can determine for themselves. In exchange, the suppliers of education must provide a custodial factory system for these unemployed. The context for this scenario is increasing unemployment due to globalisation and greater efficiencies. The challenges for the education providers are, first, to reduce expectations and diminish the potential for social unrest through delaying entry to the work market and, second, to transmit middle class social values to this potentially volatile population. The myth to which all concerned subscribe is that there will be employment opportunities for those who serve their custodial sentences and behave with minimal disruption and controversy. In addition there will be discouragement towards measurement of the value of the product; volume and not utility is what counts. The custodial experience must not be too taxing intellectually, which means a lowering of standards, so that everyone does well. Through extolling the virtues of lifelong learning some *prisoners* may even be encouraged to undertake life sentences to extend their stay in childhood, gain higher qualifications, further postpone workplace entry and allow others to shoulder the responsibility for society and the economy.

If the exchange here described is to take place successfully a number of conditions must be satisfied. First of all, there must be a convincing explanation or there will be a public outcry. Secondly, the monopolistic market must be engineered so that the manufacturers of educational products become their own consumers, a point also expressed by Illich. Thirdly, an apparent level of competition must be demonstrated, for example, through league tables or the provision of different suites of courses. An opposing and ongoing public debate is stoked, with the government selling education as the key to jobs and social progress for all while the providers badger the government for more and more resources.

> In this way the government pretends to regulate the education economy by imposing fees on the real consumers while, at the same time, forcing those on state benefits to enter the artificial market to ensure sufficient volume that, in turn, ensures economy of scale and selling of existing capacity which would remain otherwise unsold.
>
> (p. 511)

It is important in this scenario, the authors say, that the consumers do not suspect that the market is rigged or they will not participate. In order to encourage greater and greater participation on a countrywide basis, the government promotes the following messages: only the idle and lazy refuse higher education; qualifications open employment doors; you will become a member of middle class international; there is a ladder of opportunity for all willing to consume more and more education – 'a Doctorate becoming the ultimate currency which qualifies you to join the factory which qualified you ...' (p. 511).

The threat to the success of this model, the authors acknowledge, lies in the resistance of those practitioners who wish to pursue a kind of education, which is creative and developmental for the educator and educatee alike – Freire's (1974) *Education for Critical Consciousness*, in fact. This is a minor problem for the model however, as power is shifted to administrators who ensure maximum control, minimum deviation and an alienation of real educators so that they can be replaced by pseudo-educators who are happy to 'exercise irresponsibility in the form of artificial work' (p. 511) – a situation described too by Lumby and Tomlinson (2000) who note that managerialism and professionalism are 'oppositional cultures' (p. 139). Quality control procedures are orchestrated both to corral and give direction to those who lack focus and also to silence those who oppose the factory system. And, since a superior validating authority oversees quality control procedures, no one asks the fundamental question – what is the point of quality control procedures in a factory which produces products that serve no real purpose? Rorty (1989) offers a postmodern solution to those educators who are alienated by this system – they can invoke the Jefferson compromise. This means that an individual faced with a situation with which s/he has difficulty but which is broadly accepted by the public at large, must be prepared to sacrifice his/her conscience for the sake of public expediency. Informed by pragmatism and having no *skyhook* from which to hang his opinions, Rorty seems to take no cognisance of the personal angst which may be incurred by an educator in attempting to extinguish the kind of moral accountability described by Gibbs and Iacovidou.

Chaharbaghi and Newman describe the inexorable shift towards the quantification of education which was exacerbated by the cold war where 'the volume of research papers published on both sides became auxiliary matrices to those who inspected and evaluated the relative sources of power on either side, beginning with megatonnage and inadvertently counting academic output in the same paradigm' (p. 512).

Chaharbaghi's and Newman's seductive falsification paradigm overturns the vernacular view of education. Although there is no suggestion that a conspiracy in education does, in fact, exist we must be cognisant that, as Freire (1972) insists, methodological failings can always be traced to ideological errors. Coren (2005), in an article which is less learned, but may appear to many educators to be hysterically apposite, supports the view of Chaharbaghi and Newman that higher education is politically manipulated. She suggests that this is a widespread phenomenon. Tony Blair is not the only person committed to university places for all. Her amusing insight bears witness to the unprecedented increase in the bureaucratic accreditation of learning in recent decades.

British educational theory has been, for some time, that one must chase after teenagers and throw qualifications at them, creating academic disciplines out of tourism, media and sport. If they refuse to engage, then we simply enlarge the syllabus further until it engulfs whatever they happen to be interested in. There is no hiding from qualifications, kids! If you bunk off maths and skulk behind the bike sheds listening to your iPod, we will hunt you down and give you a degree in Ipod Studies or Bike Culture.

To underline her allusion to esoteric educational courses she reports the boom in enrolment in an Austrian school following the publication of Rowling's *Harry Potter and the Half Blood Prince*. Set up in 2003 and located in Klagenfurt, this school provides education in astrology, magic and potion making. This is an example of the erosion of the boundary between high and low culture already identified by Bloland and an example of the respectability awarded to low culture through cross colonisation by academics.

Illich, the most radical of radicals (some would describe him as a heresiarch) also reflects these ideas. He describes education as an unusual industry where producers are their own consumers and which continually lobbies for more and more investment. Education today, he says, 'confuses process with substance, teaching with learning, grade advancement with education, a diploma with competence' (p. 1).

Our imagination is 'schooled' to accept service in place of value. Medical treatment is a simulacrum for healthcare, social work is seen as community development and a qualification as education. Social advancement, he says, depends not on demonstrated competence but on the 'learning pedigree by which it is supposedly acquired' (p. 16). In Illich's view, educational institutions have the effect of polarising society, grading the nations of the world according to an 'international caste system' (p. 9). Asserting that the poor need funds to enable them to learn, not to treat them for their perceived deficiencies, he dispels the illusions that school is either efficient or effective. Learning, he says, is the human activity which least needs manipulation. He may alarm well-meaning practitioners with his claim that most learning is not the result of teaching. He is not saying that people learn nothing through school but simply that what they do learn could be taught more cheaply and more effectively through another medium. For him context is immeasurably important. For example, learning a language is more likely to be achieved if one is immersed in a meaningful setting, i.e. living, travelling or working abroad. While many people learn to read at school, any love of reading they may possess does not occur *because* of school; if it did, reading as a hobby would be more evenly distributed throughout the population. Illich's claim for the effectiveness of learning outside of school is supported by Ball (1996) who draws attention to the fact that almost all children learn their first language between the ages of 1 and 5 years. We never, in our lives, do anything as clever again, he says, and it is done without the help of professional teachers across the entire spectrum of ability range. Illich is keen to point out that although current educational practice is inefficient this does not mean that planned learning does not benefit from planned instruction, both of which, he says, are in need of improvement. He deplores the unwillingness of institutions to take account of the extraordinary learning capacity of the child's first four years, a point also raised by Abbott (2002). His claims about school apply, too, to higher education. Reform, however, must start with early education; trying to achieve reform of higher education, he says, is like trying to effect slum clearance from the 12th floor up. His dark impressions of organized education conclude that it serves neither justice nor learning because educators insist on including certification with instruction. The rights of the individual to exercise competence to learn or to instruct is pre-empted by the closed shop of certified teachers. In turn, the competence of the teacher is restricted by the constraints of the syllabus. The value of education is undermined by its counterproductive action, by which a fundamentally beneficial process is turned into a negative one. Ives and Jarvenpaa (1996) offer some hope to Illich with their suggestion that the advent of e-learning will push aside certification in favour of demonstrated skills or work products and, even in so far as certification continues, it will no longer be the sole preserve of universities or professional associations.

Illich is not against schools, hospitals and other institutions per se, but asserts that beyond a certain level of institutionalisation negative returns apply. Schools reduce peoples' capacity for thinking, hospitals make people more sick. Like Chaharbaghi and Newman, Illich draws our attention to the latent functions of education systems – custodial care, selection, indoctrination and learning. What students learn at school is to subscribe to a particular worldview and to develop a dependence on experts who can search out pre-formulated answers to the world's problems – a point also made by Handy (1996). The education system, says Illich, is the 'repository of society's myth, the institutionalisation of that myth's contradictions and the locus of the ritual which reproduces and veils the disparity between myth and reality' (p. 37).

Intellectually emasculating, current education becomes the advertising agency that makes us believe we need society as it is. It is the game itself, not learning, that gets into the blood and becomes a habit. People embark on a credential collection journey and pursue more and more certificates because these labels provide the passport to enable them to fit into a world which promotes consumption as success. Their social regression is so comprehensive that they are not aware of the initiation and ongoing nature of the ritual which shapes their cosmos. 'In the schooled world the road to happiness is paved with the consumer index' (p. 40). The mind conceives of the world as a 'pyramid of classified packages accessible only to those who carry the proper tags' (p. 76).

The educational system is an example of regressive taxation, undertaken mostly by the already privileged. Poor parents, recognising that poverty is defined by the distance one falls behind in some advertised ideal of consumption, are less concerned with what their children learn than with the certificate and what they will earn.

Illich recognises that his views will be received with more alarm than enlightenment. They threaten the consumer economy, individual privilege and the self-image of the western world. Such is the level of indoctrination that any alternative to established education lies 'within the conceptual blindspot' (p. 70). The work is an easy target for institutionalised minds which cannot conceive of alternative educational processes, or perhaps, which fear the collapse of the consumption-driven world as we know it. For others, however, Illich presents a courageous, imaginative viewpoint which offers an escape from the psychic prison of systematised, confined and routinised thinking. His ideas have become an ongoing conversation (a *conspiracy*, in the etymological sense of *breathing together*) for fearless thinkers.

Current reading of Illich presents one exceptionally jarring note. Writing in 1972 he wonders if Mao's Cultural Revolution might be the first successful attempt to dis-establish school. To be fair to Illich, however, it must be borne in mind that Mao's apparent attempt at democratisation fired the imagination of many in the west at the time. The knowledge that Cultural Revolution was, at best, a misnomer which gave rise to abhorrent abuses only became known in the west in recent times, notably through the work of Jung Chang (1991).

Reflecting the assertions of Bloland, Edwards, Ainley (2000), Lyotard and others that education is now performativity driven, Chaharbaghi and Newman remind us that until the 1960s the university defended the right of the individual to free speech but made no connection between knowledge and wealth. To get on in the world the scholar first had to join it. In the words of Illich, the old university was a 'liberated zone for discovery and the discussion of ideas ... a community of academic quest and endemic unrest ... which in the modern multiversity ... has fled to the fringes' (p. 35).

Kalantzis (1998) warns, however, not to underestimate the importance of the education-work nexus but advises us to situate education on the objectives of social cohesion and individual well-being as well as a robust economy. She supports Marrington and Rowe's (2004) view that while there is no guarantee against poverty 'education is a critical path to mobility' (p. 3). Dunne (1995) also cautions against dismissing the instrumental role of education. Asserting that only a saint or a mystic could, without being hypocritical, deny the importance of financial rewards, he reminds us that such a high minded notion of education sprang from ancient Greece which, despite being the birthplace of democracy, did not itself act in a democratic fashion. Only a small proportion of its adults were citizens and free to access education, but their freedom was bought by the slavery of the disenfranchised who constituted the majority. Dunne (1995) regrets that the espousal of a production-driven society has the effect of harbouring 'colonising ambitions' (p. 61) towards education, ambitions 'casually betrayed in its language' (p. 61). Concern with the economy excludes more humanistic ones, especially the artistic and the spiritual. The problem with extrinsic rewards is that, because they are so powerful, they displace intrinsic rewards, so that education, while in one sense gaining the world, at the same time loses its soul. He warns that if educators are not vigilant in respect of the intrinsic values of education there is no shortage of other goods which will be pressed upon them. He resists the notion that educators should have to take their cues from the emergent society and bend their efforts to serve its needs. Instead, education should facilitate people to critically evaluate their own society and to shape their lives within it.

Casazza (1996) finds that the link between work and education has a long history in the American university. In the first half of the nineteenth century higher education was designed simply to develop the character of young gentlemen with Greek, Latin and mathematics in order to 'strengthen the muscle of their minds' (p. 13). As long ago as 1850 there was a call to give students practical instruction and not just a classical-literary course suitable only for the 'aristocracy' (p. 11). Indeed, such was the bias, in black colleges, in favour of performativity that funding was more easily achieved when a trade curriculum was offered – one college discovered that the only way it could offer Latin was to call it Agricultural Latin. These colleges, which were founded especially for black students, offered instruction which was at a lower level than average because black students, already suffering disadvantage, were poorly prepared for college. Despite the recognition of the education/work connection, however, a philosophy of elitism still informed many universities. There was resistance to admitting women, fearing that they would lower standards. While black men were admitted to university the policy of segregation was continued, especially in the South, and their curriculum provided, overwhelmingly, technical syllabi. According to Casazza, however, women and blacks themselves believed that success and career advancement hinged on a traditional curriculum. Reluctant classicists feared that the extension of traditional studies to include technical disciplines would lower standards. In a university which introduced a science curriculum the hope was expressed that any student who enrolled on this 'barely useful' course might become hooked on education and advance to the study of what was 'ideal and beautiful' (p. 12).

Chapter 4

Naming the Industry's Products – Education Terminologies

The meanings of the words education, knowledge, information, skill, learning, teaching and training – often used interchangeably – demand, in the author's view, some examination at this juncture. An understanding of education may be gleaned from John Masefield's 1946 address to the University of Sheffield when he described a university as

> a place where those who hate ignorance may strive to know, where those who perceive truth may strive to make others see; where seekers and learners alike, banded together in the search for knowledge, will honour thought in all its finer ways, will welcome thinkers in distress or in exile, will uphold ever the dignity of thought and learning and will exact standards in these things.
>
> (Chaharbaghi & Newman, p. 509)

Freire's thoughts on education (1972, 1974, 1998), distilled from the richness and complexity of his writings, echo those of Masefield and suggest that education is the development of critical consciousness within the individual in order to allow him to follow his ontological vocation to be a *subject* who acts upon and transforms his world, rather than simply a receiving *object*.

Chaharbaghi and Newman see education as an individualistic experience, the outcome of which is self-realization and personal growth. It concerns 'broadening capacities and understanding using a divergent, creative and meaning-oriented approach' (p. 513). They suggest that the (1997) Dearing Report (a report criticised by Trow (1998) as being unreasonably constrained because it was chaired by a civil servant who had to be cognisant of political sensibilities) sees education as a commodity which, like industry, must be made ever more efficient; the medium has become more important than the message and the aim is to pre-package the data so that only one conclusion can be made. Nietzsche, in a paragraph which finds a reflection in Freire's sentiments, sees the educator as

> a divining rod for every grain of gold which has lain long in the prison of much mud and sand; the genius of the heart from whose touch everyone goes away richer, not favoured and surprised, not as if blessed and oppressed with the goods of others, but richer in himself, newer to himself than before, broken open, ... more fragile, more broken but full of hopes that as yet have no names, full of new will and current, full of new ill-will and counter current.
>
> (in Ainley, 2000)

The quest for honesty at all costs, a Nietzschean trademark, is expressed in his thoughts about religion, which the author feels can be applied to education too. 'Do you wish to strive for peace of mind and happiness, well then believe; do you wish to be a disciple of truth, then inquire (in McDonald, 1968, p. 506).

Tomlinson et al. (1992) define teaching as an interaction which involves activity by one person (the teacher) designed to promote learning by another person or persons (the learners). In as far as learning may be defined as the acquisition of capacities or values as a result of action or experience, teaching involves engaging learners in activities and/or experience whereby they are likely to learn, i.e. acquire capacities or values.

Drawing on chaos theory, Haas (2004) describes her hope that the 'butterfly effect' (p. 13) will apply. That is, that small events which occur during a 60-minute class will change someone for the better, for a lifetime. This hope sustains her when her pedagogical idealism takes a beating, when she is attempting to teach students who see education in a reified way, those students who 'seem convinced that while buying the books is compulsory, reading them is optional' (p. 13). Murray (2005) draws on Ricoeur to describe the meeting of minds or *intertextuality* which results in a *story*. A psychologist is created by clients and a writer only becomes a writer when read.

In the same way a teacher can only become a teacher if a student learns.

Abbott says that learning is a consequence of thinking, not of instruction. The whole brain, including the emotions, has to be engaged – a point also underlined by Chia (1999), Dilthey (in Moncayo) and others. He suggests that technology can be harnessed in order to free up resources for better use – the curriculum need no longer be constrained by the speed of paper and pencil – a concept also discussed by Sambataro, Ives and Jarvenpaa, and Ball (1996). For example, technology can reduce six weeks of class teaching to four and a half minutes. But, he says it is not being used. UK 'A' level students are still spending the same number of lessons studying a subject as they did forty years ago. Abbott says that real learning is about being able to negotiate one's environment. He deplores the neglect of the child's most productive learning phase, 0–4 years and agrees with Eric Heffer MP that the system of education in the United Kingdom, upside-down and inside-out, serves to over-school but under-educate. He draws on his experiences as a teacher who brought students to Saudi Arabia on geography and geology trips. A Saudi guide was incredulous and asked why these students were not learning about the world from their fathers. This loss of learning opportunity has the effect of beginning the pruning of the human brain as early as age four, with completion at age seven, with the result that adolescents are not equipped to handle the life and learning changes which require responsibility. Abbott suggests that there is considerable political and institutional inertia locked up in current educational systems, a point also made forcibly by Illich and by Chaharbaghi and Newman.

O'Donoghue and Maguire (2005) note the perceptible shift, evident in official texts and rhetoric (Delors, 1996; European Commission, 2001) from education to learning and from lifelong education to lifelong learning. They define learning as an individual process unique to the learner, whereas education is an organized set of activities. Lifelong learning is life long and life wide and encompasses all learning that takes place in all settings, formal, informal and the workplace. A central goal of education is the development of individuals who are capable of lifelong learning, their development as self-directed learners who are capable of assessing their own learning needs and taking the necessary steps towards satisfying those needs. The current obsession with linking economic goals to technical knowledge and skills has the capacity, they say, to restrict lifelong learning to a narrow conception that accords little value to the development of higher order skills. The authors further distinguish competence and competency. The latter, a skill or function including the underlying knowledge and ability necessary for its performance, they see as very narrow. Competence, they say, is much broader, representing the totality of knowledge, skills and abilities (or competencies) necessary for professional practice. It also implies a minimum threshold in performance.

Collins (2005) challenges the notion that we know what people need to learn and recognises the significant disjunction between the idealistic concepts of education described in the literature and the reductive nature of what is actually taught. He advises that we should not draw too far away from Fromm's definition of knowledge as 'nothing but a penetrating activity of thought'. Echoing Freire (1972), for whom literacy means reading the word and reading the world in order to achieve greater democracy, he feels that knowledge is concerned with creating an active interrelationship between the person and the world as the person searches for meaning in life.

Ainley (2000) distinguishes *teaching* from mere *telling and instructing*, suggesting that *teaching* involves negotiation of meaning between the teacher and taught whereas *telling and instruction* requires that the taught accepts the teacher's meaning without negotiation. He, however, defends telling and instruction at foundational level, in order that necessary information and competence may be acquired so as to provide a launch pad for deeper knowledge and holistic skills. At the same time he emphasises that teaching – as opposed to telling – is closer to both a creative art and the processes of research than it is to a technical process. Illich divorces learning from teaching and claims that most learning occurs outside of an organized educational system. To learn means to acquire a new skill or insight, he says. Of all human activities, he continues, learning requires the least manipulation.

In a treatise, which could just as well be applied to higher education, Murray (2004), reflecting the Steiner school of education, describes the function of toys in teaching children to explore their natural potential. She suggests that simplicity is the key. A doll, for example, should be silent so that a child's inner voice can be heard; so that it can play a role determined by the child and not the limited, repetitive, computerised, one-dimensional role defined by its adult inventor. Play is not play if it is always passive – a car which propels itself instead of spinning in a direction chosen by the child,

> costumes which are custom made instead of the creative pilfering of household objects to create persona . . . Symbolic play is crucial to development. A developmental link is made when the young child uses an object as representative of another object: when the box becomes a car or a tractor . . . when a rug becomes a cloak.

She draws on the work of Piaget who has researched the importance of matching toys to age and developmental sequence. Montessori, she says, reminds us that our task for the child 'is to touch his imagination and to enthuse him to his inmost core'.

Freire would have agreed. Necrophilous toys he might have called the objects of play which stimulate adults to admire the ingenuity of the adults who develop them, little realizing that their real cost is measured in the compromised ingenuity of the child. Play, like much education, now comes in a capsule.

Marrington and Rowe (2004) distinguish between two primary classifications of learning, i.e. what things *are* and what things *do*. The former implies stasis – the defining of a *thing* outside of temporal space, for example 'cat' – and the latter describes a *movement* from one state to another. Implicit in transitive learning (i.e. movement) is the notion that one must first break free from the knowledge in which one is embedded in order to connect or re-embed with different/more knowledge. This application evokes Picasso's precept of 'creative destruction' – a more intellectual take on the common aphorism 'you can't make an omelette without breaking eggs'. This disembedding and/or boundary crossing induces fear in the learner. The authors express a similar view to Freire (1972) that our 'perceived boundaries impact on our ability or desire to learn beyond what is known' (Marrington & Rowe, p. 455). They draw on Bergson (1913) in an attempt to explain this phenomenon. Bergson differentiates between intellectual knowledge and intuitive knowledge. Intellectual knowledge has us placed on the periphery – we are on the outside looking in. 'We know about something, we have the language to define it in relation to prior learning, it fits with our codification' (in Marrington & Rowe). It may sound, too, like Freire's (1972) banking system. Intuitive knowledge, on the other hand, requires what Chia (1999) refers to as 'intellectual auscultation' to facilitate an absolute engagement with an object. Dilthey appears to agree with this view, suggesting that knowledge is not limited to intellectual comprehension but embodies and articulates a variety of body-mind functions – the *jouissance* of Lacan (in Barglow). It involves an originality of seeing, amplitude, concentration and maturity. This paradigm shift, also explored by Abbott, suggests whole person involvement rather than simply brain or *black box* engagement. The personal feelings evoked in intuitive learning provoke necessarily painful experiences in our psyches with which we may have discomfort or inexperience in dealing. This, according to Marrington and Rowe, may explain why 'we separate learning from our social process at macro level' (p. 455). The potential for separation is greater the more money we have because we carry out formal learning in another place, separate from our normal lives.

In another evocation of Freire's (1972) concept of banking education as an agent of oppression, Marrington and Rowe draw on Foucault (1979) whose description of the École Militaire in Paris is that of a prison. They also draw on Winnicott (1947), who wrote before Freire and Becker (1980) and before the revelatory Zimbardo (1972) experiments, that we are all trapped in the same cognitive prison, only accepting and believing in one model. Winnicott, in a shattering challenge, which Freire would well have understood, reminds us 'There is no feeling of dependence, and therefore dependence must be absolute' (in Marrington & Rowe).

In an attempt to explain why we all cling to a dysfunctional system of education, (an explanation which might answer the question raised earlier by Chaharbaghi & Newman), Morgan (1986), reflecting many of Becker's (1980) ideas, describes the organization as having the potential to be a 'psychic prison' (p. 199), first, as a cognitive trap, but then much more interestingly, as the arena in which we act out our unconscious anxieties and drives, our repressed sexuality, our fear of death, and the need to cling to comforting rituals, the mythology of eternal archetypes. Chang's (1991) account of living in China under Chairman Mao graphically underlines the susceptibility of the individual to comply with a system, even one which causes pain and suffering. Indeed, even Habermas confesses that the awareness that Hitler's Germany was a politically criminal system came only with the Nuremburg trials (in Stephens, 1994). The metanarratives of modernism described by Bloland seem to provide a line of good fit with Morgan's view.

In an echo of Chaharbaghi and Newman's conspiracy model of education, Marrington and Rowe extract a view on education from Beer's (1989) fables of Wizard Prang. The Wizard is discussing with another person the possibility of the human race running its affairs differently, in a wise and benevolent fashion. 'The purpose of education', Wizard Prang answers his interlocutor, 'is to make sure this doesn't happen'. Illich and Freire would probably agree.

The usefulness of education and learning which is not rooted in a specific context is challenged by Chaharbaghi and Newman as isolationist. It does not create the kind of generative behaviour that Freire (1972) and Habermas (1987) see as a requirement of education for critical consciousness. If learners have no specific context for application, say the authors, they are neither sensitive nor hungry and are not ready to learn. In this imposed atmosphere the only alternative to education is entertainment – distinguished by the terms *edutainment* and *infotainment*. These are the tasteful arrangement and dramatised delivery of data to provide a pleasurable, but temporary, mental stimulus. 'Like a theatre', the authors remark with grim irony ... 'it provides entertainment but without the risk of a catharsis that might involve personal change' (p. 513). Education, they define, as an individualistic process with personal growth and self-understanding as necessary outcomes. 'Education represents a process of inquiry where the question is the answer' (p. 513).

Education is expansive and organic in its linkages; training is a repetitive use of the same method and skill is the technical competence resulting from training. Real learners create havoc with *delivered* education because of their questioning – the delivery being a feature of the educator's banking approach. This havoc supports the claim advanced by Cheng and Van de Ven (1996) that innovation and chaos are intertwined. It supports, too, Young's view of the necessity for the 'inexhaustible heterogeneity' mentioned earlier. Learning from training is incremental. Generative learning is organic and creative, context dependent and experienced psychologically or physically as a change in behaviour. *Knowledge*, they say, is concerned with content, focusing on the changing of data into information through observation or being told. *Doing* is a process, which exploits knowledge consistently where knowledge is transformed into technology.

Bloom's (1987) claim that hunger is essential to education reflects that of Chaharbaghi and Newman. 'One must spy out and elicit those hungers. For there is no education that does not respond to a felt need; anything else is a trifling display' (p. 19). He is concerned about the blurring of the distinction between liberal and technical education and the 'technical smorgasbord of the current (American) system, with its utter inability to distinguish between important and unimportant in any way other than the demands of the market' (p. 59). Bloom's writing is coloured by a strong moralistic, fundamentalist streak which may disturb those with a less modernist outlook. Nevertheless many may agree that

> hardly any (American) homes have any intellectual life whatsoever, let alone one that informs the vital interests of life. Educational TV marks the high tide for family intellectual life.
>
> (p. 58)

In his *Critical Theory* Habermas sets out categories of knowledge discovery and the bases on which knowledge claims can be warranted. According to MacIsaac's (1996) reading of Habermas, knowledge underpins three aspects of social existence – *work, interaction and power*.

Work knowledge refers to the way one negotiates one's environment – instrumental action – and is founded on empirical investigation and governed by technical rules.

Social knowledge (*interaction*) describes human social interaction or 'communicative action' and refers to the reciprocal expectations about behaviour between individuals. The third type, *power*, is emancipatory knowledge, that is, a knowledge of the self –achieved through self-reflection. It involves an exploration of the manner in which one's history and biography defines one's self-image and one's perceived role and social expectations. This emancipation, Habermas suggests, is from 'libidinal, institutional or environmental forces which limit our options and rational control over our lives but have been taken for granted as beyond human control' (in MacIsaac).

Habermas (1987) asserts that a speaker raises four validity claims – that is four bases on which any utterance can be challenged. The first challenge is whether or not the utterance is *meaningful*, second if it is *true*, third whether or not the speaker has a *right to address* the topic and fourth, if the speaker is *sincere*. Pursuance of these criteria produces what Habermas (1987) calls an ideal speech situation and enables the educator to deconstruct distorted ideology and speech. In this connection it is interesting to note the oft quoted excuse, delivered with a shrug, '*it's the system* ... ', as though the system was an immutable force of nature. Insights gained from critical self-awareness are liberating in that at least one can see the underpinnings of the situation – a transformed consciousness is achieved.

Akbar (2003) presents a quite extensive discussion of knowledge. He examines *explicit* and *tacit* knowledge and their interdependence and explores the different levels of knowledge. He suggests that, in the absence of conscious effort, knowledge levels are acquired through mistakes and failures, a subject, which, Marrington and Rowe suggest, has never been given sufficient attention. This is significant given the criticism by Gibbs and Iacovidou that examinations simply mark the student's examination performance and give no credit for ongoing diligence and application. There is further support in Jung's assertion that knowledge rests not on truth alone but upon error also. Akbar distinguishes between understandings of knowledge in the traditional epistemology – intransitive and objective truth, absolute, static and non-human – and understandings in the modern epistemology as a process of justifying personal belief in pursuit of truth. This understanding of knowledge is interesting in view of the numbers of apparently immutable 'truths' that have been turned on their heads. Isn't it now accepted as true that the world is round, not flat, that A × B is not necessarily the same as B × A, that water does not always freeze at 0°C, that potatoes are so toxic they would not be permitted on the human consumption list if they had been discovered only in recent times? Are Schrödinger's kittens alive or dead? Are measures of Gross National Product true even though they exclude all unpaid work, including work in the home? Conceptions of truth reached a watershed in Galileo's time. If the earth were not at the centre of things surely all certainties would evaporate? The world survived that revolution.

Akbar draws on Lawson (1997) – knowledge is *relative, changeable* and *historically transient* – and distinguishes between what he calls the 'ontological existence and the epistemological availability of truth'. The highest level of such truth is absolute in nature. However, while it may exist, its essential core is not explicitly available for subjective understanding, he asserts. The lowest level of objective truth, i.e. everyday reality, is explicitly available to us. In between there are different levels of objective truth with differences in levels of explicitness. *Explicit knowledge* is structured or formal and can be aggregated in a single location as hard, codified data. It is stored in organizations' rules, procedures and conduct. *Tacit knowledge*, on the other hand, is too individualistic and person-owned to be formally organized or to be available at a single location. It depends on individual skills and experiences together with subjective hunches, insights and intuition. Research has not yet identified the crucial element within tacit knowledge which allows new knowledge to be created, but, as Akbar points out, the active involvement of individuals in the *context* is critical to the internalisation of tacit knowledge – an assertion with which Illich would agree. Akbar also draws on Inkpen and Crossan (1995) who suggest that learning begins with a recognition of a mismatch between our beliefs and perceptions and it progresses as we modify our beliefs to resolve our dissonance – the necessary *hunger* described by Chaharbaghi and Newman, and Bloom.

Akbar distinguishes between single loop, double loop and triple loop learning and integrates them with the concepts of know *what*, know *how* and know *why*. Single loop learning, such as that attained by the banking system, results in incremental change – the basic mastery of a discipline through training and certification, i.e. know *what.* Know *how* is the transformation of book learning into effective execution – double loop learning. Know *why* is the deep knowledge of the underlying cause and effect relationships. It involves learning about previous contexts for learning and seeks to deconstruct the underlying purposes or principles in an effort to better understand – the disembedding already referred to by Marrington and Rowe. It is called triple loop learning. Know *what* and know *how* represent a rudimentary level of knowledge where an individual's knowledge lacks coherence and is cursory and disjointed and is retained as discrete and independent entities.

While it is likely that there will be a *movement* along a person's knowledge trajectory over time, a *shift* to a higher trajectory occurs when different levels of objective phenomena are viewed as explainable by a common denominator, i.e. information is given meaning through the process of sense-making. Akbar draws on Lefrancois (1972) who describes this process as one of grouping into classes objects/events on the basis of their underlying equivalence, rather than their apparent uniqueness – a characteristic long ago identified in Ecclesiastes 'there is no new thing under the sun' (Eccl. 1:8).

Unlike Akbar, Salisbury (2003) does not distinguish between levels and trajectories of knowledge. *Novices,* he says, are trying to increase their expertise and therefore require factual knowledge. Most of their cognitive effort relates to memory and understanding. For *practitioners,* most of their cognitive processing relates to application and analysis. For *experts* involved in new knowledge creation most of their cognitive processing relates to evaluation and creation.

Carroll (1998) emphasises the difficulty of achieving learner understanding, suggesting that teachers enjoy the risky reward that 'complete learner understanding is somehow not 'required until the assessment is due. And even then, sometimes not' (p. 116). He asserts that teaching methods, which require participation, interaction and thinking on the part of the student should almost certainly facilitate the surfacing of learner problems – the kind of *havoc* indicated earlier by Chaharbaghi and Newman. 'If learning is to be developed', Carroll says, 'then some learning problems or learner resistance should be expected' (p. 114). In a reflection of the views of Freire (1972) and Illich he suggests that most formal education has had the

effect of breeding dependence on the part of the learner. This dependence is fostered through unreflective teaching methods, doing too
much for the student and allowing mumblings and half-truths to
go unquestioned. Education should have as its outcome increased
choice. Anything that does not achieve that, he asserts forthrightly, is
not education. Like Freire (1974), Carroll declares that teachers must
be learners too. 'If they have lost that capacity for learning they are
not good enough to be in the company of those who have preserved
theirs' (p. 127). This view is supported by Rhys (1994). 'We cannot
effectively help others to develop skills which we ourselves do not
possess, nor encourage them to pass through processes from which
we shy away' (p. 110).

Robotham (2003) suggests that a crucial element in the process of
learning how to learn is the development of metacognition, where
individuals are able to metaphorically stand back and observe their
learning. He draws on Chickering and Claxton (1981) who suggest
four principles, which underpin learner competence in an educational context:

- competence is internal and external, situational and personal,
- competence is limited by a person's perception, neurological
  system and character,
- competence attainment requires diverse learning styles and,
  lastly,
- competence is a motivational force.

Reflecting Newman's (1943) concept of knowledge – 'not to know
the relative disposition of things is the state of slaves and children'
(p. 157) – Robotham declares that a competent learner is one who
can discover and create new knowledge for him/herself, can communicate it to others, can retain it long term and can use it to solve problems. He/she can construct linkages between old and new knowledge
and always wants to know more. Kember and Gow (1994) categorise
concepts of student learning in a five-level hierarchy:

- learning as a quantity of knowledge,
- learning as memorising of facts,

- learning as the acquisition of procedures that can be retained or utilised in practice,
- learning as an abstraction of meaning and, finally,
- learning as an interpretative process which facilitates an understanding of reality.

Hunt (2003) identifies a vital dimension of knowledge, the certainty of the individual that s/he is correct. Earlier, Pears (1971) suggested that according to the behavioural paradigm of knowledge (capacity to act), a person's pre-disposition to act depends on the extent of his/her certainty. Hunt draws on the 1829 wisdom of Colton (in Seldes, 1985), 'malinformation is more hopeless than non-information; for error is busier than ignorance' (in Hunt, p. 106). Not alone does misinformation lead to bad decisions and errors in practice, but also removes the foundation for more advanced learning and inhibits the capacity of the learner to realize the presence of and/or the extent of the misinformation. This inhibitory factor is reported as the *stubborn-error* effect in Marx and Marx (1980).

Spender (1996) acknowledges that the literature on knowledge, learning and memory are inconsistent in many ways. He suggests that the prevailing notion of knowledge seems naively positivistic and that of learning simply mechanical – that knowledge is made up of 'discrete and transferable granules of understanding about reality which can be added to an extant heap of knowledge' (p. 64). No modern epistemologists hold this view, however. They assert that knowledge is less about truth and reason and more about the ability to intervene knowledgeably and purposefully in the world. Like Akbar, Spender draws on Polanyi (1962, 1966) to distinguish between objective and tacit knowledge. Tacit knowledge is gained experientially, is personal and non-communicable through language. It is inseparable from the processes of its creation and much of it is picked up by osmosis. The relationship between data and information is not immediately obvious, according to Spender. 'In an uncertain, non-positivistic world, where there is no privileged access to truth, there are always problems of meaning' (p. 65). While data is defined as that which can be communicated and stored, meaning cannot be stored unless data are treated as facts.

Skilbeck (2001) defines education as 'systematic processes of learning and teaching aimed at the continuing growth and development in individuals and society of skills, knowledge, values, standards of conduct and understanding' (p. 19).

His definitions offer a subtle distinction between tertiary education, which he sees in terms of advanced *applications* and uses of knowledge and university education, which he sees essentially as knowledge *creation* through research and enquiry. His distinction seems to be understood by students in a third-level educational institution, who, when asked for suggestions on redesigning their course, would, overwhelmingly, request more practical than theoretical subjects (Graduate Survey DkIT 2005). Holland (2007) reports that Irish universities rely on the Institutes of Technology to offer access to students from the lower socio-economic backgrounds, thus allowing them (the universities) to retain their elite status.

Thornhill (2003), in an address to Irish business leaders, agrees with the importance placed on the relevance and connectedness of the education system to economic and social development. He claims that the concept of *relevance of education* is one that induces apprehension in educationalists. His challenge asks 'Who would seriously propose that education should be irrelevant?' He goes on to describe education's role in serving some very important higher order functions.

> An important core function of education is its role in enhancing the capacity of individuals to live fulfilled lives and to develop their own potential, both as individuals and as members of communities and of society. Trying to posit a choice between applied and pure education is a distraction

– a reflection of the view already put forward by Kalantzis (1998). He reiterates that education includes developing in students a capacity both for citizenship and participation in the economy. He is perturbed that debates on education tend too much to be confined to educationalists and feels that the inclusion of all interest groups is necessary. He defends schools and colleges which are often lampooned as bastions of restrictive practices, academic detachment and amateurish management, and reminds us that the management strategies and styles of many third-level institutions are now being copied by advanced knowledge industries – a description which might find little favour among those who are concerned about the application of a business market model to the education field.

Armstrong (2004) offers a link between education and religion. Although she does not use the terms single loop and double loop, she deplores the trend towards oversimplification of knowledge, which she sees as an outcome of time pressure and the impending advent of technology use in 'A' level examinations. She advises that we need to 'counter the culture of the sound bite and the instant opinion' and, instead, teach that some truths are not instantly accessible. Tick-box questions do not test students' powers of reflection or their appreciation of complexity. The proposed e-assessment of 'A' level students will be faster, more flexible and more efficient, but at the expense of creativity and insight, she warns. Some kinds of insight can only be attained after a long interval of patient attention – what Keats called 'negative capability – when man is capable of being in uncertainties, mysteries, doubts, without any irritable reaching after fact and reason' (in Armstrong) – an alien passivity in these times when knowledge is instant and geared to performativity. Habermas also counsels us to engage in the 'forgotten experience of reflection' (in Stephens). The tendency towards extreme instrumentalism – if not assessed it is not important – on the part of students is identified in the Nuffield Review (2006). This review, based on focus group interviews with 21 universities, claims that, although the presentation and computer skills of students have improved in recent years, there is an alarming decline in literacy and numeracy standards. The review reveals that students cannot write in sentences, cannot spell, cannot be understood, yet graduate with a 2:1. The 'A' level system, according to the report, no longer meets its original objective of preparing young people for studying at university. Despite achieving academic success at 'A' level, learners are increasingly coming into higher education expecting to be told the answers. This reductive pragmatism is evidenced also in Holden's (2005) interview with a maximum points Irish Leaving Certificate student, headlined as follows: 'There's no point in knowing about stuff that's not going to come up in exams'

(p. 13). Collins (2006) testifies to the fault line in education. 'Education systems, generally, are driven by their assessment processes. That which is assessed is that which is attended to and is accorded value. If it is unassessed it is unvalued' (p. 12).

Using religion as an example, Armstrong cautions against the imposition of orthodoxy, suggesting that we can do damage to our minds if we habitually turn them away from their natural inclination towards a search for truth. She reminds us that during the scientific revolution of the sixteenth and seventeenth centuries 'western people started to regard religious dogma as empirical fact and to insist on an orthodoxy that consequently seemed incredible'. No wonder, she remarks, that Confucius, Buddha and the Koran had little time for theological conformity.

In what could be a parallel of the distinction between education and qualification, Moncayo distinguishes between *spirituality* – an immediate, intrinsic and direct experience, and *religion* – extrinsic, institutional and conventional, a mechanism for social affiliation and control. Mystery is the ideological mechanism through which priests cling to power with religion fostering illusions and dogmas, which are unverifiable in principle. Symbolic or spiritual forms need to be understood, not as dogmas, but as 'evocations of that which lies at the limit of the visible and invisible, as prismatic perspectives on truths which are enigmatic by their very definition' (p. 3) – the Lacanian desire *to know the unknown* (in Barglow). Moncayo's ideas on spirituality vis à vis religion reflect those of Freire (1974) concerning education for critical consciousness as opposed to banking education. Religion, which is reduced to a simplistic ritual, argues Moncayo, reinforces conformity and a repression of authentic personal psychic experience. His modernist perspective sees prayer in a hierarchical fashion, viewing contemplative prayer as superior to the more archaic prayers of petition to parent-like figures. Contemplative prayer is prayer of aspiration and realization of the sacred as 'the emptiness that lies beyond representation' (Moncayo, p.4).

This is an interesting metaphor. Moncayo appears to issue a warning not to be deceived by a simulacrum but to be prepared to engage with a power which is emptied of physical representation. Freire would probably agree and would hardly be astonished by the statistical findings of Franzblau (1934), Vetter (1958) and Gorsuch and Alashire

(1974), among others, who have shown positive correlations between the practice of conventional religion and negative characteristics such as bigotry, prejudice, racism, indifference to social problems and even dishonesty. Authoritarian conventional religion, with its concomitant prayers of petition and concrete, rather than metaphoric, beliefs, has also been shown to correlate positively with intolerance of uncertainty, ambiguity and doubt. This is hardly surprising, since the great western religions are posited on modernistic, positivistic principles – it is telling that both words *posited* and *positivist* have the same etymology. This distrust of doubt would surely unnerve Freire (1974) and Habermas (1987, 1989), who do not see doubt as an enemy but as its contradistinction, a subjective position wherein knowing emerges from the void. Metaphor, Freire (1974) says, reflecting Moncayo, always gifts us with the echo and evocation of something that is beyond word and logic.

Hannabuss (2001) also shows a link between knowledge and religion. He distinguishes information – statistical, financial, performance related masses of data – from knowledge, which, he argues, many religious systems claim will lead to wisdom. Such wisdom contains self-knowledge and knowledge of knowledge or meta-knowledge. Notwithstanding postmodernism's claims that *meta* cannot exist, Hannabuss points out that, despite the high esteem in which wisdom is held, it has had a poor press and we never hear of 'wisdom management'. In a swipe at religions, he remarks how odd that is since religions 'have traded in wisdom for centuries and they are experts at both managing and stage-managing at least the external signs of wisdom' (p. 358). He recognises how seductive is the rationalists' paradigm of knowledge – systematic, orderly and capable of being exteriorised by examinations and observations. On the fringes and periphery of this cognitive neatness hovers the less clear experiential and intuitive realm, which, he asserts, is supported more by eastern than by western philosophy, suggesting, like Whyte (2004), that knowledge is closer to religion or faith in eastern philosophy. He lays the blame for our reluctance to examine self-awareness and authenticity at the door of the Protestant work ethic and a western culture of blame and guilt. Any embrace of the transcultural and pluralistic contexts of knowledge inevitably, he says, leaves us with a continual dynamic dislocation and a need to redefine at all levels.

Illich draws on Durkheim's realization that religion has a propensity to divide social reality by pre-determining what is to be considered sacred and what profane and asserts that this polarisation is caused by current education also, a point made, too, by Hayakawa et al. (1990). Illich sees the same distinction between the Church and salvation as between schooling and education.

Mirroring Hayakawa et al.'s (1990) view of the fluid nature of the meaning of language, Illich asserts that some words, including *school* and *teaching* have become so flexible that they cease to be useful. 'Like amoeba they fit into almost any interstice of the language' (p. 25). Classification, say Hayakawa et al. (1990), is not a matter of identifying 'essences'. 'It is simply a reflection of social convenience or necessity – and different necessities are always producing different classifications' (p. 108).

Society regards as *true*, he says, those systems of classification which produce the desired result. Sifting through the array of definitions on learning, knowledge, teaching, education, information and data does not result in clear meaning, considering the degree of interchangeability of understanding and the dependence on one or more to provide a circular set of definitions of the others. Thus a thesaurus will provide, as synonyms for *knowledge*, education, enlightenment, learning, wisdom, cognisance, information. The danger here is that we may fall into the trap of the synchronic articulation of what is a diachronic structure. As Becker (1980) and Hayakawa et al. (1990) warn, any information we receive, other than by direct experience, is really a *model* of some real idea or thing, and language is just such a representation, allowing us to communicate facts and ideas to others – a representation which must necessarily accommodate myriad interpretations if we are to avoid the 'infantilism' (Hayakawa et al., 1990, p. 103) of thought against which they caution. They sum up the problem by drawing on the succinct observation of Bridgman (1927). 'For of course the true meaning of a term is to be found by observing what a man does with it, not by what he says about it' (Hayakawa et al., 1990, p. 104).

Chapter 5

Postmodern Consumer Culture – The Effect on Education

It is clear that the study of consumer culture is pushing its way towards the mainstream of social science. The desperation to consume is at the heart of postmodern consumer culture. Featherstone (1996) argues that the emphasis on the commodity and the process of reification has directed attention away from a focus on production towards consumption and the process of cultural change. That is, consumers are more and more drawn to the passing, novel and changing experience, and see that experience firmly rooted in the process of consumption rather than production. Postmodern consumer culture constructs a situation in which *being* depends on consuming rather than on producing. Baudrillard (1998) asserts that postmodern society, through the agencies of advertising, the media and consumption, presents us not with reality, but with hyper-reality or neo-reality. The mass media have, in fact, neutralised reality. Commodities, through advertising, become signifiers, or codes – shared systems of meaning without material underpinnings. His views on waste oppose those of Durkheim's functionalism (in Baudrillard, 1998, p. 5), which presented the traditional view that waste within consumer society is 'a kind of madness, of insanity, of instinctual dysfunction which causes man to burn his reserves and compromise his survival conditions by irrational practice' (p. 43). Williams (1976) provides us with one of the earliest uses of the term consume, 'to destroy, to use up, to waste, to exhaust' (p. 68), a definition which sits easily with Durkheim's approach. Baudrillard's perspective on waste as consumption presents us with a paradoxical concept in an economic system, which, for so long, has seen the need to control and channel production in order to overcome scarcity. Instead, Baudrillard illustrates an individual who is defined by his consumption. This reading requires a revision of traditional concepts of utility, scarcity and choice, which have rationalistic origins, and their replacement with the understanding that waste, not only begets employment, but, through the economic multiplier, fosters more wasteful, useless expenditure on which future employment prospects may depend.

The objective of wasteful expenditure lies in the social logic of the achievement of status through the consumption of social signifiers. Baudrillard (1998) asserts that a foundational human drive is to achieve status – the status of aristocratic birth being the pinnacle of such hierarchy and which is closed to most – 'a status of grace and excellence' he calls it (p. 60). The consumption of objects confers status –'salvation by works, since salvation by grace is unattainable' (p. 60). Antiques, a sign of heredity, invoke a particular prestige, elevating one nearer to the envied ascribed aristocratic status. The deconstruction approach of postmodernism subverts the notion of the purchase of antiques as an urbane, sophisticated and unique attempt to define separateness and superiority and reveals it, instead, as a manifestation of a motivation to social-climb, a motivation with which the general mass of society appears to be inoculated. The author notes the irony that the postmodernist, who eschews hierarchies of any sort, may, unwittingly feel superior in intellect to the modernist still locked in the iron cage of truth and pursuing a better life and higher status through the consumption of commodities which are peddled to him/her through advertising.

Baudrillard (1983) sees that increased commodity production, coupled with information technology, has led to a victory of the culture of signs which distorts determinism, so that social relations shift with cultural signs; we can no longer be sure of social stratification. The kaleidoscope of images and information threatens our sense of reality. The dominance of sign culture creates a simulational world in which the surfeit of signs and images has erased the boundary between the real and the imaginary. We live in a hyper-real world in which the accumulation of signs and images – like Becker's flimsy canopy – provides the road map for our journey through life. For Baudrillard this means that 'we live everywhere already in an aesthetic hallucination of reality' (p. 148).

Perhaps Baudrillard's most striking contribution to postmodernism is his concept of the simulacrum, which devolves from the implosion of boundaries and meaning. He dips into ancient writings and extracts a reference from Ecclesiastes to the simulacrum. 'The simulacrum is never that which conceals the truth – it is the truth which conceals that there is none. The simulacrum is true' (1988, p. 166).

An extensive trawl by this author through the Book of Ecclesiastes, however, failed to reveal such a quote. This reference itself, therefore, appears to be a simulacrum. An implosion simply means that the boundary between a simulation and reality collapses and the basis for determining the real is gone. There is nothing simple about the result – the eradication of boundaries and the destabilisation of meanings.

Baudrillard suggests that the simulacrum evolves in four stages. These four stages are described by Appignanesi et al. (1995). In stage one the object reflects a basic reality, in step two the object masks and perverts a basic reality, in step three it marks the absence of a basic reality and in step four the object bears no relation to any reality whatever – it is its own pure simulacrum. In stage four, they say, 'reality becomes redundant and we have reached hyper-reality in which images breed incestuously with each other without reference to reality or meaning' (pp. 54–55), a stage many feel may have been reached in higher education where the boundary between qualification and education has imploded. The pervasiveness and exceptional authority of the simulacrum found extraordinary expression as recently as December 2005 to confound the possible settlement of Northern Ireland's 36-year war. Unbelievably, Dr Ian Paisley would have chosen a film image as evidence of decommissioning over the evidence of the eyes of two clergymen observers, notwithstanding the biblical proposition that 'the testimony of two men is true' (John 8:17 in Caraman, p. 88).

In a reference to the tourism industry, Featherstone asserts that the postmodern tourists are not interested in authenticity but revel instead 'in the constructed simulational nature of contemporary tourism' (p. 102) which they know is only a game. Even museums, he says, are abandoning their commitment to education and cultural imperatives in favour of a more populist ethos. He draws on Baudrillard (1982) who describes the Beaubourg Museum in Paris as a hypermarket of culture. The masses simply wish to touch, manipulate and consume and have no interest in looking, studying or analysing. Their attraction to the exhibits has, in Baudrillard's words, 'all the semblance of housebreaking or the sacking of a shrine' (Featherstone, p. 103).

Baudrillard (1998) emphasises the difference between the usefulness of a product and its symbolism, and asserts that the postmodern consumer is more interested in the symbolic aspect of the product rather than the real. In the postmodern marketplace the social meanings and symbols which attach themselves to products are supplied by advertising and marketing agencies. Without such agencies, products would be perceived by consumers as items of utility but devoid of cultural significance, i.e. products would be bought for their functional benefits only. Declaring that everyone is equal before objects as use value but not before objects as signs and differences which are profoundly hierarchical, he emphasises the pursuit of *signs* that denote difference. 'At the level of signs there is no absolute wealth or poverty, nor any opposition between the signs of wealth and the signs of poverty; they are merely sharps and flats on the keyboard of difference' (p. 91). He cautions against being seduced by a change in the form of distance between classes and confusing it with democratisation, a caveat which may well apply to the massification effects of education. Education, which is apparently available to all, mutes, but does not disguise, the class differences between the already arrived and the arrivistes. Bourdieu (1986), agreeing with Baudrillard, also suggests that the lack of symbolic capital which betrays a person's origins is only barely masked, irrespective of one's trajectory through life.

Williamson (1978) claims that one of the primary functions of promotion and advertising is to create 'structures of meaning' (p. 12). Jhally (1989) coined the phrase 'the theft and re-appropriation of meaning' (p. 221) to explain the process of influencing the demand for commodities. That is, an item of clothing becomes Levis, sports shoes become NIKE, a timepiece becomes a Rolex, all badges of elitism. Function takes second place to psychological characteristics. Lee (1993) agreeing with this concept sees, in the commodity, the thread linking all the changes of the 1980s. He sees the 1980s as the decade when image attained superiority over the real, when there was a 'shift away from notions of substance and content towards packaging, aesthetic form and the 'look' (p. ix). He sees the commodity as, not alone the focus of material economic wealth, but 'an important material and symbolic resource by which ordinary people could, both materially and culturally, reproduce their life' (p. xi). People *become* what they consume, what they wear. They become their image. In an unusual twist, Lee draws on the work of Karl Marx. He shows that the historical rupture between labour and needs is now exacerbated by the fact that the object which is created is consumed for its symbolic rather than functional characteristics. This theory may have serious implications for education if students pursue accreditation rather than learning. The education field has not escaped the impact of consumerism and commodification. Significant issues may arise when education is seen as a commodity which can behave like any other commodity in the marketplace.

There is a striking synchronicity in the emergence of the terms massification, managerialism and marketisation in advanced capitalist societies. Pritchard's (1994) suggestion that the advent of massification has reduced education merely to a saleable commodity is supported by the similar view of Maguire et al. (1996). The terms *education market, student as consumer,* and *student as customer* have crept into the vernacular. Many writers have attempted to discern the positive and negative changes that may result if a marketing approach towards education is adopted, i.e. if students are considered as customers or consumers. The vocabulary of consumerism is increasingly applied to the campus.

While there are distinct differences between *consumers* and *customers*, the literature does not distinguish between them, with many writers using the terms consumer/customer in the same paper. The term customer implies an exchange relationship. Modern marketing management urges the business to develop satisfactory exchange relationships with customers. Exchange means that both sides give something which is accepted by the other in return. The Webster dictionary defines a customer as a purchaser or buyer. A consumer, on the other hand, is a user of commodities or services as opposed to a producer. A customer will measure the price s/he has to pay against the utility to be derived from the product or service. A consumer who is not also a customer, does not pay any price, therefore the value which is placed on the product or service may be in some doubt. In motivational terms, the distinction between consumer and customer seems, to this author, to be considerable. Irrespective of the educational merits, or otherwise, of using marketing analogy and marketing concepts in the education field, it is amazing that the terms customer/consumer are used without definition and sometimes interchangeably.

There are as many writers opposed to the notion of student as customer/consumer as there are those who support it. Laskey (1998), for instance, cautions against taking a polarised view on the marketing approach. She suggests it would be ill-advised to turn a third-level institute into a degree mill in a misguided attempt to please customers. On the other hand, it may be equally ill-advised to base criticism of the market analogy on a 'misleading and stereotypical perception of the customer focused operation'. By rejecting the customer analogy completely, she suggests, institutes may well be incubating another destructive stereotype: the bureaucratic ivory tower which is deaf to the real needs of its students. Laskey suggests that making a marketing analogy is useful because it allows a third-level institute to make a decision about its positioning in the market and in this way can both influence its customer base and educate the customers it attracts. This is an interesting observation since an objective of education is to *create* a mature critical thinker who is capable of objective appraisal. Schmoker and Wilson (1993) believe it is useful to assign the term *customers* to students because the use of the word *customer* thwarts the misperception of students as 'passive receptacles'.

Interestingly, students judge the quality of their educational experience by the level of satisfaction they feel as consumers. That is, perceived quality of education is a *consequence* of consumer satisfaction, not a *cause* (Athiyaman, 1997). It, therefore, seems logical that students, as consumers, will be happier with higher grades, will judge the quality as high and the grade spiral may continue – satisfaction enhancing perceived quality, perceived quality attracting more customers (students) and so on in a cyclical fashion. Athiyaman's study shows that the attitude of the student pre-enrolment has little or no direct effect on post-enrolment attitude. An implication of this finding, put forward by Athiyaman, is 'that all service encounters should be managed to enhance consumer satisfaction' (p. 528). This in turn will enhance perceived quality. Hill (1995) also found a significant mismatch between students' expectations and perceived quality but did not investigate the effect of student satisfaction on perceived quality. Telford and Masson (2005) find that there is generally no student dissatisfaction on issues where stakeholders do not share the same values. This would seem to infer that students are getting their own way on these issues.

Le Grand and Robinson (1992) refute the notion of student as customer and the suitability of the market as a mechanism for distributing education. Using the principles of welfare economics they cite specific characteristics in the market, in particular, imperfect consumer information, capital market imperfections and externalities – points made, also, by the Expert Group on Future Skills Needs (2007) – which render the market unsuitable as a mechanism for distributing education. They warn, too, of the dangers of persuasive advertising if students are viewed as customers. Laskey, on the other hand, supporting the concept of *student as customer*, takes no cognisance of imperfect consumer information. In attesting to the presence of the educated and discriminating customer, she asserts that just as an airline would never let its customers dictate safety standards, a responsible college would not let students determine curriculum or grading policy. Laskey's metaphor seems strikingly thin. She seems to imply that customers, in this instance, passengers, would dictate lower, rather than higher standards – an interesting observation in its own right. A further inference is that students are as exercised by education policy matters as air passengers are about air safety. Should airlines regulate their own safety procedures on an internal basis, the customer, despite imperfect consumer information, might have cause to be anxious at the absence of external regulation. Given that external regulation is fast disappearing from academe and is being replaced by academic autonomy in more and more education institutions, students might be justifiably anxious if they are denied the right to dialogue as espoused by Freire (1974), the right to speak on their own behalf, although this right if exercised, would appear, in Laskey's view, to result in lower standards.

Resistance to the notion of student as customer comes from other writers also. Walsch (1998) does not distinguish between customer and consumer. However he agrees that the *student as customer* paradigm is without merit, that the relationship between student and teacher is unique – because of the length of the interaction and because the student is part of the collaborative process in improving the final product of education. Cheney et al. (1997) mount a more rigorous opposition as they warn against the dangers of becoming imprisoned within the framework of the *student as customer* metaphor. 'If we consider students as customers, all we need to do is find out what they want at any given moment and give it to them. With this kind of market-oriented emphasis popularity and profit can reign'.

They warn that the *student as customer* metaphor actually has the effect of distancing students from the very educational process which is supposed to engage them. The definition places the student outside of the institution. The student is, therefore, not part of the process that transforms inputs into outputs – but is placed in the role of 'the patron at the fast food window'. S/he may thus be viewed in an external role for his/her entire duration at college. This student, who assumes a passive role in the education process, views the lecturer as the bestower of education grades, rather than viewing him/herself as learner and earner. Cheney et al. suggest that the polarisation of student and institution places the student on a continuum that 'progressively becomes more adversarial'. The net result of this is that lecturers may practise defensive education. The authors further suggest that students, while they are students, may be satisfied with courses which make few demands on them and confer on them a qualification which enables them to get a job – 'the educational equivalent of a cheap and cheerful shopping spree'. A survey of perceived quality among alumni might show a different perspective altogether, a factor not taken account of in Athiyaman's study but noted in the Graduate Survey (2005) already mentioned.

Customer satisfaction, according to Cheney et al., may index only a gut reaction. They further quote Barzun (1989) and Postman (1988), 'satisfaction often results from sheer entertainment instead of intellectual challenge' – a concept already referred to in Featherstone, Baudrillard (1982), Lee, Ainley (2000), and Chaharbaghi and Newman. Garrison (1997) claims that teaching students to distinguish between this unreflective gut reaction and what they ought to desire after reflection is the ultimate goal of education. 'It is an education that lies beyond knowledge alone' (p. 126).

Banning (1985) suggests that espousing the view of student as client or consumer tends to have a narrowing effect on the work of lecturers whose services and programmes become passive. He reflects the view of Cheney et al. (1997) that the language of the market can also restructure the student/lecturer relationship.

Wallace (1999) attempts to put forward a balanced discussion of the student-as-customer debate. He recognises that there is a distinction between customer and consumer but fails to make the case clearly. He does, however, make the point that customers have responsibilities. It is certainly clear that a customer who buys a car has a responsibility to have it serviced and maintained or else lose the value of the investment. Similarly, students have responsibilities to study, attend class, complete assignments, take tests and so on. How well a student fulfils these obligations has a significant effect on the usefulness of the educational outcome. Wallace seems to take no cognisance of the fact that the perception of the outcome may be different if the student is customer than if he/she is simply consumer. He does acknowledge that imperfect consumer information exists in the education marketplace but asserts that, just as in other markets, suppliers set the expectations of customers. He makes no reference however, to the seriousness of the obligation on the supplier in the education field. He appears to be *content* rather than *process* centred and focuses heavily on qualification. A further failing is that he does not advise on how to encourage customers (students) to fulfil their obligations in a rapidly dwindling, increasingly competitive education marketplace. The dangers outlined by Cheney et al. might well be borne in mind.

In his *More Means Different – Revisited*, Ball (1996) takes a positive stance on education as a market and students as clients or customers.

He does not hold an elitist view of education, believing that 97 per cent of the population can benefit from higher education if they are sufficiently motivated. He sees intelligence in terms of 'learning speed (which can be increased), metaphoric power (the capability of making connections, which can be developed) and intuition' (p. 9).

Agreeing with the application of the concept of productivity to education he suggests, like Sambataro, Ives and Jarvenpaa and Wood et al., that the use of information technology and increasing learners' responsibility for their own learning should facilitate economies on the most expensive factor in academic costs, the academic staff themselves. Referring to the title of his paper Ball asserts that it refers to the creation of *more* opportunities for a *different* kind of education plus the *means* to achieve those ends. *More* is a reminder to place the needs and wants of potential students, whom he calls clients, before the service – the suite of courses offered by the educational institution. *Means* implies that private funding must become the first priority and core resource. *Different* implies that key skills – self-reliance, flexibility and breadth – must form the core of the curriculum with disciplines placed on the periphery. Those who hope to succeed, he says, will, first of all, master the hidden curriculum (the acquisition of the key skills) and then 'add a sequence of (temporary and disposable) specialisms' (p. 8). He seems to have faith in the ability of the student to demand the kind of courses he wants rather than simply choosing from the suite provided by academics but takes no cognisance of Illich's claim that students have learned to conform to the marketable values which have been set out for them by changing government policies.

Kelsey (2000) mounts a very strong attack against the concept of market driven education and sees the real value of education as 'nation building'. Writing about the current situation in New Zealand, she warns that 'the physical and intellectual infrastructure has been run down so badly that just to restore the quality of twenty years ago would require sustained long-term investment and more political will than is apparent at present'. She asserts that the government has a responsibility to treat education 'as an intrinsic good and not a tradable commodity'. She cautions that market-based education which

is founded on the ethic of consumption concentrates on immediate gratification with short-term benefits only – a concept already
expressed by Athiyaman, Cheney et al., Walsch, Seligman and others.
Kelsey offers criticism of the Finland and Ireland model of education –
a model which is 'devoid of any sense of a nation . . . interested only in
a knowledge economy, as if that could be detached from knowledge
relating to the social, cultural, indigenous and political context in
which it operates'.

Her fellow New Zealander, Grace (1989), agrees, reminding us that
Newman's *The Idea of a University* was a

> powerful counterblast to the arguments of the Utilitarians. We note,
> however, that they have emerged again in the service of the Treasury.
> These new Utilitarians, sensing that certain forms of economic anal-
> ysis are growing in power and influence everywhere, are currently
> attempting to commodify education.
>
> (p. 213)

Grace claims that

> education is a public good because it has the potential to strengthen
> the democratic and egalitarian features of the society over and
> against any tendencies towards authoritarianism. It is a public good
> because it gives us the intellectual resources to see through the
> Treasury's argument.
>
> (p. 217)

As far back as the late 1970s, John (1977) was alarmed at the advance
of the vocabulary of consumerism in the campus. 'Catalogues and
handbooks constitute advertising (and) students, as buyers, enter
into contractual obligations with institutions which are characterised
as sellers. Institutional representatives who talk with prospective students fall into the category of salesmen' (p. 39). Illich agrees, 'the
language of the schoolman has already been co-opted by the adman'
(p. 50).

Shanahan and Gerber (2004) testify to the power of advertising
in forming perceptions of quality. One stakeholder admitted that in
judging the relative quality of (Australian) universities, it was the one

with the 'glossy pictures' that won out. 'I can't help but subconsciously believe that this is a higher quality product, no matter what the words inside are' (p. 168).

Gewirtz et al. (1995) also emphasise 'glossification' – colour rather than black and white, promotion rather than information, pictures rather than text, and high specification style and production formats – in the effort to enhance customer appeal in this newly established education market. 'Not only is imagery becoming more important but the focus and content of imagery is being transformed, in the process creating new semiologies' (p. 126).

Acknowledging the tension between information giving and impression management, Ball (1999) is concerned that the lacuna between them may be colonised by 'fabrication' as educational institutions become increasingly aware of how they represent themselves. He presents a telling vignette in the description of the refurbishment of the reception areas of educational institutions. With sofas, posters, plants and up-lighting there is a shift in imagery from bureaucratic to business-like which defines the fissure in the traditional understanding of education as a public good and skews it towards its new designation as a consumption good. Pugsley (1998) refers to the use of 'dramaturgical metaphor' (p. 98) in facilitating impression management in the educational field. Testimony is also given by Shanahan and Gerber (2004) to the importance of PR and the promotion of a public image in generating positive perceptions among stakeholders – 'successful leadership stories need to be told in an overt, systematic and widespread fashion' (p. 168). The findings of these writers support the irony of the old adage 'get the name of being an early riser and you can stay in bed till noon'.

The themes of content and commodity in an education market find expression in the work of Illich. Education institutions, he says, sell curricula – a bundle of products developed according to the same process and having the same structure as other merchandise. It comprises a collection of 'planned meanings, a package of values, a commodity whose balanced appeal makes it marketable to a sufficiently large number to justify the cost of production' (p. 41).

Consumers (i.e. students) learn to make their choices conform to marketable values and learn to feel guilty if they do not achieve the necessary grades and certificates which would entitle them to a place in their chosen job category. Students see their studies as the investment with the highest financial return, a point also made by Le Grand and Robinson and by the OECD (2004). The educational institution 'initiates the myth of unending consumption' says Illich (p. 38), and teaches that learning depends on attendance, that the value of learning increases with increased input and that the resultant value can be measured and documented on certificates. Education is the world's biggest employer and the fastest growing labour market, presenting 'unlimited opportunities for legitimated waste' (p. 46). Massive resources are expended to teach the answers to predetermined problems in a ritually defined setting. The issuing of certificates serves as a form of market manipulation and is 'plausible only to a schooled mind' (p. 15). Illich warns that we need to query the assumption that valuable knowledge is a commodity which, under certain circumstances may be force fed to the consumer. Otherwise, he says, society will be more and more dominated by 'sinister pseudo schools and totalitarian managers of information' (p. 50). As long as education is perceived as a commodity by supplier and consumer the only advance will be to develop new educational packages for more accurate delivery. This effort will simply seek 'to optimise the efficiency of an inherited framework – a framework which itself is never questioned. This framework has the syntactic structure of a funnel for teaching packages' (p. 70).

Wagner (1998) asserts that Higher Education is increasingly led by demand with all types of institutions having to reshape themselves to students' requirements. Governments, too, have to readjust their policies, he says. Donnelly agrees with this proposition, a proposition which would find little favour with Illich whose strong thesis it is that students are not the architects of their own needs but have simply learned to conform to the marketable values which have been set out for them by changing government policies.

Gewirtz et al. (1995) have much to criticise about the market approach to education. Their research shows deep unhappiness and a sense of dislocation among many educational practitioners. Politicians, they say, are in thrall to the power of the market which, theoretically, provides the discipline of accountability that the producer

cannot escape. If things go awry, then misguided consumers or care-
less producers are to blame, never the politicians. The market offers
to politicians a seductive washing of hands. The forces of the market,
goes the ideology, sifts out the weak and inefficient – only the good
will survive and everyone will prosper. The attraction of the market
is the provision of an apparent solution to the social and educational
problems of education policy. Using equality and efficiency as its pass-
words, it releases the government from its collective responsibility,
embedded in the welfare state, for education provision. It allows the
replacement of professional control with a form of managerial control which uses finance as its compass. Their primary research distinguishes between acceptable forms of marketing which do not involve
compromising traditionally held educational values and principles
and unacceptable forms of marketing which do. One educationalist,
in an effort to resolve her cognitive dissonance, acknowledged a positive aspect to education promotion. She distinguished between marketing with a small 'm', which is muted and gentle and marketing with
a big 'M' which is 'glossy, aggressive and relatively expensive' (p. 104).
Some are horrified by the application of marketing principles to education but recognise that without them they will not survive. Other
respondents express disquiet that there should be winners and losers
in education – a point also made by Dunne (1995) – society cannot
afford to run on those sorts of principles, they say. Another describes
the renting of the campus for financial purposes and the 'joy and
bliss when we got a Greek wedding ... with the marquee and we got
loads of money for it ... It didn't have anything really to do with what
we were there for' (p. 102).

The market, according to Gewirtz et al. is a 'middle class mode of
social engagement' (p. 181). They distinguish between three types of
market choosers who differ on two major indicators – the inclination
to engage with it and their capacity to exploit it to their advantage. The
first group they call *privileged/skilled choosers* who are almost exclusively
professional middle class people and who exhibit a marked capacity
to use their economic, social and cultural capital in order to decode
market messages. They tend to orientate towards elite, select educational institutions. The second group comprises *semi-skilled choosers*
who come from a variety of backgrounds but are distinguished by
a motivation to make the most of opportunities. Lacking sufficient

cultural and educational capital themselves, they lack the capacity to thoroughly exploit the education market. Perceiving themselves as outsiders, they depend on the opinions and perceptions of others. Immigrant families are among those who fit this profile. A third group is the set of *disconnected choosers* who are almost exclusively working class. Disadvantaged by the constraints of expectation and experience they tend not to participate in the market which they perceive as irrelevant. While they do make active and positive choices they do not do so in ways that reflect the value of competitive consumerism embedded in the education system. Their choices are much more influenced by their attachment to their locality and they seek to pursue education in the company of friends and family. The model of choice put forward by education markets represents just one form of provision which is understood and embraced by skilled choosers, embraced, but less comfortably understood, by semi-skilled choosers and is quite irrelevant to disconnected choosers. The culture of provision fits better, therefore, the culture of the skilled user than it does any other group – it reflects the ideal of cultivation of the dominant group (Williamson 1981). As Bourdieu (1986) asserts, the dominant class possesses the required cultural capital to unlock the code of the cultural arbitrariness of the market. He suggests that attitudes to class are deeply embedded and may 'function below the level of consciousness and language' (p.466). The market and family choice in that market is a class strategy:

> The definition of the legitimate means and stakes of struggle is, in fact, one of the stakes of the struggle, and the relative efficacy of the means of controlling the game (the different sorts of capital) is itself at stake, and therefore subject to variations in the course of the game.
>
> (p. 246)

The operation of a market in education is a classic example of what Bourdieu and Passeron (2000) term 'symbolic violence' (p. 13). This is a force exerted by the ruling class by establishing themselves and their ideas in *legitimate* systems.

A looming threat to the traditionalists' perspective on education is the advent of globalisation and, in particular, the possible influence of GATS (General Agreement on Trade in Services). Globalisation in the education field, the positive objective of which is to increase access, faces a number of challenges. Donnelly, writing in the context of higher education in Ireland, acknowledges that the recruitment of foreign students can become an entrepreneurial activity 'designed to generate revenue for universities with sagging budgets and the quest to maximise enrolment can mean a decline in quality' (p. 353). With its embrace of the Bologna Declaration (1999) Higher Education appears to be prepared for GATS. The Declaration's goal of increasing the international competitiveness of European Higher Education has, according to Donnelly, resulted in at least three developments which are having a direct influence on the design of third-level programmes. First, the Declaration is promulgating a system of easily readable and comparable degrees to promote European citizens' employability. Ireland has adopted this system in its National Framework of Qualifications (NQA). This is a single, nationally and internationally accepted structure through which all achievements in learning may be measured and related to each other in a transparent way and which can be used to describe the relationship between all training and/or education awards. Second, a system of credits is being developed to facilitate student mobility. Third, the Declaration is promoting co-operation in Quality Assurance with a view to the development of comparable criteria and methodologies.

The resultant convergence of policies which can be seen throughout the educational world is described by Levin (1998) as a 'policy epidemic' (p. 131). This convergence is due to a common set of problems which beset Higher Education worldwide. Donnelly, noting that growth has been unbridled and chaotic, reminds us that, in the United Kingdom, participation has doubled over the past 15 years against a concomitant drop of 40 per cent in costs. She describes the genesis of these problems as

> the process of shifting from elite to expanded, mass HE under severe resource constraints and with the burden of a legacy of persistent inequalities in access and outcomes, inadequate educational quality, low relevance to economic needs, and rigid governance and management structures.
>
> (p. 354)

Cheng's (1999) perspective on globalisation sees it as the development, adaptation and transfer of norms, knowledge, technology and behavioural values across countries and societies to communities, institutions and individuals. Other concepts used to describe this phenomenon are standardisation, normalisation, politicisation, diffusion, socialisation, cultural transplant, multiculturalism, colonisation, hybridisation, and networking (Waters 1995, Pieterse 1995 and Brown 1999). Cheng emphasises the positive influences of globalisation on education – the elimination of space and time barriers through web-based and internet learning, learning through video-conferencing and international partnerships in teaching and learning in addition to the rooting of curricula in social, technological, political, economic and cultural contexts. Sketching the distinctions between the traditional paradigms of learning, teaching and schooling and those of what she calls *new century curriculum and pedagogy* Cheng suggests that, in the traditional paradigm, students and teachers are part of the reproduction, perpetuation and imitative process, geared primarily to sustain society – particularly its economic and social structures. Characterised by control and by receiving and delivering, rather than by sharing, the process is undertaken in a geographically bounded environment for the purpose of gaining external rewards. Standard curricula with their accompanying textbooks, materials and methods alienate the teaching/learning process from fast changing local communities or international contexts. The school, an isolated island, is bound by teaching and learning activities in a very narrow fashion. There is no unanswerable requirement to effect strong community links as school is the major source of knowledge and qualifications with parents and communities playing the role of receivers of educational outcomes. Like Freire and Illich, Cheng sees traditional education as a disciplinary social process necessitating close supervision. The new paradigm she promotes considers teaching as a process to initiate, facilitate and sustain students' self-learning and self-actualisation. This paradigm proposes the recognition and application of CMIs –contextualised multiple intelligences – and the embrace of the concepts of triplisation, that is, globalisation, localisation and individualisation. By this Cheng means that all learning should be relevant to the individual and understood in both local and international contexts.

Hartley (1997) defends what he sees as the inevitability of low standards in education with his assertion that the significant changes which have taken place in culture and in the global economy cannot be accommodated within the traditional form of education and require a new paradigm. His claim finds voice, too, in the view of the World Bank and UNESCO (2000) statement that the expansion – unplanned, unbridled and often chaotic – has been accompanied by a deterioration in average quality and persistent inequalities. Robinson (2005) issues a strong cautionary note on the negative consequences for education if a GATS formula is adopted. He acknowledges the positives – increasing access and opportunity, consumer sovereignty, increased cost savings, greater efficiencies and economic growth and development. Against this list he suggests negatives which far outweigh any advantages. These are increased inequality, lower standards, diminished quality, the undermining of academe and the loss of traditional educational values. The fundamental difficulty with GATS, he says, is a clash of values and principles. 'GATS sees public services at best as missed commercial opportunities, at worst, as barriers to trade'. GATS covers all modes for delivering education and it is very unclear that there is any protection whatsoever for public service provision.

Back in 1776 Adam Smith recognised the human predisposition to develop markets wherever possible.

A profitable speculation is presented as a public good because growth will stimulate demand, and everywhere diffuse comfort and improvement. No patriot or man of feeling could therefore oppose it. [But] the nature of this growth, in opposition, for example, to older ideas such as cultivation, is that it is at once undirected and infinitely self-generating in the endless demand for all the useless things in the world.

(in Handy, p. 1, cit.)

One may wonder what this prescient observer would make of the current proliferation of products in the education industry.

Looking at the Irish situation, the OECD (2004) review of Higher Education commissioned by the Minister for Education, notes that

Ireland has embraced the international trend towards the application of market-based principles in the public sector with a view to improving efficiency through competition. The report suggests that there is still room to exploit more greatly the benefits of the market. It questions the heavy subsidisation of education on the grounds of both efficiency and equity and claims that the private rate of return is much higher than the social rate of return for those possessed of a university degree. Noting its success in other countries it supports the introduction of a government backed loan scheme. Flynn (2005) reports on a key address to the Irish Universities Association where a senior third-level figure underlined the frustration within the financially compromised university sector which sees itself, he claims, drifting towards a 'yellow pack' (p. 3) university system as it struggles to cope with lack of funding.

Skilbeck (2001) identifies a shift in orientation in the education market which will see the student as learner and client in a constrained resource environment. He suggests that 'the cultural state is being displaced by the market place' (p. 16) in a world where there is growth in demand for credentials of value in employment – the performativity value already described by Lyotard (1984), Bloland, Ainley (2000) and by Chaharbaghi and Newman. Skilbeck draws attention to the repositioning of the student as customer or client in the Australian education system and to the recurring concern in the USA regarding the quality of teaching and the standards attained by students. Against this backdrop he describes the shrinking market in Ireland – between 1998 and 2012 there will be a drop of 36 per cent in school leavers, from 74,000 to 47,000. Quoting de Boer, Goedegebure and Meek (1998) he acknowledges that the richness and diversity of academic life may be in danger of being fractured and trivialised by the adverse affects of massification. 'Leisurely reflection and scholarly contemplation have been replaced by rote learning' (in Skilbeck, p. 72), a development also referred to by Armstrong. Skilbeck forecasts the emergence of the 'virtual' learning institution, which delivers resources for learning and teaching but may have practically no academic staff of its own. He further warns that the logic of the marketplace has been superimposed on the 'dispassionate quest for knowledge and the disinterested pursuit of truth' (p. 23).

Supporting Coombs' (1968) observation that countries tend to emulate models from other countries even if they are conspicuously ill suited, Ireland has, historically, tended to reproduce the English educational paradigm. Clinton (1975) provides a description of non-university third-level education in Ireland.   Until 1960, university education was largely confined to the elite. That year, Ireland, having attended the Washington OECD conference, was chosen as the location for an in-depth analysis of the supply of skills and future demands for education. The subsequent report, *Investment in Education*, appeared in 1965. Soon came the announcement of a watershed development – the building of Regional Technical Colleges (renamed Institutes of Technology in 1998) to provide non-university third-level education. Several factors bolstered this decision – the skills deficits likely to occur in the 1970s, the great inequalities in Ireland, the disjunction between subjects and career needs and the gaps in the efficiency of use of educational resources. The Commission on Higher Education (1960–67) recommended that the Regional Technical Colleges should focus on the supply of technicians' courses at lower levels. The Steering Committee on Technical Education, reporting in 1967, was dismayed at the proposed dichotomy between the existing universities and the new institutions, a dichotomy, which in Skilbeck's view – with his distinction between tertiary and university education – has come to pass. The University and Institute of Technology sector have presided over an unprecedented expansion in education. Together they provide higher education to 55 per cent of school leavers. The Report by the Expert Group on Future Skills Needs (2007) says that this proportion must increase to 72 per cent by 2020. The Group further recommends that, by this date, 93 per cent of the Irish population should have qualifications at or above Leaving Certificate and that 48 per cent of the population should have a third- or fourth-level qualification.

Chapter 6

Measuring the Grade and Quality
of Education

Laskey's opinion that a responsible college, like a responsible airline, would never allow students/customers to determine quality is
contradicted by other writers who assert that grade inflation pervades (American) universities nationwide (Rakoczy, 2002; Rosovsky &
Hartley, 2002; Edmundson, 1997). Seligman (2002) suggests that
'grade inflation is especially pervasive at elite institutions where customers have high expectations and high tuition bills'.

Stone (1995) asserts that 15 per cent of current college degree
holders of Tennessee State University would not even have earned a
diploma by the mid-1960s standards. As long ago as 1985 it was clear
that, to the student, the credential matters more than the course.
The top priority for most students is to get through higher education with the highest grades and the least amount of time, effort and
inconvenience, he notes. Addressing this issue, Bloom believes that
students are 'morally unpretentious ... their primary pre-occupation
is themselves, understood in the narrowest terms' (p. 83). He adds
that students understand Tocqueville's belief that in democratic societies each person is consumed with the contemplation of a very petty
object – himself. Stone's study is a damning indictment of the concepts of education as a market commodity and students as consumers.
Writing about the American context he describes the indicators of low
academic standards that pervade higher education. The prime cause
of lower standards and grade inflation, he claims, is enrolment-driven
funding which makes grade inflation 'bureaucratically profitable'. An
insidious development is that while colleges were traditionally influenced by independent faculty, they are now typically large bureaucratic institutions which are governed by the personnel who exercise

budgetary control. Although ideas and submissions by academics are welcomed, it is the case, he says, that they are heard and acted upon only selectively. It is not that administrators do not espouse objectives of educational quality, it is that their notions of quality relate to numbers of students, organizational size, and programme and systems development whereas it is the accomplishment of students that is the quality indicator for academics. Illich agrees that this is how an organization evaluates its worth – by its level of output. In the case of the educational institution this is the throughput of graduates and the breadth of the suite of programmes offered.

Academic departments which achieve the greatest growth, says Stone, are recompensed with an increased share of resources. Departments that fail to grow remain under resourced and may actually be 'cannibalised' with their share of the budget going to areas that show greater potential for growth. Other reasons for lower academic standards, he says, are the admissions of poorly prepared students, allowing students to repeat failed assessments, and the practice of using student evaluations of lecturers as a basis for merit, promotion and tenure. A lecturer who insists on holding the line on standards will get a negative evaluation compared with one who is less stringent in doling out good results. S/he soon learns not to call down such a severe judgement on him/herself – the simple solution is to lower expectations. Quoting Mieczkowski (1995) Stone suggests that underneath an invisible layer of networks and relationships lie the subtle but persuasive rewards for academics who hold the 'right' views. These academics are accorded a warmer welcome than dissenters, their input is actively sought, they are afforded leadership roles that enhance their reputation throughout the organization, they are seen to be the management's chosen ones and are judged by management to be more reasonable and co-operative. They place their career interests above academic imperatives. They understand the unspoken rules. As Gee put it, *those in the know get the meanings free* – 'once you are a member of the group, once your behaviours count as meaningful within the social practice, you get the meanings free' (p. 10). On the other hand, those who engage in the kind of 'courageous conversation' advocated by Whyte (2004) and seek to address the issue of lower standards are sidelined by the management which considers them to be difficult and not team players, a point also made by Freire (1972). Faced with the leviathan of such informal but insidious discomfort those with discrepant views learn to keep their opinions to themselves.

Foy (1994) mirrors much of Stone's work in relation to declining academic standards in American universities. She also draws on the findings of the Wingspread Group on Higher Education (1993) to reveal that, not only are many college students deficient in basic literacy skills but they also lack the ancillary skills that are considered a prerequisite in students. She describes the shocking finding of the 1993 National Adult Literacy Survey that more than half of US college degree holders lack functional literacy skills such as the ability to synthesise information. This, despite the fact that the cost of education for the average American student is at least five times the median life earnings of over half of the world's population (Illich). While laying the blame at the doors of primary schools and those high schools which allow students without sufficient skills to graduate, Foy challenges colleges which also allow these students to graduate with undergraduate degrees. Although it is not usually considered the job of a higher education lecturer to teach functional literacy skills, it is, she says, the educator's duty to teach from the level at which students are functioning, not from the level where they ought to be. This contrasts with the stance of the professor who informed Ezra Cornell, founder of the eponymous university, that 'faculty wasn't prepared to teach the alphabet' (in Casazza, 1996).

Recognising the problem of poor literacy skills, Rockman (2004) stresses the need for the development of information literacy among students and to integrate it into teaching. Information literacy is understood as the acquisition of the skills required to intelligently and systemically find, interpret, organize and critique information for a specific purpose. Learning is, therefore, rooted in context. Such a skill provides a foundation for lifelong learning and is common to all disciplines, all levels of education and all learning environments. Like reading, it is not a skill which is acquired once and for all. Rather, it is a complex mix of knowledge, skills and attitudes – competencies, which, although they can be learned, must be actively taught and practised and not left to the chance of absorption through academic experience. Information literacy is not to be confused with expertise in computer technology which allows students to manipulate data and create documents without necessarily demonstrating any understanding of the subject matter. Students, according to Rockman, are entering the Californian State University without core literacy skills such as the ability to think critically, to make decisions and to direct their own learning. They are over-dependent on web sources and sources accessed through search engines rather than relying on conventional sources, such as library catalogues. Information literacy straddles the divide between technical computer competence and conventional textual literacy which enables an individual to read, critically evaluate, write and analyse various forms of literary works. Rockman asserts that while students may have the skills to send electronic mail, chat and download music, many have not learned how to 'effectively locate information; evaluate, synthesise and integrate ideas; use information or give credit for work used' (p. 10). She draws on Goad (2002) who notes that there is no escape from the requirement for information literacy. 'Information literacy – the ability to recognise the need for information, to locate, access, select and apply it – was once an academic matter. Nowadays, the critical array of skills concerns anyone working in a knowledge-based environment' (in Rockman, p. 12).

Casazza's (1996) study of remedial support for unprepared freshmen in American universities finds that it has a long history, dating from the eighteenth century. When Cornell asked could the college's freshmen read he was told by a professor that if he wanted faculty to teach spelling he should have founded a primary school, not a university. During the early eighteenth century the President of Vassar complained, with a tinge of oxymoron that the 'range of student achievement extends to a point lower than any scale could measure' (in Casazza, p. 8).

In 1871 Harvard freshmen exhibited 'bad spelling, incorrectness as well as inelegance of expression in writing, (and) ignorance of the simplest rules of punctuation' (Casazza, p. 19). In the 1890s, Harvard linked poor writing skills with a lack of clear thinking and laid the blame for both at the door of second level schools. In 1892 a committee set up by the National Education Association of the United States reported that students of eighteen or twenty years of age lacked the habits of observing, reflecting and recording – habits which they should have acquired in early childhood. By 1907 more than half of college entrants to the prestigious institutions of Harvard, Yale, Princeton and Columbia were unable to meet the entrance requirements.

In 1968, Coombs suggested that if higher education institutions were to be judged exclusively by the measure of enrolment there would be no question about quality or content, he says. If, however, as we must, judge that 'institutions exist to teach students, not to produce statistics' (p. 104) we must ask what, how much and how fast students are learning. The essence of Coombs' suggestion questions how higher education can reform itself so that 'respectability, quality and prestige' (p. 102) can be evenly distributed throughout its parts so that there would be no division of first class and second class citizens among its student cohort.

Like Stone and Seligman, Foy takes account of the trap in which lecturing staff may find themselves – that is the likelihood of receiving a poor evaluation from students who find their course too difficult due to the effort on the part of the lecturer to maintain high standards. She proposes a set of initiatives designed to reverse grade and literacy drift. These include remedial foundation courses, the award of no more than a D grade if there are spelling or grammatical errors, the requirement to achieve high literacy skills before graduation. Additionally she suggests counselling, peer and software support for students.

Singal (1991) courageously dissects many political hot potatoes in his exploration of declining standards in American education. Like Foy he is aghast at the low literacy standards and declining SAT (Stanford Achievement Test) scores among college freshmen. He quotes Paul Copperman, who in 1983 wrote in *A Nation at Risk* that, while in the past each generation had exceeded the education and literacy achievements of their parents, the education achievements of current generations will not even come close to those of their parents. This reflects the 2004 OECD Ireland study which showed declining standards overall. Interestingly, while US SAT scores of the lower socio-economic and ability groups have risen, the scores of the more numerous higher ability groups have fallen, thus bringing down national averages. This 'thrusting of mediocrity on the talented'

(Brubacher & Rudy, p. 268) was deplored at Harvard as early as the nineteenth century.

Singal refutes the notion that the cause is students' laziness and lays the blame instead at the door of the prevailing social mandate that confuses egalitarianism with a diminution in excellence. Like Stone, he recognises that the 1960s' democratic thinking saw excellence in education as elitist – 'the reigning ethos of those times was hostile to excellence'. This ethos underpinned a demand for schools that aimed to foster social co-operation and equality at the expense of training for the mind. While the tide of the 1960s has receded it has left mediocrity in its wake. The effort to reduce possible feelings of low self-esteem among the academically less able is paid for in the compromised education of the more able students who learn to coast through the system at 'half speed'. The preoccupation with not stressing students has resulted in not stretching them. In an interesting aside Singal suggests a possible link with suicide because young people are so sheltered from stress that they are not taught how to cope with it. He deplores the reluctance to use opportunities presented by education to develop personal responsibility in students. Give them time to 'smell the roses' is, he says, a constant refrain, notwithstanding the fact that they are more likely to be ensconced in front of a TV or 'cruising a shopping mall'. He assures us that the pursuit of social equality and academic excellence are not mutually exclusive. He calls for changes in education which may topple some sacred cows and offend those with (misplaced) social sensibilities. Unlike Foy, he makes no mention of remedial support at college but suggests changes to be made at the high school level. First of all he calls for the imposition of a heavy reading load. Distrust the term *age appropriate reading*, he says, which is very often junk masquerading as literature – the reading of which results in an impoverished command of English. Reading is the 'primary vehicle by which students absorb the rhythms and patterns of language' thus facilitating analytical writing. Secondly, teach history that is integrated with knowledge of culture and power relations. Thirdly, introduce flexible ability streaming which allows all students to reach higher levels of excellence. Schools which stream students on the basis of ability have higher SAT scores than those who do not stream. Fourthly, attract brighter students into teaching and resist the practice of teacher training which forces the teacher to focus on constructing a lesson plan. Such lesson plans are measurable outcomes delighted in by 'quality' auditors but practitioners question their value. Freire, too, would probably have a problem with teaching education to a formula – education which is confined rather than organic. Singal issues a strong warning against mini-courses and electives and what he calls a 'spotty' approach to education, the *technical smorgasbord* referred to by Bloom.

Cross (1983), like Singal, would not lay the blame at the students' door. She describes the type of student who comes to university because of the greater open-door policy. They are, she says, often passive towards learning and they bring with them a fear of failure. Their fear of failure is deeply embedded in them because of their long experience of non-achievement. The disadvantages of attempting to meet students' expectations by providing bespoke programmes present, however, a double-edged sword, she says. The concomitant of this freedom of choice is the 'opportunity to fail' (p. 198). Casazza draws on Gleazer who exhibits impatience towards those who ask whether a student is *college material*. 'We are not building a college with the student. The question we ought to ask is whether the college is of sufficient student material. It is the student we are building and it is the function of the college to facilitate that process' (Casazza, p. 23).

Casazza's study, which supports the widespread implementation of what are now called development courses, fails to find a positive echo in Stone, Seligman, Foy or Singal. Seligman supports Stone's view that those most at risk from student evaluations are young non-tenured lecturers but suggests that many people in the education field are not fazed by grade inflation – 'it makes students happier, teachers more popular, parents less inclined to notice the inflation in tuition charges'. The warning sounded by Gibbs and Iacovidou that the adjective *quality* is not the same as *good* – although 'it might be used irresponsibly as a simulacrum of it' (p. 113) – is supported by Chaharbaghi and Newman and by the findings of Shanahan's and Gerber's primary research that not alone do measurements, but also perspectives, of quality become simulacra for education.

In the case of Ireland, it seems evident that the country can no longer lay any claim to the descriptor 'The Island of Saints and

Scholars'. Holt (2004), in a column cleverly entitled *Consuming Academia*, criticises school and university rankings as 'ideology dressed up as expertise' (p. 2). What we have, he says, is a 'culture in which brutal (in every sense) calculation and measurement displace cultivation and passion' (p. 2). He draws on a reference from an academic who testifies to the silence in Irish academia – 'the 'good' academic is encouraged to become increasingly silent' (in Holt, p. 2).

In the context of awards, the National University of Ireland made a recent decision to introduce a new marking scheme which will ensure higher grades for students of NUI, who, the report claims, have traditionally been awarded fewer first class honours than their counterparts in British universities (*Irish Times*, March 2002). In the Institute of Technology sector, the requirements for progression up the ladder from certificate to diploma to degree have been reduced. This policy, it is forecast, will have a profound effect on student retention. There is an assurance that this action will not devalue awards – an ideology which seems fundamentally at odds with reality. O'Grady (2007), O'Grady and Guilfoyle (2007) and O'Grady and Quinn (2007), reflecting much of Stone's thinking, provide evidence of grade inflation in both Institutes of Technology and Universities in Ireland. These authors assert that grades awarded through the third-level system in Ireland do not now represent the standard of ability or achievement that they did in the past. In 1994 the percentage of first class honours awarded across the Universities was 7 per cent. By 2005 there was a significant increase to 17 per cent. Over the same period in the Institutes of Technology, despite a significant decrease in the CAO points of entrants, the number receiving first class honours degrees increased by 52 per cent. O'Grady and Guilfoyle draw on Manhire (2004) who insists that grade inflation is unethical and is contrary to traditional ethical tenets concerning good educational practice. O'Grady enumerates twenty factors emanating from structural changes in NCEA/HETAC which have contributed to grade inflation and O'Grady and Quinn explore the social and institutional forces which also exert pressure on grades. O'Grady and Quinn suggest that declining social distance is a factor as academics experience discomfort in disappointing students by awarding poor grades. Unlike Ball (1996), they eschew what they call the Pygmalion myth that all humans are equal in ability and that factors such as teaching methods can be manipulated in order to successfully educate any student who presents in the system. Like Brubacher and Rudy, they bemoan the squandering of the capabilities of the more academically talented in a society where the educational process is becoming increasingly degraded.

Declining standards in the Irish secondary system are revealed in the OECD (2004) report. Out of 29 countries Irish 15 year olds rank 13th in science and 17th in maths with more than 17 per cent scoring at the lowest level in maths. While these pupils rank 6th in reading skills, the news is not good since 11 per cent score at the lowest level and, overall, standards have dropped since the 2000 study. Considering that at least 54 per cent of secondary school pupils will go on to higher education this represents a bleak outlook for success at college. Holland (2007) quotes Collins who remarks that second-level students 'come to university singularly unprepared for the intellectual challenges of adult life . . . They think like powerpoint. They find it difficult to construct a narrative: they return exam scripts in bullet points' (p. 5).

Greer's (1998) study of the Irish higher education context reveals seriously compromised literacy competencies. His study, mirroring much of Foy's American outcomes, finds that most students can be categorised as average to below average in basic reading skills and that there is no correlation between success in examinations and their comprehension skills or vocabulary. Furthermore there is no improvement in reading skills over the three-year study period, their writing skills are inadequate for the tasks normally required of third-level students and they have a preference for reasoning at concrete operational level. In an effort to achieve the twin aims of course coverage and student retention, the traditional positivist teaching model (the banking system eschewed by Freire) is employed. 'Consequently assessments take the form of objective measures of regurgitated material' (p. 355). Greer's findings assert that 'reading and writing skills do not appear to be required for success in examinations, but without them the student remains underdeveloped' (p. 351).

Flynn (2006) reports on the finding that third-level students have low levels of understanding of maths despite having taken higher level maths in the Leaving certificate. They lack a basic understanding of arithmetic, algebra and geometry. Even more astounding is the suggestion that many second-level teachers of maths, themselves, have no in-depth understanding of the subject. Fitzgerald's (2005) voice is a lone one in its praise of standards of education in Ireland. He claims that the rapid increase in the numbers who have third-level qualifications – from 300,000 to 650,000 in the decade from 1991 to 2002 – has been achieved without a lowering of standards such, he says, as has been the case in Britain, both at secondary school level and in some universities. In Britain, he says, because of the variety in standards, employers discriminate between universities in making career appointments. If anything, he adds, the comments of external examiners of the National University of Ireland suggest that standards in Ireland may actually be on the high side. Expansion continues. By 2007, half of those in the 25–29 cohort who have completed their education will have third-level qualifications, two-thirds of them at degree level.

O'Leary (2005) cautions against confusing correlation with cause when he asks why the Irish are so determined to believe that their education system is among the best in the world. He answers his own question – 'it's the economy, stupid! How could we have produced the Celtic Tiger, the best growth rates in the world, the fastest growth in employment and all that without a world-beating education system?' (p. 5). He argues that the increased demand for education is very likely a consequence rather than a cause of economic improvements as higher standards of living occasion increases in demand for all products. Deconstructing the accepted wisdom that the rising level of educational attainment has contributed about 1 per cent per annum to the growth during the 1990s, he reminds us that educational attainment, in this context, refers to the length of time the average individual spends in education, not to any improvement in the quality of educational outcomes.

In the United Kingdom a report carried out by Dr Ruth Lea (2005) on behalf of the Institute of Directors reveals a belief among top business leaders that students are leaving university with qualifications that do not make them fit for jobs, 'the labour market cannot satisfactorily overcome very fundamental basic skills deficiencies in

literacy and numeracy'. The report describes endemic grade inflation at both the second and third levels and claims that employers
are becoming increasingly wary of degrees from many new universities, a point also made by Fitzgerald (2005). Blake (2000) claims that
in the rush to meet performance indicators, institutions of education
have made the meeting of such targets their overwhelming priority: success and quality are synonymous with meeting such targets.
Warner and Palfreyman (1996) also emphasise the changed role for
higher education managers. Obliged to shift their focus from the academic issues which had previously concerned them, they direct their
efforts instead towards external matters such as market positioning
and mission statements. Halsey (1995) identifies some of the cause
of discontent in academe. He suggests that both the institutions and
the academics are suffering an identity crisis, a suggestion which is
supported by the work of Bruner (1957), Tajfel (1981), Tapper and
Salter (1992) and, most recently, Bruner (1993).

Resistance to treating education as a reified, measurable product
comes, too, from Dunne (1993), Fielding (1998), Lander (2000),
Srikanthan and Dalrymple (2002), Knight (2002) and Saito (2002).
Saito argues that the limitations of quality measurement 'are symp-
toms of nihilism and cynicism, of the flattening and thinning of our
ethical lives' (pp. 248–249). Kistan (1999), asserting that the concept
of quality is always influenced by political and economic developments, sheds some light on the varying understandings of the concept.
He draws on Harvey and Green (1993) who offer five possibilities –
quality as exceptional, as perfection, as fitness for purpose, as value for
money and as transformative. Such fluidity of definition would find
little favour with Illich. Reflecting the sentiments of Dunne (1995),
Ball (1999) describes the implications of a system guided by market and performativity criteria. '(It) bites deep into the practice of
teaching and into the teacher's soul ... specific and diverse aspects
of conduct are reworked and the locus of control over the selection
of pedagogies and curricula is shifted'.

The changing relationship between education and production
demands, he says, that we address the modality that has largely been
ignored, that of values. Advocates of the market paradigm often
approach the issue of values in either of two ways. First, the market

can be seen as value-neutral – simply as a mechanism which delivers education more efficiently, effectively and responsively. On the other hand it can be suggested that the market can act as a transformational force in the lives of students as, it is claimed, it possesses a set of positive moral values in its own right – those of effort, thrift, self-reliance, independence and risk-taking. Decrying what Bottery (1992) calls the pauperisation of moral concepts in the public sphere, Ball (1999) asserts that a new moral environment is being created for both consumers and producers. In this environment educational institutions are being inducted into a culture of self-interest while the pursuit of positional advantage over others by individual students is legitimated and even celebrated, a reinforcement of Bloom's view that the tide of egalitarianism brought in its wake calculating individualism. The fall-out from this competition and culture of self-interest, says Ball (1999) is that a society which is rich tends, in fact, to behave as if it were poor. He draws on Bauman (1992) who asserted that the society of the post-modern community does not require supportive social relationships. The concept of a deliberate, planned quest for the common good and for the values of civic virtue becomes almost meaningless on the postmodern playing fields of competition and survival. 'The spaces within which reflection upon and dialogue over values were possible are closed down,' Ball (1999) reminds us ominously. Gibbs and Iacovidou also courageously question the moral implications of an education which is posited on the ethical vacuum of market imperatives. They assert that, although we must be vigilant lest we fall into the trap of 'puritanical modernism' (p. 118), it is essential to recognise that an education that is not founded on a framework underpinned by what is decent, moral and ethical is unworthy and inauthentic. Spivak (2005), while acknowledging the crisis in education, maintains that teachers must continue to believe that there must be ways in which they can help, although she does not specify how. Otherwise it is not possible to carry on. She draws on Gramsci 'pessimism of the intellect, optimism of the will'. Disillusionment, she says, is not something that teachers can afford.

Pollitt's (1990) review of managerialism in the UK public sector describes a framework based on exacting financial controls, the efficient allocation of resources, the rigours of the market and the widespread use of performance criteria as evidence of quality. The framework also asserts the need for management control and the manager's right to manage. Scott's (1989) accountability framework suggests that colleges must have *political accountability* to account for public funds and *market accountability* to answer the demands of stakeholders. In addition, they must have *professional accountability* for maintaining the highest possible academic standards and *cultural accountability* to develop new knowledge and insights. Randle and Brady (1997) argue that the managerial approach places student enrolment and income generation above concern for student learning – managers, they say, are informed by a different set of values than academic staff. Telford and Masson (2005) discover that, although all the stakeholders in their study felt that lecturer commitment was of almost paramount importance, neither management nor students thought that student commitment was at all important whereas this was a major factor for the lecturers. Managers were more concerned with treating students as adults, attached less importance to teaching and no importance at all to teaching styles, they find. According to Warner and Palfreyman (1996) such a *them-and-us* mentality can be found in organizations where there is a bureaucracy that must interact with professionals. Raelin (1985) describes the cause of conflict; it lies in the clash of cultures. Managers are attuned to corporate culture, concerned with efficiency and financial constraints. Professionals, on the other hand, who according to Raelin are by nature individualistic, will resist the conformity to regulations imposed from outside the profession. They tend to ignore procedures which attempt to standardise decision-making. The ideal, says Raelin, 'is that one day professional accomplishment will become consonant with managerial proficiency' (p. 220). Jarratt's (1985) nettled response to demands for collegiality in chartered university governance claims that academics sometimes 'see their academic discipline as more important than the long-term well-being of the university which houses them' (p. 33). His assertion is borne out by Warner and Palfreyman who draw on Merton's College's evidence to the 1966 Franks Commission of Enquiry – 'education in general and university education par excellence are worlds in which the administrator should be kept in his place' (p. 6).

Newby (2003), alone of his peers, praises the rate of return in UK education – over the past 15 years the student participation rate has more than doubled against a backdrop of a sector which has absorbed a cost reduction of nearly 40 per cent, a statistic also reported, but with misgiving, by Donnelly.

The impact of managerialism in education is manifested in the promotion of NPM, New Public Management. According to Hammersley (2002) the goal of NPM is to introduce forms of organization within the public sector which replicate as far as possible the 'discipline of the market' (p. 4). This market form is designed to subject Higher Education to the dynamics and culture of competition and business. Ball (1999) describes the concomitant of this approach – the performativity criterion already described. Management activities impress the pragmatics of performativity on to the work practices of lecturers and on to the social relations between them. Performativity criteria make management 'ubiquitous, invisible, inescapable – embedded' in everything the lecturer does. Actions are judged on the basis of their contribution to the organization's overall performance rather than on anything that derives from authentic principles or values. As a consequence the possibilities for metaphysical discourse are closed down. The judgement of the professional and the values of service and altruism, which have so long underpinned the work of many, are displaced. Survival, under the pervasive gaze of performativity, replaces professionalism and ethics with pragmatic self-interest. In such an 'enchanted workplace', says Lyotard (1984), 'administrative procedures should make individuals *want* what the system needs in order to perform well' (p. 62) [author's italics]. In a telling dismissal of performativity, Ball (1999) claims that such a management criterion eliminates emotion and desire from teaching, rendering the teacher's soul 'transparent but empty ... [as the] ... humanistic commitments of the substantive professional – the service ethic – are replaced by the teleological promiscuity of the technical professional – the manager'.

Richter and Buttery's (2004) study of Australia's higher education system also exposes the challenge to the integrity of education posed by the worship of economic rationalism over scholarship. Australia, they say, firmly belongs in the second tier. There is every sign, they add, that while athletes would not be happy to train on fast food 'students are quite happy to train on fast Masters' (p. 126). Harman (2002) sees a shift in Australian universities from collegial to more corporate styles of management. This raises concerns for academic heads who may have to choose between loyalty to their vice-chancellors and loyalty to their academic colleagues.

Many writers on education emphasise the importance of student engagement, the development of student responsibility and the promotion of a learning community. The uses of external measures of quality and the attempt to treat students as customers are inimical to such processes. Illich warns against the illusion of numbers. Personal growth, which is what constitutes real education, is not a measurable entity. 'It is', he says, 'growth in disciplined dissidence' (p. 40). Gadamer (1975) and Carr (1987) also assert that education is not just about technical competence. Such competence must be rooted in phronesis[1], they say. In the Irish context Donnelly expresses concern that universities may be neglecting to exhibit in contemporary society their unique intellectual and moral leadership, a view also emphasised by O'Toole (2007). Carr claims that education cannot be rendered intelligible if it is guided by fixed ends and governed by determined rules. Lomas (2004), in an examination of the United Kingdom's outcome-based approach to education, exposes the opportunity costs of such an orientation. Audits, data collection and other quality related measures cost the UK higher education sector approximately £250 million a year – a sum that, according to one estimate, could fund the employment of 8,300 new lecturers or the provision of 50,000 extra higher education places (p. 159). Harvey (2002) further queries the value of quality monitoring. He reports that delegates to a 2002 quality conference were sceptical that external monitoring had any positive effect on student learning or programme quality. Yorke and Longden (2004), too, question the reliability of performance measures and the tendency to interpret them for largely political ends.

Handy also warns about our obsession with counting and measurement, an obsession which derives from the importance in management of the accountant at the expense of other professions.

---

[1] phronesis: moral accountability.

Accountants are society's auditors, he says, trained to look backward rather than forward, to shun risk and to count only what they can put their finger on. The goodwill of accountants is not an issue, he says, he is simply concerned about what they count. Their way of thinking is entirely appropriate for auditors but not for leaders. People are counted as costs, not assets, and no value is placed on intellectual assets, effort or diligence. He reminds us that although Adam Smith is usually remembered for his concept of the *hidden hand of greed* as the prime mover of the economy, he is entitled to be remembered also for his often forgotten exhortation that a proper regard for others is the basis of a civilised society. Despite Einstein's reminder that 'not everything that can be counted, counts and not everything that counts can be counted' there is, nevertheless, a built in bias in favour of savings rather than value. Handy claims that cost control is a necessary but not sufficient condition of success. 'The bottom line should be a starting point not a finishing post' (p. 75). Caulkin (2007) reminds us of the potentially catastrophic consequences that attend the alignment of policy with targets. He points to the death of between 20 and 30 million people in China during the Great Leap Forward when fictitious figures were presented to the authorities because the targets for grain production could not possibly be met. Acknowledging that this is an extreme example, he, nevertheless, quotes Hope (co-founder of the Beyond Budgeting Roundtable) who describes the budget as 'a management tool of mass destruction' (Caulkin, p. 40). Analysing the fallout from companies such as Enron, Tyco and WorldCom, Hope asserts that the problems can be traced back directly to aggressive targets, linked to incentives, which drive short-term actions. Caulkin claims that, on a small scale, China's fictions are being repeated every day as the imposition of targets induces corrupt practices in organizations which use the budget as their overarching management tool. Several decades ago, Schumacher (1974) voiced concern about the central role of economics in policy making. 'In the current vocabulary of condemnation', he says, 'there are few words as final and conclusive as the word "uneconomic"' (p. 34). He acknowledges a generally accepted distinction between economics and finance but suggests that this distinction is a smokescreen. Finance unashamedly looks merely at the bottom line, economics claims to take other factors into account by carrying out a cost/benefit analysis. Schumacher is scathing about such a pretence.

> This is generally thought to be an enlightened and progressive development, as it is at least an attempt to take account of costs and benefits which might otherwise be disregarded altogether. In fact, however, it is a procedure by which the higher is reduced to the level of the lower and the priceless is given a price.

(p. 37)

If an activity is judged as uneconomic its right to existence is not only questioned but energetically opposed and anyone who clings to a thing which is shown to be uneconomic is considered either a fool or a saboteur. Schumacher claims, however, that decisions based on economics are fragmentary in the extreme as they are concerned only with whether or not the undertaking yields a profit to those who undertake it. There is no concern with benefits to society as a whole and such a deficit is all the more a problem as financial decisions are weighted towards the short term rather than towards the long term. Schumacher recognises that while every discipline has apposite applications within its own proper limits, it becomes evil and destructive when it transgresses them. The destructive nature of inappropriate quantification becomes all the more hazardous as education shifts from Masefield's ideal towards its new function as an agent for social placement.

Chapter 7

Education – Agent for Social Placement

Historically, higher education was linked to elite, professional careers. The idea, first identified by McGregor (1960), that the efficiency and effectiveness of organizations is heavily dependent on the quality of human resources still pervades contemporary organizational thinking (OECD 2004). The significance of education lies in the perceived need for more technical, professional and managerial workers in an increasingly competitive globalised world. Brown and Scase (1994) assert that the belief in education's ability to deliver economic goods has not been seriously questioned, and that furthermore, the belief still persists as part of the conventional wisdom among politicians, parents, employers and students that education is a form of investment. Brown and Scase identify two competing explanations of the relationship between education and occupational stratification – the technocratic theory and the social exclusion model.

The Technocratic Model describes the requirements for skills acquisition as a result of rapidly increasing technological change. This is mirrored in increasing expansion of higher education and a shift to a professional society. This model rests on a number of assumptions, notably that swift technological change is an inevitable feature of advanced industrial societies. The model further assumes that, in consequence, a much greater proportion of jobs require extensive periods of formal education and training and that the proportion of semi-skilled and unskilled jobs declines over time. The expansion of higher education can be explained by the pressure placed on governments to increase funding for higher education in order to ensure a continuous stream of professional, managerial and technical workers. The labour market is therefore a structure with a hierarchy of occupations mirrored in the competition for academic and professional credentials. This competition for educational credentials of access reflects a political ideology which would equalise opportunity so that talent will rise, irrespective of gender, colour or class barriers. The argument underpinning this ideology is that advanced societies can no longer afford to squander the talent of marginalised groups.

The Social Exclusion Model, in contrast, questions the technocratic model on both theoretical and empirical grounds. On theoretical grounds it faults the assumption that it is possible to read the structure of higher education simply in terms of the needs of the economy. This model assumes increasing competition between occupational and social groups against a background of little change in skill level, or even, perhaps, de-skilling. The expansion in higher education is indicative of credential inflation and the middle class continues to monopolise superior jobs. This model claims a multiplicity of facets in the ideologies, traditions and content of education systems and a complexity in their interrelationships and power plays. At the empirical level an argument is mounted that there is little evidence of dramatic rises in skill levels in the second half of the twentieth century, and in fact, that, on balance, there is greater evidence of de-skilling – a suggestion supported by Braverman, (1974), Bowles and Gintis (1976) and Ainley (2000). There is also little evidence to support the view that college graduates are more productive than school leavers. Like Illich, Collins (1979) asserts that schools have little effect on learning apart from the reproduction effect identified by Bourdieu and Passeron (2000). That is, schools strengthen the structures of the cultural styles endemic in the higher social classes while examination results simply reward middle class cultural discipline. Collins (1979) asks why the technocratic ideology of American education fails to translate into open occupational opportunity. He answers his own question, suggesting that social groups are concerned with acquiring and controlling career power and income. Educational credentials become the virtual, but powerful, building blocks of specialist professional and technical enclaves, with hierarchical division of labour. Collins' (1979) conclusion is that the expansion in higher education is pivoted more on the struggle between social groups for scarce credentials than a need for more technically competent workers. Bourdieu and Boltanski (1978), echoing Collins (1979), link the

increasing demand for education to social structure. Credentials are
pursued by the middle classes in order to reproduce and reinforce
their social advantage, protecting them from downward mobility during recession phases of a rapidly changing economy. At the same time
access to credentials is the essential driver of working class mobility
especially in advanced economies where traditional working class jobs
have largely disappeared.

Brown and Scase, while agreeing in principle with Collins' (1979)
view, take a less polarised approach. They suggest that the demand for
more educated labour may devolve as much from the changing organizational model as from rapid technological developments. They
also identify a further source of demand for education, that is, the
skills that employers think they need, which may be different from the
skills they actually need, a subject which has received scant attention.
In the past, claim Brown and Scase, educational qualifications were
confidently embraced by employers as a good general predictor of
career competence for the reason that there was a close connection
between education and work experiences. Public and private sector
organizations alike, bureaucratic in outlook, valued the mastery of
knowledge content, the meeting of deadlines and the discipline of
compliance with authority – all values exhibited by successful adaptation to the study life of the student. The current organizational
paradigm suggests a different set of values – creativity, innovation,
'habit breaking rather than habit making' (p. 25) – values which
provide a line of poor fit if educational credentials are used in recruitment. How habit breaking, themselves, the managers of these organizations may be is open to query. Research shows that when recruiting
for their fast-track graduate development programmes they continue
to consistently target the established universities despite the willingness of new universities to reshape curricula and assessment in order
to produce the more rounded candidate whom organizations claim
to want.

The organization of higher education in England has traditionally blended neatly with the bureaucratic paradigm of work which, in
Fordist fashion, perceived a clear distinction between conception and
execution, thus ensuring that the proportion of employees requir-
ing advanced academic or technical education remained low, the

preserve of the elite. In the United States, by contrast, college education was a usual prerequisite for entry into technical, administrative and professional occupations. Despite many nods in the direction of student autonomy in higher education, the reality is that the bureaucratic model is still strong. Students have little or no say in the content, pacing and grading of the learning process, the choosing of texts, methods of assessment or in the management of the institution. Brown and Scase suggest that students quickly learn that

> there are certain hoops to jump through, such as the completion of assignments by a specified date, or the regurgitation of lecture notes in written examinations, which demand rule following behaviour and an acceptance of the academic authority of the teaching staff. There is little mileage to be gained from challenging the status quo, which leads to the label disruptive rather than innovative or creative.
>
> (p. 39)

The latest phase of expansion and reform of higher education in England owes its thrust to this apparent mismatch between education and the economy; it is underpinned too by a political awareness of the success of the Asia/Pacific region whose competitive advantage is associated with a high proportion of employees possessed of advanced academic qualifications. In this phase an effort was made to give apparent authority to the ideology of a level playing field. Therefore, the costs per student, higher at the universities than at the polytechnics, were standardised at the lower cost, with the polytechnics renamed as universities. As is the case in the United States of enrolment related funding, the creation of a single market in education forced higher education institutions to increase enrolment in order to survive. Ball (1996) suggests that more means different. Ainley (1993) concurs that a new hierarchy will devolve, with research concentrated in centres of excellence at the top and teaching-only institutions at the bottom, where narrow skills related to employment will be taught. In between these levels will be courses to serve the cultural needs of more privileged students who will access employment in artistic, intellectual and conceptually orientated occupations. Brown and Scase draw particular attention to the attempt to assist the student to develop a measure of cultural capital. Much of what students learn at university, they say, is learned through the informal curricula of campus and college activities, the kind of tacit knowledge referred to by Akbar, Spender and Polanyi (1966). An attempt is made to compensate for the absence of such extracurricular activities at new universities through the provision of skills courses.

> The so-called 'personal transferable skills' are then taught separately from the culture of which they form a part, because personal and transferable skills are inherently social and generic. Therefore efforts to acquire these social and generic skills by formal teaching, rather than as part of the culture of the informal curricula of college and campus, could result in an opposite effect to that intended.
>
> (pp. 43–44)

The idea that such skills can be taught piecemeal and to all strata is highly questionable. What Coombs (1968) would call 'the papering over a mass of students with a common cultural face' (p. 102), it ignores the reality that many middle class students may already be possessed of these skills as a result of their family and previous education socialisation. Bourdieu et al. (2000) assert, too, that even if not all middle class students possess these skills, their previous experiences form ready foundations for them, foundations not available to working class students. The provision of formal transferable skills training in the less prestigious institutions takes, therefore, according to Brown and Scase, the shape of a 'deficit model' (p. 44); it is for those who do not already possess the necessary cultural capital and have not been able to acquire it.

With its focus on the upgrading of professional skills, technocratic theory is billed as the facilitation of *embourgeoisement* – the shift to a professional society. Braverman's (1974) and Ainley's (2000) opposite view, that there is evidence of deskilling, supports the theory of enduring class divisions and the proletarianisation of white collar occupations. Brown and Scase argue that the use of skills or qualifications as a proxy for class, prospects, rewards, security and life chances no longer holds. In this they are supported by the prescient observation in Marshall's (1963) forecast that 'the ticket obtained on leaving school or university is no longer for a life journey' (p. 113). Brown and Scase report that, in terms of career satisfaction, the rhetoric of the adaptive organization fails to deliver, with employees maintaining a clear division between their private life and their work life in a bid to cope with occupational frustration. The adaptive organization is particularly sensitive to the presence or absence of cultural capital. Brown and Scase describe a typical *Essex girl* (p. 141), who despite a first class honours degree, creates a problem for her organization and its clients with her accent and style of dress. Emphasising that recruitment into adaptive organizations is 'pregnant with social significance' (p. 142), they explain that it is never expressed explicitly that playing tennis and rowing indicate energy and contribution while playing pool does not. Employers will not admit that girls with Essex working class accents who are not into power dressing 'are inevitably excluded, irrespective of their academic abilities' (p. 142). The claims advanced by some organizations that objective screening tests neutralise the social realities of gender, class race and ethnicity are, in the opinion of Brown and Scase, untenable. The bureaucratic organization, in its selection process, has traditionally relied on the certification of expert knowledge and on particular characteristics of external behaviour which demonstrate compliance with formal authority. The recruitment and selection patterns of the adaptive organization represent the commodification of the whole person identified by Fromm as early as 1949. The physical characteristics – speech, value system and interests – are incorporated into a package, saleable on the job market.

Tapper and Salter (1992) claim that one of the key social functions of higher education is to control both individual and social mobility. A second is to control change in the status of professions. Additionally, its near monopoly of high status knowledge and culture gifts it with a third, unique kind of power, ideological power, the authority to make authoritative statements about values. A shift in ideology is a precursor to the resistance or facilitation of change. Despite the varying pressures for change since the nineteenth-century Russell Commission, the old universities, armed with their unassailable claim that they represent the first incarnation of the liberal idea of education and its concomitant culture, continue to dominate the hierarchy. The dominant position of Oxbridge in the higher education hierarchy is mirrored in the status symbolism of the British élites. This separate specialness was traditionally a privileged route to centres of political, economic, church and court power. This very uniqueness gives the old universities a clear marketing advantage in their competition with other institutions for higher education government funding. Their uniqueness, historically embedded, is inalienable and allows them unrivalled influence over the way in which universities carry out their functions and respond to change.

The education system experiences pressure from the economy to produce both manpower and knowledge useful to the economy's needs. Historically, the traditional approach of the higher education sector was to resist such a nexus. For many decades the upper strata of society and state shared the universities' value system. In fact, it was perceived that the British elite was a single, homogeneous group with a common value system and shared cultural identity.

Tapper and Salter claim that the strength of an ideology can be assessed in its ability to ignore, or selectively interpret, the reality with which it is confronted. The Robbins Report (HM Government, 1963), underpinned by the principle of social demand, was the driver of mass education. The report insisted that the unlimited massification to which the principle gives force, should be guided by a high-quality and expensive form of élite education. However, as Tapper and Salter, with irony, point out,

> the fact that the reality and the ideology are fundamentally irreconcilable made no difference to the attempt to legitimate the former with the latter. The need to justify ideologically a policy juggernaut which no one knew how to control had to be fulfilled and this need coincided with the universities' desire to maintain their hegemony of the higher education sphere.
>
> (p. 13)

The authors acknowledge, however, that the relevance of the traditional values to a mass higher education system could not escape challenge. The inexorable problem lay in the belief that education is, at root, an economic resource which should be exploited so as to maximise its contribution to the economy. This economic ideology of education is fundamentally at odds with the traditional values of education as a public good. The link between education and industry has a long history. However, it was ignored by the higher education sector until the 1980s because the economic ideology of education, advanced by the state, found its answer in the technical colleges of further education, traditionally characterised by vocational education and links with local firms. The traditional universities, meanwhile, were in a position to pursue education for citizenship, education as a public good. This was particularly the case for prestigious universities such as Oxford and Cambridge. The fundamental objective of the binary system was, in Fulton's (1991) words, an attempt to 'outlaw academic drift – even if the term had yet to be invented; that is, to create a diversity of institutional types which would perform different but, hopefully, equally valued functions' (p. 593).

Although it appealed to a large majority who felt that something is better than nothing, it was opposed by egalitarians for whom *nothing but the best* is the only appropriate life position. Because of the higher costs involved (unit costs do not compare favourably with other universities) and because teaching quality is difficult to assess, it may be difficult, according to Tapper and Salter, to substantiate the claim that an Oxbridge undergraduate education represents value for money. There is a powerful structural interpretation of prestigious education since such an education is part of an elite network of interlocking institutions. Tapper and Salter ask if the mutual benefits so derived result from merit or from ascription. They describe an air of resignation in the university to the increasing encroachment of the state and society whose understanding is that 'autonomy at the expense of the taxpayer is no longer an option' (p. 245). Beloff (1990) suggests that the pressure experienced by the higher education sector emanates, not from the policies of governments and civil servants, but from the 'indifference of the general public to university values' (p. 3). In his opinion, the only escape from state-financed mediocrity lies in independence from state funding, although Tapper and Salter remind us that the most cursory glance at the figures is convincing proof that such a scenario is a pipe dream. They counsel against becoming imprisoned by nostalgia and advocate the development of a new vision which, cognisant of political realities and the acceptance that higher education institutions differ dramatically from those of the past, could nevertheless embrace the best of the past. The alternative is to settle merely for the pursuit of competent leadership and managerial efficiency.

The massification of higher education in England, according to Halsey (1995), took academics by surprise. He muses on the timidity of what were seen as radical forecasts in the 1960s, when Fulton developed the first *new* university in Sussex with an estimated optimal size student population of 3,000. Kerr's (1963) description of the magnitude and structure of the University of California, with its 100,000 students and its 200,000 students in extension courses, left English academics more disbelieving than amazed, informed or prepared.

When the medieval universities were founded in Europe there were only two possible opportunities for change – who should be allowed to enter and what s/he should learn. By the 1960s the universities had not strayed beyond this perception of newness. They accepted the established wisdom on both counts. Newman's idea of a university saw the most intellectually able academic as a prototype in the guise of sage, literatus or expert, incorporated into the university to ensure the continuity of intellectual work and culture. Kerr (1963), the last in the line of a succession of modernists, tipped the balance of the idea of a new university towards people of new rather than established, universal knowledge. Thus ensued a battle for hegemony over the mode of cultural transmission and between the preservation of old, and the provision of new, knowledge. A further battle was founded on the question of who should learn. Halsey draws on Durkheim who suggests that the only way to find a homogeneous and egalitarian education is to retrace man's development to a prehistoric era before the existence of hierarchies and stratification. This means, he says,

> that the existence of higher learning presupposes a degree of complexity in the division of labour and a level of economic and political development that affords the possibility of 'idleness' for a scholarly class. Consequently, universities have always played a role in social stratification, controlling access to highly valued cultural elements, differentiating the capacity of individuals to enter a hierarchy of labour markets, and therefore being intrinsically inegalitarian institutions.

(p. 18)

Newman's idea of a university as a place for the distribution of universal knowledge fits the bureaucratic organizational paradigm. In contrast, Kerr's (1963) willingness to explore new structures and new sources of knowledge is mirrored more by the adaptive organization. Since Victorian times, there has been expanded debate about the definition of *educable*; this debate continues today in the context of a higher education system based on populist rather than elitist perspectives. Halsey reminds us that widening educational opportunity provided a safety net for a society almost fractured by the polarisation of the ownership of wealth. A new polarisation in the distribution of cultural capital is the current threat to society, he maintains. Therefore, a more inclusive educational policy would appear to be a necessary underpinning of a more integrated society.

When Kerr articulated his vision of the multiversity in 1963 few universities in Europe had more than 5 per cent of the relevant cohort. France was the first to reach 15 per cent in 1972 – the threshold of massification, a threshold defined by Trow (1974). With what Neave (2002) claims was much manipulation of the statistics, the United Kingdom reached this figure in 1985.

The removal of the binary divide in 1992 in Britain marked a strong shift in the orientation of the university sector from the elite paradigm to a mass system. Coterminous with this development was the huge philosophical shift in the perception of the role of higher education. According to Daniel (1993), until late 1990, 'British politicians had used the term "mass" with apologies, embarrassment or distaste' (p. 197). The outcomes of a mass education model are post-entry selection, variable standards and a high level of wastage. The elite paradigm on the other hand (with a participation rate of less than 15 per cent) has rather different outcomes – pre-entry selection, uniform standards and a low dropout rate. Trow (1998), in a response to the Dearing Report, concludes that higher education institutions have been faced with a dilemma of market expansion versus standards. Like Beloff, he asserts that the academy needs to recapture autonomy in order to move beyond mass education to create a learning society. Drawing on the differences between these two systems Ball (1996) suggests that 'the traditional model of university education is itself an impediment to expansion' (p. 5). Brown and Scase (1994) declare that what was once a privilege for the elite few (in the early sixties only 6.55 per cent of the population went into higher education) has become an expectation for the majority. While, as Trow (1998) claims, the shift from an elite paradigm of education to a mass model has occurred within a political rhetoric of equality, Halsey et al. (1980) assert that 'the system of (mass) education was neither a class solvent nor an engine of meritocracy. It added educational to class rigidity' (p. 213). Emphasising this point, and drawing on Willis (1977) who asked why it was that working class kids (*sic*) went into working class jobs, Pugsley raises the question why is it that in the nineties they get working class degrees? Warmington et al. (2005) call educators to task for abdicating responsibilities in respect of falling standards. They recognise that the concept of educational standards has been transformed by successive Conservative and New Labour policies from a social goal to a consumer option for aspirational individuals. In this environment, the media have free rein to engage in 'discourses of derision and idealisation' (p. 13) regarding education. They call on educators to embrace agency and not to abandon the debate to polemicists and politicians.

Despite Pugsley's assertion that by mid-1991 the term *mass education* was accepted at all levels and absorbed into the cross-party political vocabulary, the commitment to expansion was not met with commitment to funding. In fact, according to Fulton, there was a suggestion that successive governments were determined that expansion would only be financed 'on the cheap' (p. 602). Pugsley suggests that the sector is expected to compete for funding in order to meet the expansionist aims of the government while seeing its funding decrease in front of its eyes. A further punitive response by governments is to cut funding allocations or to have funds already received clawed back if institutions do not meet targets. This major shift in the political paradigm is underpinned by two fundamental elements. First, the belief that the free market is the most efficient way of effecting social policy and second, the rhetoric that minimal state intervention grants greater autonomy and democracy.

The Conservative Government persistently engaged a political ideology founded on classical liberalism which promoted the view that 'the state is an anachronistic institution whose regulative functions will be replaced by the market' (Harris 1989, p. 1). Since the mid-1980s, Pugsley claims, the idea of public service has been replaced by provider/client contracts with consumer pressure increasingly determining what services public enterprises are to provide. Dill (1997) agrees that the higher education policies of the 1990s were shaped by antistatism and consumer ideologies. The fundamental rationales were 'the drive for economic efficiency, coupled with value for money and the incentive to make the academy more adaptable and innovative' (p. 14). Le Grand and Bartlett (1993) recognise the strong arm of politics in the restructuring of higher education with clear evidence of the political creation of regulation and competition. They argue that, in consequence, a quasi-market rather than a true market now exists. This quasi-market differs from conventional markets on both supply and demand sides. Provision from competitive institutions has replaced provision by state monopoly. Introducing a market allows the government to effectively opt out of education provision. Instead its role has become, in Dill's words, that of 'a purchaser of services from independent providers who compete with each other in an internal quasi-market' (p. 182).

The basic rationale behind the Education Reform Act of 1988 is the improvement of the quality of education by creating a system in which high-quality provision is financially rewarded. The essence of this quasi-market system which emanated from the Reform Act was that the budget allocation to an educational institution depended on the numbers it can attract. This arrangement is described as a quasi-market, because although there are providers and consumers, no money changes hands. Thus, the budget, and not phronesis, becomes the default management tool of third-level institutions. Caulkin's warnings that the imposition of targets induces corrupt practices has particular resonances in an education field which has seen an inexorable shift from the elite model espoused by Masefield to the current model of mass provision.

Chapter 8

From Masefield to Massification

In his reflections in *The Future of the City of Intellect: A Brave New World – European Style,* Neave (2002), offers his views on the impetus and origin of higher education reforms. Higher education reform, he says, tends to originate from without the system with governments often using a contextual interpretation such as fear of unemployment as a moral lever to counteract resistance – a point made also by Chaharbaghi and Newman. Foreign examples – America for the United Kingdom, the United Kingdom for Ireland – serve as precedents for policy drives. Governments also add impetus to their demands by hinting at difficult consequences for the common good if higher education does not fall into line. Kerr (2002) suggests that the future for what he calls the *City of Intellect* will be located in the major research universities. The use of the term research university is, says Neave, a grammatical redundancy since all universities were once assumed to engage in research. The separation of teaching and research, he claims, is one of the significant features of massification. Identifying two distinct phases of massification, he describes the first, from 1963 to 1977, as posited on a neo-Keynesian ethic by which the university functioned as an instrument for a more egalitarian distribution of wealth. The second phase was launched on a market philosophy bolstered by competition between institutions and the rise in consumer sovereignty. Neave would find an ally in Bourdieu and Passeron (2000) when he suggests what he considers might be perceived as a heretical interpretation, that governments have sought to protect elite education while simultaneously acquiescing to popular demand. The outcome was a structure of educational stratification, another hallmark of massification. Degree level, terminal courses were provided, geared to transporting the student into industry rather than into postgraduate study.

The second phase of expansion entailed two changes of major strategic significance. The first was a shift to enrolment-driven funding. The second saw a shift in the focus away from the public sector towards an expanding private sector. Governments, in effect, slipped away from their responsibility for the financing of higher education which they had acquired with the welfare state, under the democratic guise of devolving power to regional authorities. At the same time they put in place a complex weave of systems for institutional assessment. In Neave's words: 'the welfare state mutated with varying degrees of haste and frenzy into the evaluative state' (p. 27).

Like Chaharbaghi and Newman, Neave suggests that governments' apparent gift to the institutions to determine their own mission and direction merely shifted attention away from the real issue – the shift in control from output onto product. The addition of more sophisticated evaluation instruments served to ensure that higher education appeared to be responsive to public demand and scrutiny.

At the same time as governments were abandoning funding for degree level courses to the ingenuity of the individual institutions a parallel but opposite change was occurring at the postgraduate level. Greater control and standardisation of procedures accompanied a skew in the directing of research funding into areas of commercial rather than academic interest as governments sought to exploit research resources to achieve international advantage. Governments' special treatment of research universities neutralises to some degree the democratic impulse of massification as such universities can withdraw to an elite intellectual high ground, a point also made by Holland in the Irish context. Thus the remainder of the educational institutions pick up the diverse crosses of new suites of courses to meet the increasingly differentiated needs and ambitions of a socially and intellectually differentiated student cohort. This new model, elite on the one hand and differentiated on the other, was introduced and implemented as a national template, conceived by governments and grown, however unwillingly, says Neave, in the womb of compliance of the City of Intellect. The idea of the research university, inevitable though it may be, is, in his words, 'a reductionist, if not an exclusionist development, not an expansionist one' (p. 30).

Neave expresses much dismay and anxiety about the possible impact of globalisation and the encroachment of European harmonisation. Despite the Maastricht (1992) pledge that higher education would be a matter for each state, the Sorbonne Declaration (June 1998) and the Bologna Declaration (June 1998) illustrate the degree of harmonisation being imposed by Europe. These structures, seeking to develop a European educational architecture, attempt to normalise the length of undergraduate studies and, in Neave's (2002) words, to

> perform a similar disservice for the access and duration of postgraduate studies ... the notion of harmonisation is creeping in through linguistic sleight of hand. The barriers of sovereignty in the university world, despite formal treaty guarantees, are becoming as permeable as sand and about as strong.
>
> (p. 21)

This change signals the shifting of decision-making in education to a place beyond the nation state. Neave claims that the emergence of a European system of education marks the end of a long historical epoch which saw higher education incorporated into public and national service in Europe, although it long remained a private, property owning corporation in England.

Higher education has shifted from being a public good to being a product, from direct provision by the state to provision by pseudo or quasi-markets, steered by governments by remote control. The competition for SOCRATES and LEONARDO programmes, skilfully dressed in the clothes of some of Europe's great civilising figures, are instruments of policy which require the higher education system to become a conduit by which such policies will be achieved. Thus the university and the nation itself lose their identity as ethics, values and culture – the foundations of the university's traditional formation as social observer – fall by the wayside. Veblen (1918) would surely resist the idea of higher education becoming a mix of entrepreneurial and service institutions as bonds are formed with business – the equivalent, says Neave, of selling the family silver. In true Confucian mode, Neave expresses concern about the trend towards globalisation which sees the decoupling of conditions of service for university staff from the public sector structure towards a competition-based local decision-making entity. He complains that the burden of adjustment falls on the university which is shotgunned into an uneasy marriage between 'amor scientiae' and 'amor pecuniae' (p. 34). His baroque metaphor suggests a shift from the 'Palace of Kings' Counselors to the Glass Towers of Merchant Princes' (p. 34). The reader may perceive it ironic that academe, which occupies the high moral ground in the higher education debate and which repudiates any alliance with commerce, is willing to fight to retain its own share of mammon which only a thriving economy can provide. Such a perspective may be as anachronistic as musicians kept by princes.

Coombs (1968) writing almost forty years ago presages the debate on the current crisis in education. The crisis of which he speaks is a crisis of maladjustment between education and society, brought on by the failure of educational systems to match the needs of its external environment. He forecasts a deepening of the crisis as education is pincered between its rising unit costs and the depreciating rate of growth in its funding resources. Neave (2002), discussing the same (current) crisis claims that the burden of adjustment falls squarely on the shoulders of the academic. In 1968 Coombs offered avenues of adjustment in the shape of educational innovations. Merely to continue to remake old systems, he argues, would invite disaster, a claim supported by Abbott.

The genealogy of Coombs' findings is of some importance. His is not a lone voice but the accumulated considered concerns of 150 delegates, education ministers, university heads, professors, researchers and sociologists, who attended, in a private capacity, at a conference in Williamsburg in 1967. While education systems, says Coombs, seem to exist in a symbiotic relationship with crisis – shortage of everything except students – the crisis facing the world in 1968, expressed in the increase in illiteracy which paralleled population growth, was underpinned by four major factors. These were the increase in popular aspirations, the continuing shortage of resources, the inherent inertia of educational systems and fourthly, the intrinsic resistance to change of society itself. Coombs employs an apposite metaphor in pinpointing the need for change. 'No more than a grown man can suitably wear the clothes that fitted him as a child, can an educational system successfully resist the need for change itself when everything around it is changing' (p. 5).

An educational system, he says, must not cling to conventional practices merely to honour tradition or 'lash itself to inherited dogma in order to stay afloat in a sea of uncertainty' (p. 5). He reports a number of recommendations from the Williamsburg conference including the gathering, analysis and dissemination of information on teachers, students, income and expenditure. Urging continuing self-appraisal and friendly external scrutiny, he wrote too early to see that sophisticated evaluation techniques can be a smokescreen (Gibbs & Iacovidou; Neave). In an effort to promote interest in education, Coombs makes a novel suggestion – the employment by the media of competent education reporters who would accord it the same level of attention as it does to sports and financial reports. Such an innovation might go some distance in alleviating the problem of *imperfect consumer information* identified by Le Grand and Robinson. The Williamsburg conference further recommended that managers and specialists should be concentrated in the ranks of teachers and professors – an occurrence which is not always the case in the United Kingdom. Pugsley illustrates the substitution of the title Chief Executive for the established President or Director – a situation which has, to date, not occurred in Ireland.

The lowering of standards which accompanies expansion of the educational system would have found little support in Pattison (1868). Although he was at the forefront of the Victorian early attempts to expand the university, his view of higher education is singularly elitist and quite radical, in a timeless sense. His view was a demanding one – that a student should be willing to so devote himself to the acquisition and understanding of the available knowledge about the world and about himself that he would be willing to forego any material reward that might be expected to devolve from such a serious and sustained intellectual effort. Such a high-minded ideal, expressing itself in antipathy to the idle aristocracy, many of whose sons populated Oxford, would find little favour either with the lower classes who could not afford to ignore the education-work nexus. His dedication to university reform was posited, not on the notion of social egalitarianism, but on the recruitment of a student population singularly consumed with the purest pursuit of knowledge. Marshall, in 1872, provided the orthodoxy for a century of educational reform. Unlike Pattison, he perceived no difficulty in coupling high-minded education to material wealth in order to create more wealth, to narrow income differentials and enhance cultural progress. American support for Pattison's esoteric, elitist view was put forward by Veblen, a Norwegian-American sociologist, who wrote in 1918 that the only pursuit of the civilised man which truly justifies itself is the acquisition of knowledge. This he saw, as the single incumbent duty of the modern university, the seeking of knowledge, not for profit or any utilitarian purpose, but simply to satisfy idle curiosity. Astoundingly, he dismissed the underpinnings of the medieval universities as mere training centres for ecclesiastical and courtly placements and viewed them as irrelevant stages in the evolution of a barbarian civilisation. He treated the education of engineers and doctors in the same dismissive fashion, asserting that they should be educated apart from university life; otherwise they might convey the impression of a 'specious appearance of scholarship and so invest their technological discipline with a degree of pedantry and sophistication' (in Halsey, p. 42). Such a vanity, he perceived, would be aimed solely at producing a sense of awe in the vulgar. He believed that it is the quest for knowledge which must constitute the main interest of the university; utilitarian impulses and applications are alien to that aim. Neither Pattison nor Veblen, with their utopian dream, could have conveyed any hope of social progress to the working classes.

University expansion was by no means universally supported and concern was raised about falling standards. In an amusing excerpt, which reflects so well the anguished thoughts of current times, Halsey draws on the observations of the American Abraham Flexner (1930). Flexner opined, and applauded, that English tutors were excessively conscientious, and more parsimonious than their American counterparts, in issuing credentials – between 1882 and 1929 only 6,473 bachelor degrees and a mere 74 PhDs were conferred by Manchester college. By contrast, looking at the American higher education scene, which had already undergone an expansionary phase which England would not begin to enter until the 1960s, he deplored 'a wild, uncontrolled and uncritical expansion ... the quacks emit publications that travesty research and make a noise that drowns out the still small voice to which America should be listening' (in Halsey, p. 39). Flexner was happy to assume at the time that the English exhibited no signs of emulating the American system of expansion or of espousing the American ideology that higher education was indiscriminately good for all. He complimented the English who appeared to recognise that the majority of youth is unable to assimilate higher education, and offered them technical education instead.

Following the expansion in England of higher education in the wake of the Robbins Report came the refrain, constantly maintained and renewed, that more means worse. Halsey draws on Miller, a director of a polytechnic, who in 1974 resurrected Flexner's ideas and attacked what he saw as the false vision of mass higher education.

> A great number of people will, one hopes, remain able to observe that most people, in any nation, are simply not capable of the intellectual effort to take in the stuff of higher education and would therefore be much better off without being dragooned into it.
>
> (in Halsey, p. 39)

A wry reader, acquainted with Illich and Wizard Prang, might observe that education's chief function is to be an industry, not to educate.

The vision of Veblen was never realized; expansion in America led to the multiversity described by Kerr (1963). In England there developed in the aftermath of the war a social consciousness that new beginnings were possible. Since war had been fought for human principles and not merely for political or material expediency, there could be no return to the pre-war status quo. Instead, society would have to be reconstructed along more egalitarian foundations. In his *Crisis in the University* (1949) Moberly identified a spiritual gap as the major problem, and, in a quote which would not be out of place in the twenty-first century, remarked that 'all over the world, indeed, the cake of custom is broken, and old gods are dethroned and none have taken their place' (p. 16). His analysis advanced questions which are still being debated today. What is the function of the university? What impact should it have on students? What are its responsibilities to the outside world? His description of students finds many an echo in current times. They are, he says,

apathetic and have neither wide interests nor compelling convictions . . . expressed or felt (little) respect for dons having opened up for them a whole new attitude to life . . . If they find prophets at all it is outside the university . . . out there in the street is something new in the making, which will shatter all the syllogisms and formulas of the schools.

(p. 23)

Moberly saw the chief function of the university as the production of good citizens, an elite which would provide future leaders. Like Newman, he saw the university as a community and the role of teacher as both paternal and pastoral. Seeing that the Christian church's hold on the university was slipping away, Moberly embraced liberalism, his 'naïve optimism' (in Halsey, p. 47) perceiving that emancipation from the church's influence would eliminate parochial constraint and unwarranted interference with free enquiry. He took for granted the ability of a moral perspective to survive without institutional structures and overall, sought to embrace liberalism rather than to fight it. Like Flexner, Pattison and Veblen his liberalism suggested that enquiry matters more than teaching, that learning for learning's sake is what counts, that a university must deal only in intellectual aristocracy and must eschew mediocrity at all costs. The social importance of a subject or faculty should never be an issue, he said; what matters is simply its intrinsic intellectual worth. The observation by Confucius (in Halsey et al., 1980) that it was not easy to find a man, who had studied for three years without aiming at pay, seems to have escaped these four writers.

Moberly observed that the sun was setting on the idea of a liberal university and that a new democratic approach, fuelled by post-war social optimism, saw the university primarily as a pragmatic endeavour to conquer nature and to advance scientific discovery for the satisfaction of human needs. This new culture condemned the liberal outlook as elitist rather than democratic, removed rather than embracing and as deifying sterile, monkish intellectual pursuit over useful human needs applications.

Kerr's 1963 description of the history and future of the university traced its ancestry to the medieval university which he likened to a village with priests. The university of Victorian and post-Victorian times he saw as a one-industry town with its intellectual oligarchy. The university, on the cusp of birth in 1963, he saw as a city of infinite variety, homogenous and anarchic at once, pluralist in outlook, encompassing both intellectual excellence and a tolerance of intellectual stratus – the latter being a metaphor for large numbers of less educated, less able entrants. He foresaw the organic community of the university giving way to an industrial complex and, in a contemporary criticism, suggested that the university is a mechanism held together by administrative rules and fuelled by money, adding, to the reader's amusement, that it could be described as a loose collection of faculty entrepreneurs held together by a common grievance over parking. He urged generosity in judging what was justifiable in teaching, research, selectivity and service to the community and advocated openness to student admission and the balance of private and public funding. Kerr's (1963) Californian dream was an extravagant one at the time when the Robbins Report appeared in England.

Halsey documents reaction to university expansion in both America and England. He describes the findings of the American Carnegie Commission, which reported finally in 1980, having been inaugurated in 1963 and having changed its name in 1974. Despite acknowledging the pessimism and cynicism towards higher education identified by Nisbet (1971) and later epitomised by Bloom (1987), the commission, under Kerr's chairmanship, remained upbeat. It completed its study with renewed optimism for the value of higher education to American society.

Halsey describes the lowering of standards of both entrants and graduates as numbers increased and the negative rate of personal return on education as the numbers pursuing PhDs accelerated. The pursuit by minority groups of equality of opportunity followed by the regularising effects of affirmative action may have compromised the principle of intellectual, individual effort on which academic excellence had been traditionally founded. As expansion continued, the average age of staff rose, distancing them in outlook from students, who, informed by the logic of consumerism, made increasing and novel demands on faculty. Commentators of the time, says Halsey, estimated that the degree as a career investment would become more rather than less important. The Carnegie Commission, he says, offered no solutions to these problems and changes apart from an exhortation to professors, students and public to

> be their best selves ... the public should ... maintain its enthusiasm, students should pursue higher education for its own sake as well as for its market advantages. The universities should redouble their efforts to be excellent, to be responsive to social needs, and exemplars of moral probity and devotion to science and scholarship.
>
> (p. 53)

Halsey recognises both the value of these aspirations and the difficulty of putting them in place. The inflexibility occasioned by tenured staff, he says, and their defensive stewardship of academic ideals militates against initiatives from other origins – governments, unions, presidents or their own administrations – a point also raised by Ives and Jarvenpaa.

For an exposé of the English higher education system after Robbins, Halsey draws on Scott (1984) whose argument is that, if there is a crisis it has its roots in a liberal-democratic secular society, not in its experience under a Thatcher administration. Such an outlook would demand a detailed analysis of the complex mix of values, purpose and principles which make up the intellectual culture of a nation. Scott sees the evolution from traditional, through liberal and modern to a postmodern paradigm expressed in shifts from elite through mass to universal provision. He views higher education's action on the labour market as that of a sieve, concluding, like Halsey, that education's rate of return to individual graduates is bound to decline as the number of graduates increases. The impact of mass and universal education has been so seismic that he concludes another Robbins is impossible, a forecast refuted by Marris (THES 1984) who asserts that since the economic rate of return on education is so enormous, a case exists for another Robbins-style expansion. Scott, who shares Moberly's earlier view that the crisis in the university is a spiritual one – neither of these observers describe the crisis as one of economic resources – also shares his fear of erosion of the values of the university and the loss of a moral social order which is a prerequisite of both freedom and progress.

Scott's singular contribution to the debate is the re-interpretation of knowledge as product rather than process. Such a scientific, rather than cultural interpretation of knowledge, emphasises research over teaching and intellect over sensibility. A reshaping of university life replaces humanism with academicism and education with technology. This boundary collapse, already identified by Bloland, sees the university as less separate from the mainstream of ordinary life and therefore more serviceable as well as more flexible to the power of the state. Scott's acceptance of the idea of expansionist-teacher and expansionist-researcher contrasts, however, with Moberly's narrower elitist-teacher and elitist-researcher. Scott's embrace of the wider concepts inevitably faces him with a greater complexity of issues involved in attempting to understand the genesis and state and future direction of higher education. Halsey draws our attention to the use by both authors of the word *crisis* and suggests that it may be a misnomer for what is a 'chronic peril' (p. 57). Offering hope, he suggests that intellectual life, despite its service to production and consumption will also demand its freedom and its privileges. Perhaps it is this very demand that occasions an identity crisis for some practitioners in higher education.

Some of the history of higher education is sketched in its evolving hierarchy. Shils (1955) describes the embarrassment on one side and the disappointment on the other if a young student, asked whether he was an Oxford or a Cambridge undergraduate, could assent to neither proposition. Oxford rewrote her status, traditionally derived from social connection, to status derived from intellectual excellence. All other universities scrabbled for a place below Oxford. In Halsey's words: 'wherever two or three are gathered together there also shall be a sociological commonplace: invidious comparisons will emerge' (p. 58). In the British system of merit precedence goes to longevity. Underlining this outlook is Pugsley's description of the aspirations of prospective students revealed in an interview with a Chief Executive of a new university. This interview illustrates the importance of branding.

> I'd like to go to a *real* university . . . if we can't go to a real university, then we'll go to a new university. If we can't go to a new university, *then* we'll go to a college of higher education.
>
> (p. 83)

As the civic universities, then the Open University and the polytechnics achieved recognition, Oxford and Cambridge shifted from near monopoly to pre-eminence. Their exceptional status, born of the Boat Race and the Varsity Match, found new expression in the stratosphere of academic excellence. The assumption of a constrained pool of ability which informed many commentators on higher education was accepted as a rationale for preserving class privilege by diverting students who had limited claim to class or ability into the new institutions.

Cushioned by the legacy of its colonial past and the inheritance of North Sea oil, England's higher education system was able to sustain the cost of don/student ratio of 1:8 in the prestigious universities at the same time as it advanced its unprecedented expansion by, first of all changing the definition of higher education, and then locating it in colleges which had previously been allocated and administered under the system of further education. Part-time attendance and short-term courses multiplied. However, as Ainley (2000) testifies, much of what passes for higher education has, in fact, the stamp of further education. Pondering why this expansion, carrying the twins of increased but devalued opportunity, has been embraced by successive English governments, Halsey reflects the views of Chaharbaghi and Newman's equally astounding suggestions. He asserts that the government's aim is to avoid one kind of idleness, unemployment, in order to beget another, legitimate form of idleness, leisure. Higher education, reveals Halsey, justifies idleness without stigma. He draws our attention to an insidious form of idleness, that of over-manning ' . . . the perpetual tea break, sleeping bags on the midnight shift. The parallel in academia is clear—the 1:8 ratio, the sabbatical, the long vacations, dons don't keep hours . . . ' (p. 107). Unemployment means failure, says Halsey. He recognises that a challenge was inevitable for the justification of a system which had nine out of its every ten pounds paid by the state. Education was believed to have a higher rate of return – estimated by Le Grand and Robinson at around 14 per cent – than factories or machines. Renewed expansion saw the lot of the academic change – status, tenure, identity, funding and working conditions. Halsey asks if these changes represent a trend towards a proletarianisation, a condition foreseen with foreboding by Weber as far back as 1918. He defines proletarianisation as 'a three fold reduction in the power and advantage in the work and market position of a class or occupational group: in autonomy of working activity, security of employment and chances of promotion' (p. 125). The profession in general, but dons in particular, have seen their prestige, salaries, autonomy and resources much humbled. Whether the quality of teachers and researchers has risen or fallen is, according to Halsey, an open question.

The staple themes of today's discontents in higher education are to be found in the separate writings of Weber and Veblen in 1918. Weber emphasised the demand of a modern economy for specialised manpower, the application of the bureaucratic paradigm to all forms of social organizations and what he called the proletarianisation of the university research worker and teacher. Additionally he held up the American higher education model as a portent of higher education's future in Europe. Veblen, also in 1918, wrote a protest against 'the conduct of universities by business men'. He recognised that the American university was, in fact, a business enterprise in competition with other universities. Its aims were prestige and advertising at the expense of intellectual pursuits and at a cost of a vast competitive waste of resources.

The author of Ecclesiastes would not be astonished to find the same laments about education being revisited over the centuries. In 1213, the Chancellor of the University of Paris complained that in the days before universities were named as such, or had structured governance, lectures were more frequent and there was more zeal for study: ' . . . now that you are invited into a university, lectures are rare, things are hurried and little is learned, the time taken for lectures being spent in meetings and discussion'. (in Moodie & Eustace,

1974, p. 11). Even earlier, in the third century BC, Ptolemy asked Archimedes if there was any easier route to geometry than that of Euclid's Elements. Archimedes (287–212 BC) is reported to have replied 'my lord, there is no royal road to geometry'. Legend has it that he escaped with his head.

At this juncture a question must be asked regarding the degree of dilution to which education may have been exposed. This matter was the subject of an international case study on third-level education by McArdle (2007). The findings of this study are presented in the following three chapters.

Part 2

Chapter 9

Higher Education as a Consumer Experience

An international study[1] encompassing the administration of surveys and in-depth interviews, carried out among lecturers and students, provides compelling evidence that higher education is a consumer experience and, in line with consumer culture, tends to be delivered in capsule format. The countries involved in the study are Ireland, Australia, South Africa and France. Ninety-five lecturers and seven hundred and seventy-eight students took part in this survey. The findings offer insight at local, national and international levels. The purpose of undertaking an international study was to reduce the likelihood of attributing local or national causes to what might be a general trend. A statistical analysis was carried out on the survey data to discover salient variables embedded in the surveys and to identify common responses among the student and the lecturer cohorts.

A striking finding of this survey is the number of students who do not have the essential or supplementary texts for their course. The first four statements in the student survey deal with possession of texts and how often students consult them. Under half of the surveyed population has essential texts for four or more subjects, almost 42 per cent have texts for between one and three subjects and one-tenth have no essential texts whatsoever. The country with the highest rate of possession is South Africa at 83 per cent. The situation is worst in an Irish institution where 18 per cent have no essential texts, 56 per cent have them for between one and three subjects and 27 per cent have texts for four or more subjects.

---

[1] McArdle, D. (2007) *Capsule Education: Cultural Influences in Education Provision* Ph.D. Thesis, Education Department, National University of Ireland, Maynooth.

Students were asked how often they consult texts – even in the library, if they choose not to purchase them. The rate of consultation varies considerably between institutions. Again, South Africa scores highest with 74 per cent consulting often, 20 per cent rarely and 7 per cent never. The picture is worst in Ireland where 29 per cent consult often, 47 per cent rarely and 24 per cent never. As regards supplementary texts just 7 per cent, overall, possess four or more and 71 per cent have none whatsoever. At 15 per cent South Africa has the highest rate of possession and, at 21 per cent, the highest rate of consultation of these supplementary texts. Overall, the rate of consultation of supplementary texts is very low – just over 10 per cent consult them often and 66 per cent never consult them.

The reluctance on the part of students to purchase or consult texts is reflected in statement 14 of the lecturers' survey which examines the propensity on the part of lecturers to give comprehensive notes and handouts to students – 64 per cent do this and 30 per cent do not. In the Irish institution with the lowest rate of possession and consultation of texts 83 per cent of lecturers agree that this is their response. As many as 79 per cent of lecturers overall feel that students would probably underachieve if they did not give them comprehensive notes and handouts. The response to this statement carried a 100 per cent agreement rate from one of the Irish institutions surveyed.

Three quarters of students perceive that it is the lecturers' duty to provide all the information (notes and handouts) that is needed for a student to succeed in examinations. At 80 per cent the agreement response is highest of all in an Irish institution and lowest in Australia at 63 per cent. Such a high agreement response offers strong support for the belief of lecturers that students are becoming more demanding of them.

A statement which suggests that lecturers examine a set of notes rather than a subject, finds almost 60 per cent agreement. Agreement is highest in France at 79 per cent and, at one-third, it is lowest in South Africa. The statement that students appear to want information to be packaged in notes and handouts, rather than having to undertake independent reading, draws almost total agreement from respondents. A statement which suggests that students appear not to want information that is not needed for exam purposes elicits a very high agreement response of 80 per cent overall. When students are asked a similar question on their survey it elicits more disagreement than agreement. Those who disagree number 49 per cent while 44 per cent agree. In a similar vein there is a finding that almost 70 per cent of students overall assert that examination questions which require them to study information not covered in detail in class are unfair. At 84 per cent the figure is highest in Ireland. There is an even higher response to a related question which suggests that only material fully covered in class should be a question on an examination paper. Overall almost 80 per cent of students believe this. An institution in Ireland reports the highest agreement at 90 per cent and South Africa has the lowest level of agreement – 63 per cent. Almost 40 per cent of students agree that what is covered in class is all they need to succeed in examinations.

A statement on the lecturers' survey, which asks if students have a clear understanding of the 'big picture' of the programme meets with the agreement of fewer than a third overall; in the Irish institutions the rate is as low as 18 per cent. The poor grasp by students of their course is revisited in another statement which asserts that students know discrete facts about a subject rather than having an integrated understanding. Overall, there is agreement of 80 per cent with the statement. Agreement in Ireland is even stronger at 92 per cent and is lowest in France at 68 per cent. The statement that students are willing co-creators in their own learning meets with overall disagreement; only 36 per cent agree. Alone, of the institutions studied, France, with an agreement rate of 63 per cent, assents to this proposition. Supporting this view is the response that 65 per cent of all students agree that they feel they should do extra reading apart from lecturers' notes and handouts. This figure is broadly replicated in all institutions surveyed. Interestingly, interviews with students will reveal in Chapter 11 that, while they *feel* they should do extra reading they do not, in fact, do it. Supporting the perception that students exhibit low levels of interest in the course is the statement which shows that 67 per cent of them are resistant to the use by lecturers of language which they do not understand. Another statement claiming poor student engagement is the statement which suggests that the term 'capsule education' is an appropriate one to describe the students' attitude to learning. Overall, the agreement response is 83 per cent with South Africa having the lowest response at 68 per cent. France presents

100 per cent agreement while Ireland shows an agreement rate of 86 per cent.

In addition to the low rate of text ownership and the low rate of consultation of texts, lack of engagement by students is also shown in poor attendance. Only France has general attendance of more than 70 per cent (attendance is compulsory in France). In Ireland lecturers estimate that over 50 per cent of students attend half, or fewer, of their lectures while almost all Irish lecturers agree that students skip lectures in order to study for continuous assessments. Interviews with students will later reveal that they consider attendance amazingly low; some of them admit to attending as few as 50 per cent of the lectures and others attend as few as 20 per cent.

More than three quarters of lecturers – 100 per cent in the case of France – perceive that students are becoming more demanding of them. Overall, 83 per cent of lecturers agree that students expect extensive guidance regarding topic areas in studying for examinations. Lecturers respond to increasing student demands by preparing notes and handouts and by ensuring that they do not set an examination question that has not been fully covered in class or flagged in some way in advance. An overwhelming 90 per cent agree (half of these agree strongly) that this is how they respond.

Perceiving a wide range of abilities among the student population, another response by lecturers is to pitch their teaching towards the lower rather than the higher ability students. (In true modernist tradition, there is no query about the valuing of these parameters.) Overall, the agreement rate is 55 per cent. This bears out the tendency of mass education to have the effect of 'thrusting mediocrity on the talented' (Brubacher & Rudy 1976). Agreement is highest in France at 68 per cent. There is slightly more disagreement than agreement with the suggestion that teaching and learning are fragmented by the semester system. Overall, 37 per cent agree and 40 per cent disagree. At 47 per cent agreement is highest in Ireland. The lecturers' concern about declining standards is not reflected in the perception of students. As few as 3 students out of the 20 interviewed have concerns about standards. The others feel that standards are high.

The purposes for which students undertake higher education is examined in the lecturers' survey. The vast majority of lecturers – 85 per cent – perceive that students are more interested in obtaining a qualification than in learning. The placing of qualification before learning is examined in the student survey. Almost half – 48 per cent – of students agree that obtaining a qualification is more important than what they learn. This would appear to support the view that education is a consumer experience. Agreement is highest in Ireland at 69 per cent and lowest in South Africa at 23 per cent – the only institution to disagree with the statement. Students rank a qualification in first place, job prospects second and interest in their course third. As few as 21 per cent overall see interest in their course as the most important aspect of higher education. In Ireland the figure is even lower at 12 per cent. Australia and South Africa register relatively greater levels of interest in the course at 20 per cent and 32 per cent respectively.

More than three quarters – 78 per cent – of lecturers surveyed hold the opinion that students see education as a commodity rather than an enriching experience. South Africa has the lowest agreement level at 69 per cent. Students' abilities to cope with concepts and metaphor are also examined. Only 38 per cent, overall, agree that students are quite adept at understanding concepts although agreement is lower in an Irish institution at 28 per cent. Approximately 43 per cent of lecturers in both South Africa and France agree with the statement. A smaller proportion, 25 per cent overall, believe that students can understand metaphor. Belief is lower in one Irish institution at 19 per cent and even lower in South Africa at 14 per cent. In another Irish institution agreement is considerably higher at 36 per cent. France shows agreement of 42 per cent and an extraordinarily high no-opinion result of 58 per cent. No respondent in France actively disagrees with the statement that students have difficulty in understanding metaphor.

The perceived difficulty which students experience in dealing with concepts is supported by students' own responses to suggested definitions of learning and teaching. A significant feature is that responses are characterised, for the most part, by high levels of no opinion. There appears to be little discernment of difference between the various concepts put forward. In general, students offer high levels of agreement – some as high as 87 per cent – with all suggestions. South Africa is distinguished by having the highest levels of agreement with all but one of the ten definitions offered. There is 87 per cent agreement that learning is *understanding how to solve problems*. More than three quarters believe that learning is *adopting a special way of viewing things and events* and 67 per cent believe *that learning is changing one's attitude and approach to life*. A significant number, 54 per cent overall, believe that learning is *remembering a body of knowledge*. Interviews with lecturers indicate that students are concrete thinkers, that they shy away from metaphor and have difficulty embracing concepts, a finding supported by Greer (1998).

While 72 per cent of students seem to know the rhetoric that learning is *making meaning for oneself*, fewer – 67 per cent – agree that teaching involves allowing them to *participate fully in selected situations and activities*. In terms of definitions of teaching there is some hint of dependency and confinement. The highest recorded agreement – three quarters – believe that teaching is *presenting a body of knowledge*; this contrasts sharply with the rather lower number, 54 per cent, who subscribe to the quantitative view of education that learning is *remembering a body of information*. Over 70 per cent believe that teaching is *training in methods to solve very specific problems*. However, in an apparent contradiction, an equal number believes that teaching means providing challenges in a rich, resourceful environment. Dependency is again suggested in the 63 per cent of respondents who see teaching as *providing a set of instructions to change the way* [they] *see things and situations*.

Students' apparent lack of interest in learning causes frustration to 76 per cent of lecturers. Eighty-four per cent of French lecturers agree with this statement. In France there is not a single respondent who disagrees with the statement. The lowest figure comes from an Irish institution which reports 55 per cent agreement. Surprisingly, this institution scores a much higher level of agreement – 82 per cent, half of it strong agreement – with a related suggestion, that low levels of response from students have the effect of de-energising lecturers. In France there is 100 per cent agreement while, overall, agreement is 76 per cent. Interviews with lecturers later will reveal that lecturers are stressed, exhausted and de-motivated because of lack of engagement by students and increasing student demands.

Despite low rates of text ownership, low rates of consultation of texts and a generalised reductionist approach towards education, over 81 per cent of students (a figure replicated fairly closely in all institutions) express confidence that they will succeed in their examinations. The level of disagreement with the assertion is no more than 5 per cent in any institution. Coupled with responses from students during in-depth interviews about the short time they devote to study, this seems an extraordinary result.

It is interesting that, in as far as these responses are concerned, they are the responses of students who attended class on the day the survey was carried out. In some institutions 50 per cent of students attend half, or fewer, of their lectures.

Because of the large amount of data produced by the surveys, factor analysis was used to simplify the complexity of attempting to engage with such a large number of responses and to determine the degree to which items are tapping into the same concept. Factor analysis thus brings order by determining which responses are related and which are not. The factor analysis conducted here is exploratory because it seeks to examine possible relationships between variables rather than trying to fit them to any existing model.

This analysis merely identifies the major components embedded in the survey and the statements with which they are most closely associated. A narrative emerges with these components as major themes. This analysis does not attribute causality at this point. It serves merely to show association. Later an attempt is made to distinguish causes and effects using Path Analysis to identify the relative forces and direction of each component. Additionally these themes are used to provide a loose structure for interviews with students and lecturers in Chapters 10 and 11.

Six components, or themes, emerge from the analysis of the lecturers' survey as significant in contributing to understanding the thrust of the findings. Data from the correlation matrix facilitates the identification of the most significant correlation measures and allows for the labelling of the components which emerge. The first component, labelled **Non-engagement**, is associated with over 25 per cent of the survey statements. The second component, labelled **Fragmented learning,** accounts for almost 22 per cent of the total variance. Component three, labelled **Encapsulation**, is associated with just over 18 per cent of survey statements. Component 4, **Students' demands**

and staff fatigue, carries almost 8 per cent of the weight of the survey. Component 5, **Semesterisation,** is associated with almost 8 per cent of the survey statements and component 6, **Lower standards,** is responsible for just over 4 per cent of the survey. Taken together, these six principal components reflect 85 per cent of the salience in the lecturers' survey. The remaining 15 per cent carry so little individual or cumulative weight that they signify no more than would be expected from extraneous elements and/or error. Using data from the correlation matrix it is possible to identify the degree of correlation between the components embedded in the survey. The data is further reduced using Principal Components Analysis (PCA) which facilitates the identification of the most significant correlation measures. These figures indicate the relative strength of the ideas in the mind of lecturers when responding to the survey statements.

Examining the component identified as **Non-engagement,** the correlation value of 0.899 relates to statement 23 concerning the frequency of student attendance while statement 6 (0.893) relates to students' skipping lectures to study for their Continuous Assessments. Other supporting statements with high correlation values are 4 (−0.844) that students do not have an understanding of the big picture, 21 and 20 (−0.797 and −0.694 respectively) that they do not understand metaphor or concepts and 16 (−0.592) that they are not willing co-creators in their own learning.

An observation of the **Fragmented learning** component shows a correlation value of 0.928 which records the belief among lecturers that students are more interested in obtaining a qualification than in learning (statement 19) and statement 17 (correlation value 0.892) expresses the view that students see education as a commodity rather than an enriching experience. This opinion is further bolstered by statement 15 (0.729) that students know discrete facts about a subject rather than having an integrated understanding and by statement 1 (0.726) that students do not appear to want information that is not needed for exam purposes.

The third component to emerge is **Encapsulation,** a theme which forms a core element in this study. Statement 3 (0.881) suggests that students wish to have information packaged rather than undertake independent reading. Statement 7(0.697) expresses the belief among

lecturers that students would probably fail if they were not given comprehensive handouts while statement 13 (0.684) agrees that the term 'capsule education' is an appropriate one to describe students' attitudes to education. Statement 14 (0.636), which declares that lecturers prepare comprehensive notes for students, further supports this factor.

Statement 22 (0.843) illustrates the view that low levels of response from students have the effect of de-energising lecturers and statement 12 (0.715) suggests that students are becoming more demanding. Both of these variables contribute significantly to **Students' demands and staff fatigue**, the fourth component.

Semesterisation emerges as the fifth component. It is represented by statement 8 (0.885) which holds the belief that semesterisation has the effect of fragmenting teaching and learning.

The component **Lower standards** is the sixth component revealed in the statistics. It is represented by statement 11 (0.520) that lecturers pitch their teaching at the lower- rather than the higher-ability students.

Using path analysis, often called causal modelling, it is possible to determine the strength of the influence that each of the above components exerts on each other. Encapsulation is perceived by lecturers as the cause of much of the problem in higher education. Since this theme underpins this work, it was decided to test the influence, if any, the other components exert on **Encapsulation**. A path model was constructed, suggesting the above influences.

The arrows in Figure 9.1 show the hypothesised causal connections between the variables. The model moves from left to right, implying causal priority to those variables closer to the left. Path coefficients (standardised regression coefficients) are computed to provide statistical estimates of the postulated influences. The strength and direction of these influences are illustrated in Figure 9.1. The computation of standardised regression coefficients allows direct comparisons to be made in order to understand the relative weight each component has on other components in the path model.

In addition to the components within the model all the variables have further arrows directed to them from outside the model. These reflect the amount of unexplained variance for each variable

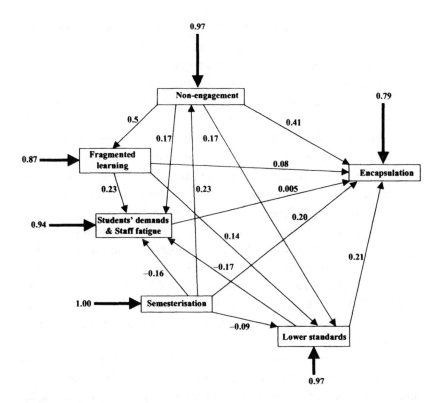

Figure 9.1 Path diagram for encapsulation with coefficients (Lecturers' Survey)

respectively, that is, the amount of variance which is caused by elements outside the model.

The model above proposes a number of direct effects. It can be seen that **Non-engagement** has a direct effect on **Encapsulation**. This is supported by a Beta value of 0.408. **Fragmented learning** also has a direct effect on **Encapsulation** although its impact is low with a Beta value of 0.076. The presumed direct influence of **Students' demands and Staff fatigue** on **Encapsulation**, with a Beta value of 0.005, is statistically insignificant. Therefore no influence can be assumed. **Semesterisation**, has a direct influence on **Encapsulation**, showing a Beta value of 0.201. Factor 6, **Lower standards**, has a direct effect on **Encapsulation** and exhibits a Beta value of 0.212.

In addition to the above direct effects on **Encapsulation** there are a number of indirect effects. **Non-engagement** has a direct effect on **Fragmented learning** with a Beta value of 0.501. This factor also has a direct effect on **Students' demands and staff fatigue** with a Beta value of 0.173 and a direct effect on **Lower standards** with a Beta value of 0.169.

Fragmented learning has a direct effect on **Students' demands and staff fatigue** with a Beta value of 0.234 and it also has a direct effect on **Lower standards** with a Beta value of 0.143.

Semesterisation has a direct effect on **Non-engagement** showing a Beta value of 0.233 and a negative effect on **Students' demands and lecturer fatigue** – Beta value −0.164. It also has a negative effect, Beta value −0.094, on **Lower standards**. It is not, itself, however, influenced by any other factor in the model, that is, all influence on this factor comes from outside the model.

The combined influence of the above provide for indirect effects on **Encapsulation**. An analysis of the combination of all internal influences, direct and indirect, on **Encapsulation** shows that almost 79 per cent of the reason for **Encapsulation** (assuming acceptance of the causal imagery in the model) comes from external factors which are not examined in the survey. This means that just over 21 per cent of the influence on this factor is accounted for by the internal factors indicated.

A further analysis of the Beta weights shows that components **Non-engagement, Fragmented learning, Semesterisation** and **Lower standards** contribute to **Students' demands and staff fatigue** but this factor contributes to no other factor in any significant way – it makes only a very marginal contribution to **Encapsulation** with a beta value of 0.005. Therefore, while this factor is bolted to the other factors it is not, of itself, contributing any significant influence.

Non-engagement has a considerable influence on **Fragmented learning** (Beta value 0.501) and seems to usher in another urgency by contributing to **Encapsulation**. The model suggests that it does not really matter what is in the 'capsule'. It can be inferred that students are not in college to learn but the capsule is demanded because of non-attendance. In the same way, **Lower standards** relieve the fatigue of lecturers – Beta value −0.172, a finding which will be supported by interviews with lecturers in Chapter 10.

Another surprising result is that **Semesterisation** appears to actually discourage **Lower standards**. However the Beta value, −0.09, is much too insignificant to assume any significant influence. Some of the reasons for the effect may be explained in lecturers' interviews later – there is a statement that lecturers in one institute are encouraged not to examine topics in the final examination which they have already examined in a Continuous Assessment. This means that students have no more than 6 weeks' material to study for a final examination, thus allowing more efficient use of memory and consequent high marks. In terms of external influences the following apply: **Non-engagement** and **Lower standards** experience 97 per cent influence from outside. For **Fragmented learning** and **Students' demands and Staff fatigue** the extent of external influences amount to 87 per cent and 94 per cent respectively. In the case of **Encapsulation**, 79 per cent of the influence comes from outside and 100 per cent of the influence is external in the case of **Semesterisation**.

There are 26 variables on the students' survey. When a factor analysis was carried out on the survey data five components emerged. Together, these carry 63 per cent of the weight of the survey. Using the data from the correlation matrix, the significant components were labelled.

The first component, **Best Educational Practice,** which accounts for almost 19 per cent of the weight of the survey, is represented by statements 18–21, 23 and 24, which deal with students' perceptions of teaching and learning; all of these variables have correlation values greater than 0.7.

Interest in Course, contributing over 16 per cent to the survey, is the second component to emerge. It is represented by statements 1 (−0.693), 2 (0.757), 3 (−0.861) and 4 (0.892). These statements show that students have few essential and supplementary texts and that they do not consult them very often.

The **Limiting Effect of Examinations**, contributing almost 15 per cent to understanding, is identified as component 4, which is best represented by statements 7 (0.831), 8 (0.820) and 9 (0.847). These statements reveal that students consider that examination questions not covered in detail in class are unfair, that only material fully covered in class should be examined and that the lecturer should provide all the information required for examination success.

The fourth factor is **Encapsulation**, which accounts for almost 7 per cent of the weight of the survey. Statements 22 (0.745) and 17 (0.721) suggest that students view teaching as presenting a body of knowledge and learning as remembering a body of information.

Career emerges as the fifth factor with a contribution of over 6 per cent to the survey. Statements 14 (−0.787) and 16 (0.679) indicate that what students value most about their course is a qualification and job prospects rather than interest in the course.

As in the case of the lecturers' survey a path model was constructed using the above components as the structure. Again, since the hypothesis in this work suggests that students are taking a 'capsule' approach to education it was decided to test the influences, if any, that the components **Best Educational Practice, Interest in Course, the Limiting Effect of Examinations** and **Career** have on **Encapsulation**. This is shown in Figure 9.2. It can be seen that **Best Educational Practice** has a small positive influence (0.122) on **Encapsulation. Best Educational Practice** has a more significant influence on **Interest** (0.357) and is itself influenced, in a more significant, negative fashion by the limiting effect of **Examinations** (−0.619). These two latter statistics fit the causal imagery of the model because it would, intuitively, be expected that **Best Educational Practice** would impact positively on **Interest** and that the limiting effect of **Examinations** would have a negative influence.

Interest has, as would be expected, a negative effect on **Encapsulation** (−0.049). The surprise is that this statistic is so low. Again, as expected, **Interest** is itself affected negatively by **Examinations** (−0.296).

The limiting effect of **Examinations** impacts negatively on **Career** (−0.160). This may suggest that students realize that content has nothing to do with career, it does not matter what is in the 'capsule'; they are trusting of the system and will study anything in order to gain certification. The factor **Examinations** has a very small positive effect on **Encapsulation** (0.071) while **Career** exerts an equally small negative effect (−0.072). The factor **Examinations** is an exogenous

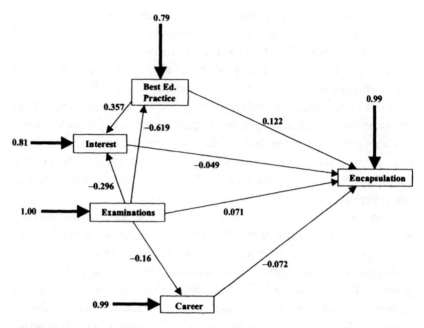

Figure 9.2 Path diagram for encapsulation with coefficients (Students' Survey)

variable; that is, it influences all the factors in the model while not being influenced by any of them. This means that all of the influence on **Examinations** comes from outside the model. The most significant influence, a negative one, in the whole model is that of **Examinations** on **Best Educational Practice** (−0.619). This statistic fits well with the causal imagery as it can be imagined that the limiting effects of examinations will have a negative effect on good teaching practice.

   Encapsulation affects none of the other factors but it is affected by all of them. So limited, however, is their combined influence that over 99 per cent of the influence on **Encapsulation** comes from outside the model.

   Further analysis of the path model illustrates that three factors are either completely (**Examinations**) or overwhelmingly (**Career** and **Encapsulation**) influenced by factors outside the model. In other words, what goes on in the classroom/lecture theatre barely influences **Encapsulation** or **Career**. In the case of **Interest**, 81 per cent of the influence comes from outside. In the case of **Best Educational Practice**, 79 per cent comes from outside. For both **Career** and **Encapsulation**, 99 per cent of the influence is external. The factor **Examinations** is completely uninfluenced by any factor in the model. This means that 100 per cent comes from outside sources.

A seminal finding in the path analysis in this chapter is that most of the influence on encapsulation of education comes from outside the institution. Learning styles would appear, therefore, not to be amenable to the efforts of individual lecturers in a teaching situation. For students, the issue of interest in the course does not appear to be a significant influence on encapsulation because they will 'learn' whatever is in the 'capsule' in order to obtain their desired qualification.

The results of the surveys administered to lecturers and students are very heavily skewed either towards agreement or disagreement with the questions posed – there are very few polarised outcomes. South Africa emerges as the country which seems the least caught up in the embrace of 'capsule' education. South African students score highest in ownership and consultation of texts – even supplementary texts – and in having interest in their course. These students are less likely than their counterparts in the other countries to want simply the bare information to pass the exam (33 per cent) and to consider it unfair if material not fully covered in class should appear on the examination paper (58 per cent). Interestingly, it is South Africa students who are least likely to be confident of examination success, although they return a positive response of 77 per cent. Similarly, from the lecturers' perspective, the survey reveals that the most positive results (in the modernist sense) come from South Africa. The least positive results come from the two Irish institutions in the survey. Text ownership and consultation is exceedingly low, yet the students here are extremely confident of success in examinations.

Chapter 10

The Testimony of Teachers

Interviews with lecturers and students were carried out for the purpose of giving comprehension, colour and meaning to the components embedded in the survey data. Both sets of interviews present a different – often polarised – perspective on the educational process. There is, however, no suggestion that either one perspective is the 'right' one since perspectives are formed by societal influences, often by previous generations. The perspectives offered by students have been formed for them by all of their experiences, including educational ones. The educational model with which they are familiar has not been fashioned by them; they have been moulded by it. It will become apparent that while lecturers experience frustration with the system of current educational practice, students, attuned as they are to the system, exhibit no such frustration but indicate a capacity to respond to it. Although it is clear that oppositional objectives can cause stress, a reading of the interviews allows for the process of disidentification (Ball, 1995) which facilitates the unravelling of what is insidious and invisible in prevailing practices. While the attitudes of students are clearly at odds with traditional views on education their honest insight provides tremendous weight in facilitating enlightenment about an educational model which is a closed book to anyone educated through the traditional paradigm. The student responses are innocent of any guile as they appear utterly unaware that those who value traditional education might find fault with their outlook. In the age old tradition of shooting the messenger, students, as is apparent in the interviews, may often find themselves blamed for creating the model of which they are, in fact, the unwitting victims.

The interviews take the form of a narrative – a story which the subjects tell about themselves, their opinions and their stance in relation to education. So natural is the impulse to tell, so familiar is the narrative as a form of communication, that we have come to rely on it as a repository of the truth as it really is, as it really happened. Far from providing an objective grid which represents certainty, however, the narrative is simply a heuristic instrument, an aid to investigation. Hayakawa's (1965) work finds echoes in White (1987) who warns against the acceptance of narrative as a neutral medium representing real events and processes. It is, in fact, says White (1987), possessed of myth, thus endowing events and opinions with an illusory content more characteristic of unconscious than conscious thought. The ideological and political implications of narrative necessarily deprive it of neutrality. While the suggestion of myth carries the risk of inducing the reader to eschew the narrative as a means of accessing truth, White (1987) asserts that, unreal as it is, it is a meaningful representation of people's lives as social beings. Narratives which can exhibit completeness or closure 'give to reality the odor of the ideal' (p. 21).

Social reality can be both lived and comprehended as a story. Far from being an empty bucket waiting to be filled with different contents, real or fabled, the narrative possesses a content prior to any writing or telling of it – the kind of content which Hayakawa (1965, 1990) asserts can result from the fusion of the intensional[1] with the extensional. The appeal of the narrative, White (1987) claims, lies in our desire to see real events demonstrate the kind of coherence, completeness and closure of an image of life such as that encountered in myth and fable. White (1987) claims that narrative may be regarded as a solution to the human problem of 'how to translate knowing into telling' (p. 1). Because of differences in life experiences and the impossibility of having a singular of view of language, he, drawing on Barthes (2005), points out that narrative continuously substitutes meaning for a straightforward copy of the events or processes told. The absence or refusal of narrative is an absence or refusal of meaning itself. In the contest between the imaginary and the actual, the narrative must be mined in an attempt to uncover the psychological impulse of the storyteller and to reveal the desires which underpin the

---

[1] That which is suggested (connoted) within one's head.

narration. Hayakawa observes that the prime function of utterance is the relieving of tension. A human being who has access to linguistic symbols is able to symbolise his experience to himself and, in so doing, effect some relief of tension. In this way meaning is achieved and tensions are brought, symbolically, under control. It is not sufficient that accounts register real rather than imaginary details; they must also be shown to possess an order of meaning. The listener or reader of a narrative is not satisfied with a mere list; she/he has expectations of explanation.

In this study the interviewee becomes the central subject about whom a story is told. However complete a narrative seems, it is, in fact, constructed on the basis of a set of events or processes which could have been included but were not. The question, therefore, is what notion of reality authorises the structure of the narrative record. Assuming that a subject wishes to give a real rather than imaginary account, the result is, in White's (1987) view, a product of an image of a reality which already bears distinguishing features of the social system in which the subject is an actor. The social system, which authorises the rankings of importance of events, features only barely in the consciousness of the subject, or, indeed is present as an element in the discourse only as far as there is an awareness of its absence.

White (1987) seems to suggest that humans are hardwired to focus on and remember negative rather than positive events, giving support to Hegel's view that periods of settled human happiness are blank pages in the chronicle. He also agrees with Hegel's assertion that an account must display, not a discrete list, but a certain form, the narrative and a certain content, a politico-social order. Given the structure of the social system, which he claims is embedded in the narrative, White (1987) suggests that it is the latent or expressed purpose of the narrative to moralise the events it describes by identifying with the social system which is the 'source of any morality that we can imagine' (p. 14).

The purpose of narrative is to give a human face and invite identification rather than to deliver the intimidation offered by a representation of events which is so complete and ordered – like an Excel spreadsheet – that it disallows human agency. The narrative summons us to participate in a moral universe which would have no attraction for us if it were not for the power of narrative form. In an implicit invocation of the moral standard, the narrator distinguishes between those events worthy of investigation and recording and those which are not. It is because events are supportive of the perceived social order, or because they do not fit, that they find a place in the narrative, thus asserting their reality. The demand for closure in the narrative, asserts White (1987), lies in a quest for moral meaning, for an understanding of events as significant elements in a moral drama. He questions that any narrative was ever written that was not underpinned by the moral authority of the narrator.

Authority for the narrative can only be claimed if at least two versions of the same events can be achieved. In the context of this work, all of the interviews reported encapsulation. Therefore, as White (1987) asserts, the accounts make the authority of the interviews the authority of reality itself. In his view, the narrative gives form to the reality and makes it appealing by the imposition upon its processes of the formal coherence that only stories possess. The capacity to assign to events a shared order of meaning requires, in White's (1987) opinion, a metaphysical principle by which difference can be translated into similarity. It requires a subject common to all referents of all the sentences of the account. This subject must be capable of acting as the central organizing principle of a story.

He suggests that in our attempts to make sense of human nature, culture, society and history we never say precisely what we mean to say or mean precisely what we actually say. Our discourse tends to be drawn away from the data towards the structures of consciousness with which we are trying to understand them – the intensional state described by Hayakawa (1965). There are legitimate grounds for different opinions on what the topics are, how they can be spoken about and the kinds of knowledge we can have about them. All genuine discourse accepts the suggestion of doubt that, therefore, inevitably attaches to its conclusions.

White (1978) draws on heavyweights such as Vico, Hegel, Rousseau and Nietzche to underpin his assertion that 'tropes and figures are the foundation on which knowledge of the world was erected' (p. 7). In attempting to analyse narrative discourse White (1978) illustrates the use of tropes – deep structural forms of thought – as determinants which have the effect of prefiguring the outcome; there is a suggestion that stages in history coincide with their dominant figurative trope. Subjects make use of figurative tropes – metaphor, metonymy, synecdoche and irony – all of which describe the possible relationships between part and whole. Tropes produce variations of speech or thought by their variation from what might be expected. They thus confer a motility on discourse which results in a slipping away from one possible, proper meaning towards another meaning of what is proper and true. Hayakawa (1965) reminds us that metaphors, far from being ornaments of discourse, are direct expressions and evaluations which occur whenever strong feelings are engaged. He cautions us to pay attention, too, to stated facts in the narrative which, at lower levels of abstraction, can be affective even in the absence of any literary devices.

All interpretation is uncertain because it would not be necessary to interpret if the meaning were clear. In attempting to derive meaning from discourse, White (1978) advocates that the dominant tropes in the narrative be identified in order to appreciate the emplotment which is prefigured in the story. For example, in the telling of events, he asserts that a constraining force in narrative is the ideological drive to claim the beautiful, meaningful nature of the past (and present), thus avoiding any choice of offering a terrifying meaninglessness as reality. Supporting this view is Becker's (1980) suggestion that all human drives are underpinned by the need to make meaning out of what might be meaninglessness. While the content of the narrative reflects the social order, the authority of the narrative as a representation of reality must also take into account the influence of dominant tropes.

The foundations for the interviews are provided by the significant components which were identified from the analysis of the survey data. The analysis identified six components for lecturers (**Non-engagement, Fragmented learning, Encapsulation, Students' demands and staff fatigue, Semesterisation, Lower Standards**). These are the same components which underpin the path analysis in the previous chapter. The intention was that interviews would be very loosely structured on the framework of these components with the interviewer playing as minimal a role as possible, thus allowing respondents to freely relate their stories. While it is acknowledged that this approach clearly exposes the narrator to a topic-governed plot, interventions by the interviewer were limited to questioning on the above topics. A summary was made of all the narratives and a statistical analysis was carried out on each.

These groups of narratives do not represent groups of respondents; they represent simply a sense of the created self at the time of the interview. According to White (1987) however, authority for the narrative can be claimed if at least two versions of the same events can be achieved. In as far as there is agreement in the narratives a claim can be made, therefore, that the narratives here offer a coherent interpretation of reality itself.

Six lecturers were interviewed, three males and three females from each of three age groups. Twenty students were also interviewed – 11 males and 9 females, five from each of 4 years, all of whom had volunteered to be interviewed. Cognisance is taken of the fact that their volunteerism may be an indicator that these students may not be truly representative of the student population as a whole. The testimony of lecturers appears in this chapter while that of students forms the next chapter.

The real meaning of the narrative is only secured by understanding the tropes, or master signifiers, in the interviews. The interviewees are the central subjects about which the story, that is the interview, is told. The desire which underpins the narration is the quest by respondents to make meaning for themselves and to bring coherence and resolution to a particular aspect of their lives. There are a number of tropes woven through these accounts. These tropes are deep structural forms of thought which, to some extent, have the effect of prefiguring the outcome.

The narrative below describes the opinions offered by lecturers during the course of in-depth interviews. In their responses, lecturers' opinions apply to the general student cohort, rather than to individual students; all recognise that there are exceptions.

In terms of engagement there is complete agreement that students are not engaged with the educational or learning process; there is doubt, in fact, that students understand the third-level paradigm. They are in higher education for purposes which are extraneous to the process itself. They seek information solely for examination purposes, they want something for nothing and they want it on a sheet in front of them. In terms of having an understanding of the 'big picture' there is the assertion that students have very short time horizons which limit any wider embrace of a subject. Students want lecturers to do everything for them, they want to receive, never give; they want the minimum information, preferably in bulleted points. They feel they can 'work x hours, miss y days' and their objective seems merely to establish what is the minimum they need to know to get 40 per cent. Many students are acutely aware of the compensation system and are aiming as low as 35 per cent. Trying to get a response from them is like 'pulling teeth'. Many students are prepared to rise only to a particular level and if that level is not 40 per cent the pressure is on lecturers to find the level 'at which everything works'. There is a risk in being so customer-focused that there is a loss in academic terms.

There is no perceived engagement with learning for its own sake, with learning as a means of self-improvement or a means of enlarging their understanding of the world. One respondent suggests that students are involved in a game only as far as they choose. Using a football metaphor he suggests that every so often the off-side flag goes up – students call it – if lecturers, for example, refuse to play in capsules. Another respondent asserts that, while realizing that students are not engaged, he no longer perceives a problem with it. With an attendance of 33 per cent at his lectures he has settled down to a modus operandi which involves giving students information geared specifically and only to examinations, which is what they want, he says. There is, therefore, no need for engagement. Education is now a market and students trade, not in comprehensive notes, but in 'bits of notes' as a medium of exchange for a qualification.

Suggestions are that students see education as a consumer experience, that education now is simply a commodity and that this applies at all levels. 'Yes, at the end of the day they want a meal ticket ... with as little input from them as possible and that in turn gives rise to a huge amount of input from us'.

The constantly recurring question from students – 'do we need to know this for the exam?' – triggers a mixture of hopelessness and mirth, although one respondent steadfastly attempts to answer the question by stressing what real education is. He tells students that it is the greatest chance they will ever get and accentuates the importance of self-development, irrespective of the link with career, although, like the findings of Telford and Masson (2005), he can see nothing from higher management that really encourages education. He believes education should be expansive, yet, paradoxically, because of poor attendance and engagement, he finds himself achieving less. This is because he repeats classes since so many students are absent and he finds that he is teaching a different sub-group of a class from one day to the next. He really wants them to understand, he says. He would prefer that they understand a smaller amount of the course than to cover the full course and have them understand very little. Students can turn in today and not tomorrow and lecturers will pick up the pieces; he feels that he is probably too 'soft' in his approach. He acknowledges that his actions discriminate against diligent students and result in a contraction of the very education he believes in.

Another describes the 'lightbulb going off in their heads' if she attempts to teach anything that is not on the examination paper. They are concrete thinkers, so she feels compelled to keep things basic. If she attempts anything abstract 'you'd just lose them' she says. There is general agreement that students are interested only if the topic is going to be on the examination paper; otherwise they do not want to know. Whatever interest they exhibit in this instance is further limited, for as many as an estimated 80 per cent of students, to its function in facilitating the passing of examinations rather than interest in the topic itself.

Many students seem to think that part-time or full-time work entitles them to miss class. They are preoccupied with work and social life to the exclusion of engagement with the educational process. Respondents attribute some of the lack of interest on the part of students to their lifestyle 'they need money for cars, insurance, holidays etc. There is no going back and we have bowed to part-time work'.

Defending the approach of students, one respondent suggests that he is not sure that students have been encouraged to make very good choices. He cites the observation of an education commentator who believes that the choices which students make, even in schools, may have the effect of screening them away from the possibility of engaging in occupations for which they might have great aptitude or in which they might find a very fulfilling career. But because they have not done particular subjects at school they do not have the opportunity or the possibility of getting near that kind of career or near the courses that lead towards it.

Attendance is generally poor. Some say that they have a floating population, regularly as few as 40 per cent, often only 20 per cent. One lecturer asserts that many students simply drift into college; they have no particular drive or sense of purpose. Puzzled by seriously poor and intermittent attendance this respondent asks every second day 'where is everybody?', acknowledging the irony of asking the students who are in attendance a question which can only be answered by those who are absent. At least 50 per cent are present only occasionally. 'It's very hard to teach people who are not there' he sighs. His finding is that attendance improves in third year because, in his college, students have the incentive of transferring to a Degree in Finance if they do well. Another, who remarks that students claim 90 to 100 per cent attendance on the quality assurance forms, would consider 50 per cent a crowd, while Friday morning is 'a non-starter', she says. Only one finds that attendance is quite good for lectures – 60 to 70 per cent, but these are mid-week, mid-morning lectures when, she says, attendance is at its best. However, tutorials seem to be viewed by her students as an 'optional extra'; typically 20 per cent will attend. Students can 'get their hands on notes' without attending, is the general feeling. These opinions are supported by the official record in one educational institution which shows that the average student attendance across all 4 years is 48 per cent.

Pincered between the drive for student retention on the one hand and the poor attendance from students and their unwillingness to read on the other, lecturers respond by preparing more comprehensive notes which become, in effect, a substitute for the course. There is general bemusement that they all respond in this way despite the absence of an explicit directive from management. Such an outcome seems to support Lyotard's concept of the 'enchanted workplace' and to provide evidence of the 'structural violence' identified by

Habermas (1989) and the 'symbolic violence' identified by Bourdieu (1986). The lifeworld of staff has been colonised by the instrumental rationality of the system. Concerns for the more profound questions about the nature of education become subsidiary to the everyday instrumental efficiencies of the system, that is, the accreditation of as many students as possible.

All cite the increasing demands of students as a major factor in their work and some question the willingness of management to support the staff. The sense of being blamed by students and/or criticised by management weighs heavily with four of the six respondents. This view is supported by the assertion of Marrington and Rowe (2004) that hierarchies tend to become blame allocation systems and by the findings of Telford and Masson that managers place little emphasis on the learning process choosing, instead, to treat students as individuals and adults. The other two respondents acknowledge increasing demands but assert that lecturers are solicitous for their students and have a tendency to want to accommodate them. These respondents experience no sense of threat from students or management. One respondent suggested that we live in a blame culture where students have an increasing amount of clout with management while members of staff have less and less. Another, acknowledging that he has capitulated to students' demands at the expense of real education, says, 'a lot of people feel that it's simply not worth it . . . and I . . . I can't really blame them . . . you know . . . they feel it's simply not worth the fight because at the end of it what do you get?' He thinks that all staff will shortly be under extreme pressure to use Moodle[2], the educational value which he doubts. In addition to the availability of course notes on Moodle there will be pressure to put up past examination papers and model answers. He is not sure if these will be skeleton or full answers but sighs that if one lecturer provides full answers everyone else will have to follow '. . . so, one could argue that in terms of stress levels you're just better off giving in to it and that's a very conscious decision that I've taken'. The Lacanian annihilation of his own separateness, the seeking of camouflage as protection by simulating death (in Barglow,

[2] Computer program to deliver course content material by electronic media.

2001) is apparent here. The logic of Moodle is to 'capture' the students who do not attend, this respondent says. They can download a set of notes and 'learn' them. This respondent has made a political decision to give students what they want. He has seen lecturers vilified by students if their results were out of line with others, has himself been ignored by students, has been called 'the hard marker', has had his marks queried by students – 'how can this be possible?' – and has been accused of costing a student a 2:1. He has chosen to see his job as 'getting students through the system' rather than offering the kind of developmental educational experience he would, ideally, like to facilitate. He may have bought into a Faustian pact, he says, but it is simply less stressful for him. He could not cope with going against the tide. He feels that students are watchful about what other lecturers are doing and subtle pressure is applied. He cites examples of colleagues being contacted at home in the wake of a student getting a fail mark in an examination. Referring to the metaphors, *student as consumer, education as a market* and the concomitant that the *customer is always right,* he agrees that students see the college as a sort of shop where they can go at any time to get what they want. Contacting lecturers at home, he reflects, is like internet shopping, not time dependent. His musings support the suggestion by Cheney et al. (1997) that such metaphors have the effect of distancing students from the very education they are supposed to embrace and of producing adversarial rather than co-operative relations between lecturers and students. The lecturer is seen as the bestower of grades. This opinion supports the finding in the survey in this study that only 36 per cent of lecturers see students as willing co-creators in their own learning. This polarisation of student and lecturer, by placing the student outside of the institution, may result in the practice by lecturers of defensive education, as evidenced in this interview. Sometimes this respondent feels a lack of authenticity but mostly he does not have a problem. He has, he says, 'morphed into the norm'. He enjoys teaching because he gives students what they want; he would not enjoy it if he had to face belligerent students who wanted X, Y and Z from him that he was not prepared to give.

There is a challenge all the way for lecturers from both students and management, says another respondent. Conscious that the whole process has become very legalistic she is aware that lecturers may have to explain themselves, perhaps even in a court of law, for example, in a dispute about marking. Many students are inclined to blame everyone but themselves for their lack of progress, she says, suggesting that many have the attitude that if they are accepted into the college they are owed a qualification and they do not have to work for it.

> They will complain [says another] because nobody else will do that with them [expect them to study from books]. You know, I would be the only person then expecting them to do that ... so I think across the board, then, if anybody tried to do anything different, they'd ... they'd see that as unfair ... you know, because we are all packaging material for them ...

A respondent who has little problem with the fact that students have become much more demanding and feels no threat from management suggests that students need notes. 'They need this kind of ... basic sort of survival rations without which they don't feel able to prepare for the exams'. He acknowledges constant and persistent pressure – 'much water will wear away a stone really' – from students for more extensive guidance over the years and has responded with the provision of more and more notes, hoping that the restrictive nature of his teaching now is not 'too much a travesty of the subject'. He adds that perhaps lecturers have become excessively pessimistic about students' abilities and that they could be more independent learners if they were not spoon-fed so much.

All respondents feel that students' experience at second level is the driver in their demands for trimmed, watered down, focused notes. They are conditioned to rote learning a 'bare set of notes', says one respondent who points to the example of a maximum points student, profiled in a national newspaper after the Irish Leaving Certificate of 2005, who famously said in an interview 'there's no point in knowing about stuff that's not going to come up in exams' (Holden, 2005). He found 'frightening' the level of detailed advice which this student delivered – 'she talked about key words, for example, in an answer to short questions which would get extra marks. ...' Students at third level continue to want a package, he says,

... undoubtedly ... if by package we mean, you know, neat notes, focused notes very much so ... forget outside, you know ... fair enough if you've got other notes move from that to focused notes where you can eliminate pages 1, 3 and 5. Then you have sample questions and, of recent times, sample answers ...

The points-driven model of second-level education is marked indelibly on their psyches; it is the only model they know. It is an indictment of the system, and not the student mentioned above, that such a high achiever can speak with pride about such a ruthless approach, based primarily on the rote learning of formulaic answers, and dismissive of anything which is unlikely to be examined. In an ideal world the first semester should be spent undoing this paradigm, says one.

In terms of management support four of the six respondents felt that lecturers would be undermined in any contest between them and students. One admitted that she chooses to deal with plagiarism issues herself rather than follow policy because she feels that the end result is a foregone conclusion, heavily in favour of the student. If the student is a foreign student it will be even more heavily weighted in favour of the student. There is an increased demand on the part of management in relation to staff, she thinks. Staff welfare is not factored into the management approach. Lecturers, she feels, are very close to the edge but could cope a lot better with the situation if management were less obviously pro-student at the expense of staff.

Acknowledging that the staff are fortunate in terms of their management in the particular school, a third suggests that undoubtedly there are differences between those who manage and those who teach and the lot of lecturers has become much, much more difficult. Management is very much geared towards students and much less geared towards teaching staff. 'Staff seem to be means to an end ... and that end is ... well ... retention and keeping students'. Such a view offers credence to Habermas' (1989) claim that the structures of institutions are not sensitive to the true nature of human social interaction and are too ready to reduce human beings to mere objects which can be manipulated. It also supports Harman's (2002) claim that there is a shift from collegial to more corporate management style.

Students are not seen as independent learners by any respondents.

> They are . . . afraid of going outside of a very narrow remit . . . I think a lot of the honours students want to do well but they're afraid of textbooks, they are afraid of them. It's very interesting . . . if they get anything different, different language, they just curl up in a ball and find it dreadful and don't want to be examined on it or whatever.

There is recognition that, while all students can read, many have difficulty in synthesising information. One respondent says that she is reduced to giving handouts to students in class because if she gives them out in advance as many as 75 per cent will not read them. If the writing is not very simple they will simply shut down or say 'I don't know what this is about'.

In general students do not either possess or use textbooks in large numbers. One respondent claims he is at a loss to express his utter astonishment that the text for his subject, which is a workbook covering the whole course and used in class *every single* day, is, nevertheless not bought by all students. Some buy it fairly early, others show no sense of urgency despite the shortness of the semester, some buy a second-hand copy although the content has changed, others eventually buy it 4 or 5 weeks before the exam but there is always 10 per cent who do not buy it at all.

Another respondent selects chapters from a book and hands these out as photocopies. Another 'just gave up' asking the students to buy a textbook in the wake of her experience that only a quarter of the class would buy it; she photocopies notes and handouts. She would worry about being able to hold a class if the students have no material but holds the line in refusing to give notes to students who do not attend unless they have a doctor's note or have a sick child or some other problem. Interestingly, this is the only respondent who feels that students attend quite well, except for tutorials, although, she muses, this may be because she is lucky to have lectures with them mid-morning and mid-week. Only 19 out of 55 have the prescribed textbook, says another respondent. This text is necessary for use in class almost every day. She will not infringe copyright laws by photocopying a prescribed text; it would also be unfair on students, she says, who go to the trouble and expense of buying their own. This lecturer prepares notes to substitute some sections in the text. Another prepares all notes herself – this she finds enormously time-consuming – to cover the whole course because the students will not read.

Only some of them have their essential texts, says another respondent. 'My impression is that those who have them ... do not use them as a primary resource ... they like to have them as a kind of lifebelt or insurance policy in the last week before the exams', he laughs. Using an analogy with a safety announcement in an airplane – 'do not open textbook before exams as to do so will distract you', – he suggests that students do not mine for information in an organized fashion – 'they send the drill bit down on a hit-or-miss basis'. He contrasts the students' ability to handle texts now with the equivalent students' abilities 20 or 25 years ago.

> ... my sense is that by and large they weren't afraid to read books and that they could research a topic ... My feeling is that people ... that our culture is now much more visual, people read less, they listen to the radio less ...
>
> ... This is my feeling ... that people did read a lot more and were a lot more literate in that sense and that they were better able to write and express themselves on paper.

There is unanimous estimate that as many as 90 per cent of students are in higher education for the sole purpose of obtaining a qualification with the objective of getting the best job possible, in financial terms. As few as one-tenth are interested in learning for its own sake. Acknowledging that there has always been a link between education and career, there is a defence, nevertheless, in the experience of all those interviewed that, during their own education, career issues were set to the side and they took the course on its merits and engaged with essence of their course wholeheartedly. The requirement to be independent learners fostered in them a sense of ownership.

Another outcome of the retention requirement is, in the opinion of all of the respondents, the lowering of standards. There is resigned acceptance that education has become merely a consumer experience, a market with many suppliers relative to buyers. It's a Dutch auction, says one. Education's an industry now and this respondent doubts that product quality is an issue any longer. Students and parents will be seduced if they see an easy way to get an honours degree 'and they're two a penny nowadays'. Another reflects on the irony that, while competition usually increases quality, in the case of education supply it actually has the opposite effect. We know, he says wryly, that the more students we have the more income we get, so that exerts pressure on staff and it would be very brave to take a decision to go against the tide. A third respondent believes that 'in order to retain we have to dumb down and anybody who says we are not dumbing down is in denial, because we are dumbing down – we have to dumb down'.

This lecturer is astonished how few students are working at honours level. Self- directed learning is crucial for a 'respectable' degree, she says. As few as one-third of honours-degree students are capable of this.

They won't fail, though, they won't fail', she continues. 'I know what I can expect from a group and I know what is expected so far as retention is concerned. I know I can . . . I can pitch the examination in such a way that the right number of them will get through. And we all do it, yes we all do it . . . we all do it.

Such a system seems unlikely to accommodate the 'moral maturity' necessary to clarify the distinction between two interpretations of merit – a formal one and a morally rich one (Gibbs & Iacovidou, 2004). A fourth respondent claims that it is unbelievably easy to get 40 per cent in her subject. Years ago, she says, no one got as low as 40 – it would be shameful to get a bare pass. Now, she says, simply writing one's name or year will merit a mark. She makes an effort to communicate to students in a concrete fashion how little they know if they get only 40 per cent and advises them that if they ever encounter a medical doctor who got a bare pass they should walk away very quickly. Even if the doctor got 96 per cent, she says she still warns the students that they would be entitled to be anxious that there was 4 per cent that the doctor did not know! This respondent alludes to the disbelief and disenchantment of some secondary school teachers, now in their fifties, who worked very hard to get a pass degree and who see students, whom they know to be weak academically, emerging with an honours degree from a third-level institution. One respondent expressed shock that an extern returned to her an examination paper which had been sent to him for approval with the recommendation that she delete the word *discuss*. He wasn't sure that students should be expected to have the ability to discuss – and these are students preparing for an honours degree, shortly to leave the college with this award. This attitude seems to reflect Moncayo's (2003) suggestion that a postmodern perspective on education tends to permute and combine without necessarily integrating or synthesising. All acknowledge that students would have difficulty with examination papers set as recently as 6 or 7 years ago. As the teaching period has been reduced by semesterisation the whole process has become rushed, contact with students has diminished and students are not required to retain learning for any length of time. With year-long courses students were, in the past, required to carry learning right through from September to May. This has now been replaced by two short 'bite-sized semesters', with students seeking reassurance at the beginning of a new semester that they will not be examined on any topic from the previous semester. 'They don't see any point in carrying forward information at all'. The encouragement by management not to examine the same topics in continuous assessment as in a final examination further permits students to jettison information on an ongoing basis with the result that students are faced, not with a comprehensive education but with what Zemsky (1993) calls convenient, digestible packages of technical and labour-related knowledge. Not alone does continuous assessment increase the workload immeasurably for lecturers but it has the effect of removing the building blocks which are necessary for the embracing of a subject if everything can be examined in the final examination, especially if the academic year is not semesterised. Little attention seems to be paid by students to Robotham's (2003) suggestion that it is crucially important for them to be able to stand back, metaphorically, and observe their learning. Students are over-assessed, lecturers are overworked and standards are being reduced. Despite the educational benefits of a year-long course all respondents believe that the current student population would not be able to carry information for this length of time; they seem to need the short-haul mix of continuous assessment and final examination after 13 weeks. The floating population and the lack of ability/lack of willingness on the part of students induces some lecturers to repeat the teaching of topics, preferring to do half the course well rather than the whole course 'with students knowing nothing'. They cite an educator's vocation to make sense of a subject for his/her audience but realize, with some hopelessness, that they are, in fact, rewarding the errant student, punishing the diligent and, overall, reducing the educational value of the course.

Two respondents used the term 'bloodbath' in connection with their attempts to maintain standards. Students need a great deal of tuition these days, they are not willing to read or study independently and, in addition, their extra-curricular work means that they do not have the time to study. Any effort to maintain standards would result in a bloodbath, said one. Another, using the same metaphor, said, however, that in an experience which he had undergone, the blood was his, not the students'. He reports a situation when a significant number of students failed his subject and had to take re-sits solely because of it. This was a source of astonishment to him because he had

> literally bent over backwards ... notes and this, that and the other and very good hints for exams which is ... dangerous ... but you do it. And I got a very distinct feeling that, you know, what had happened, you know, management were aware of that. Thereafter I took the decision well ... that's best avoided.

Acknowledging that he feels under pressure to pass students almost irrespective of what they produce in an examination, he confesses that he has taken a conscious decision to do everything possible to facilitate students to pass.

Part of the problem of diminished standards, according to some respondents, rests with the very much wider spectrum of students registering for courses. Twenty years ago or even ten years ago there was not as broad an ability spectrum at the lower end of academic or conceptual ability. Perhaps students have particular abilities in other areas such as computer games, says one respondent, but their level of conceptual ability and reasoning has become much diminished over the years. Many admit that they pitch their teaching lower to accommodate the lower ability students. In terms of writing skills, grammar, vocabulary, spelling and syntax there is agreement that, if these factors were taken into account, 'we would be failing 80 per cent of them'. One respondent almost overlooks the problem now because it has become so bad across the board. 'They can't write, can't spell, but they manage to pass exams and come out the other end. No one wants to address the issue of poor literacy skills'.

In terms of the fact that the pass rate remains very high despite this problem, two respondents, with some irony, suggested that they might be tempted to make some assumptions about the grammar levels of those who are correcting. All acknowledge that there is more tolerance now for bad grammar, bad presentation, poor sentence construction and poor language and that 'there is nothing out there that seems to support anything else ... newspapers, television, radio etc. I'm, not sure that there is anything out there ... either from government or from their surroundings that, in a way, requires it any longer'.

Writing skills have 'disimproved by a factor of a thousand', says one respondent, who also claims that the simplest mental computation is beyond most of her students. E-mail protocols are weaving their way into other communication, she says. Many managers no longer have secretaries and operate with a laptop, perhaps at an airport, typing a message on the screen. 'Does a full stop matter? An initial capital? What's an apostrophe? We live in a very fast world ...', she says. Most students, she continues, are incapable of putting together a number of concise sentences. One respondent is fascinated that employers and supervisors continually claim that what they need in their staff, above all, is the ability to communicate, to write a report, to convey meaning clearly. As educators, he says, we are not whole-hearted in pursuing that. He believes that the teaching of grammar at third level is not a realistic option because of pressure on the curriculum and because of poor student engagement. Acknowledging that the purists would say otherwise he says that he sees no widespread consensus to improve things and reckons that the future for standards is downwards in the absence of such a consensus. All feel that there is 'encouragement' from management not to fail students for poor writing skills, but acknowledge, too, that lecturers, themselves, tend to be solicitous for students and want to pass them if at all possible. There is a sense of shame and some shock that students emerging, even with an honours degree, cannot, in most cases, write well; but all suggest that students are not taught the necessary skills at primary or second level. Two respondents claim that it would therefore be unfair to punish them for not knowing something they have never been taught. Freire (1972) might suggest that students are perhaps being punished by *not* being taught.

Standards are generally perceived to be inflationary. An honours degree is now 50 per cent, not 55. The drive to increase the loading of continuous assessments to 50 per cent further facilitates a student to pass by compensation, perhaps even without a final examination. Respondents feel that education provision has become very competitive. Inevitably, there is very significant pressure to increase retention. Admitting that he feels pressure, one respondent asserts

> now I'm sure management will say that's a nonsense, that ... that isn't the case but ... for what it's worth I feel it ... to the extent that ... you know ... without being too flippant and without neglecting ok ... duty, say as an educationalist, I've taken a decision to, you know, I'll just go the route of doing *everything* possible to get them through.

There has been a persistent devaluation of the concept of a degree. Lots of students who get degrees, even honours degrees, would not have 'been near getting degrees ten or fifteen years ago'. For the level of work it takes to get an ordinary degree now, a student would have been awarded a National Certificate 20 years ago. While students are perceived to be unaware of diminished standards, there is a suggestion that employers are becoming more discerning. It used to be the case, remarked one respondent wryly, that young people could not get a job in a (named) chain store without their second-level Final Certificate. Now it is a degree. The current wide availability of jobs was mentioned by another respondent as significant. Employers are desperate and people need make no special effort to get a job. Many of these are low-level jobs, she says, a contrast to former times when a degree was linked with a profession.

Respondents generally feel that they are letting students down in their failure to facilitate the developmental education in which they believe. Faced with the demands of students and their lack of willingness to engage, however, they claim that they have no choice. One argues that, although he recognises the 'race to the bottom', it would be possible to suggest that a lecturer who did not facilitate students to pass was failing them because that is what they want and everyone else is doing it. Another respondent agrees, suggesting that three quarters of students simply want a qualification and 'our job is to facilitate that'. Their experience of second level so determines their approach 'that it would be a mammoth task to change all that'.

A respondent who has extensive experience in third-level education agrees that the sense of education as a developmental experience is being damaged.

> Yes, I think so in the sense that...if there's any truth in the old saying ... that I learn 20% of ... of what you tell me, and 40% of what I read and 90% of what I find out for myself, ... if that's true ... well then ... we're structuring our operation too much towards the front end of that and too little towards the back end of that ... proposition.

However, on balance he feels that he is doing the right thing in passing students who would not have succeeded some years ago. This respondent, speaking about the Irish context, says that we are part of the whole economic process whether we like it or not. While students with degrees may be getting low-level jobs, nevertheless it is the first time in Irish history that the economy can offer some kind of opportunity to every single person who is interested in getting a job. We are part of a process which appears to have been enjoying some success, at least at the economic level. There is a lot wrong with a system which has failed to anticipate the problems associated with excess and success, he says, but 'Joe Taxpayer would take it amiss if we were to ... you know, hijack the whole process and bend it to where the academics would like it to be'.

He is not saying that academics should have no say in shaping the process but there are many issues that need to be debated and clarified among themselves 'before they could afford to become so high minded as to be taking up ethical positions about what the students ought to be taught or what they ought to learn'.

In a telling acceptance of *student as consumer*, he defends the accreditation of students in the face of declining standards by claiming that what students are receiving is less a certificate of competence than an instrument which allows them to negotiate in the market. Using an analogy with marriage, he asserts that people who are married to each other are able to negotiate with society and be accepted on those terms, irrespective of the state of their union. In terms of third-level education, society is happy to delegate a certain aspect of the accreditation process for students, a 'stamping of passports before they set out upon their economic voyage'. This, he sees, is the function of third-level education institutions in the national, economic picture. Certainly, he feels, the academics should be permitted to add as much quality to the process as possible but that does not give them the right to be the ultimate arbiters of the ethics of their role. Another respondent, reflecting Illich's concern with education as an industry, also recognises the role of education in the economic process; she feels that lecturers have little choice but to acquiesce with diminished standards.

> ... our students are different ... you know ... we have this great big, big building, we've all this huge staff ... Now I'm not saying that we have courses ... that we keep courses, we keep students so that we keep people employed ... but ... it's a different world ... and ... standards, I mean ... what are they? I mean who decides that this is the standard and anything else below it is unacceptable ... It's a very, very hard one to call.

Many respondents, recognising the industrial nature of current educational provision, use production metaphors in describing the process. The education process is a massive 'mincing machine'. The objective is to put as much raw material as possible through it 'and get as many hamburgers or whatever ... out of the far end of the process as ... as possible and ... you know ... never mind the quality, feel the width'.

There needs to be a substantial debate among the educators about what they would do and how they would do it, says this respondent. That would be the only opportunity to re-establish educational standards. It would be important that those criteria would be established, accepted and implemented by a substantial number of lecturers. Students would probably *feel* entitled, whether they were or not, to object if one or two lecturers went on a solo run.

All respondents declare that they enjoy the profession of teaching, enjoy where they work and the interaction with colleagues but, with one exception, find that they have become demoralised and/or discouraged by their current teaching experience. The exception, the oldest respondent, while acknowledging lower standards and lack of engagement among students, nevertheless finds that these changes have the effect of providing him with a challenge which energises him, even after a lifetime of teaching.

' ... I think, basically, that I am probably as interested in the communication and as motivated now ... And it may be ... in some ways more ... challenged by the ... the difference ... .' He still feels a measure of excitement and stimulation about the prospect of standing before a group of people and trying to make sense of a topic, to present it in a way that they can relate to and will shed light on their experience.

Four respondents have seen a massive shift in their own motivation levels over careers which span from 7 to over 30 years and one respondent says she experiences, less a drop in morale, more an increase in tedium. There is more and more work with less and less return. Poor attendance, little effort and little engagement are part and parcel of education in 2006. Work has become harder. There is only so much enthusiasm a lecturer can muster in the face of an uninterested class. For one respondent the major advantage of her career is that it enables her to keep in touch with economic, business and academic matters which affect her grown-up children. Most people console themselves by looking forward to the holidays, says another, suggesting that no one could possibly cope with the prospect of working in education for another 30 years if standards do not improve.

The lecturer's workload is cited as a major contributor to stress levels. Staff are overstretched 'right to the wire', says one who does not see the situation improving. She worries that teaching time per subject will be reduced from three to two lectures per week with staff being required to teach extra modules. Staff will respond by acquiescing and there will be further erosion of standards because students will not do the work, she thinks. From her own point of view, she keeps hoping that the downward spiral will end but realizes that this is a hopelessly idealistic notion. Semesterisation is also responsible for increasing workload and stress. It means that there is literally no time for *real* education. A year-long course gives such comfort, such space. With semesterisation the lecturer is constantly benchmarking, constantly comparing progress with last year. It is an ongoing, uphill struggle. On the other hand, one lecturer suggests that despite the educational disadvantages of semesterisation it has one positive benefit in that it provides a measure of relief to lecturers – 'I do think to some extent it keeps a lid on the amount of teaching ... ' – given that students will not learn independently. Interestingly, this is a concept which is borne out in the path analysis in the previous chapter.

One respondent recognises that students probably do not want education themselves but he wants it for them and it distresses him that they appear to have very vacuous lives with

> Big Brother and celebrity and all these things they are subjected to ... so, I mean education's the last thing they want, or the last thing they think they want and it's the last thing that's *presented* to them – other than what education can do for them. The importance of a qualification is always stressed to students, but actually learning and appreciating language, appreciating ... appreciating anything ... I don't think it's encouraged.

Despite their obvious economic prosperity, he doubts that students are happy – a reflection of Baudrillard's (1998) idea that such prosperity simply has the effect of shifting inequality to a more general field where it functions more subtly, thus becoming all the more irreversible. He feels that there are a lot of frustrated, unhappy, depressed and ill people and he is tired of being told by education commentators that education is about boosting the economy. He believes that a well-rounded education would fulfil students more but he wonders if there are outlets out there for them, given the possible absence of education from their backgrounds and the amount of 'dumbing down' of standards in general.

The dominant trope running through all of the accounts is **fatalism** in the face of a monolithic institution which respondents feel powerless to change; all have acquiesced in a system with which they disagree fundamentally. This reminds us of Becker's (1980) assertion that man chooses to make a prison out of freedom. He will choose, instead of freedom, to settle down under some kind of authority which provides him with a mandate for his life. All respondents believe in an education which is developmental but, in practice, they deliver a qualification for what is little more than a memory test. Whyte's (2004) admonitions that if we do not use our voices we become victims and that too many people haunt their life instead of living it – they are sold to the system – has resonances here. Chaharbaghi and Newman's (1998) assertion, that real educators who are disenchanted with industrial style education can be easily replaced by pseudo-educators who are quite happy to exercise irresponsibility in the form of artificial work, also strikes a jarring note as does the idea of the possible 'moral relativism' of postmodern education identified by Bloland (1995). Respondents seem to have adopted the Jefferson compromise (in Rorty, 1989), that is, the embracing of an education system which seems acceptable to the public at large with the concomitant sacrificing of their own ideals.

It would not be too strong to ascribe a **tragic** trope to the accounts of four respondents, in particular to the one female and one male from the middle and youngest groups respectively. While all four exhibit a sense of hopelessness these two exhibit an extreme measure of exhaustion and fear, which is particularly poignant when consideration is given to the length of time they still must serve if they are to continue their careers in teaching. They are both politically astute and reckon that their best means of survival is compliance with the demands of students and management. Their fatalism and exhaustion are palpable, and their interviews heavily accented with sighs. There is not a trace of suggestion that either will fight for a principle or to alleviate their discomfort; it is easier and less stressful to cave in, even to what are perceived to be unreasonable demands. The male respondent believes that it is worth the price. These two are the most unlikely to expect management support. In fact, four of the respondents would not expect management support. A fifth feels he can cope without it, which may suggest that he believes it would not be forthcoming if he sought it. This respondent, however, is adamant that there is no management support for education. These responses seem to match the opinions expressed in Stone (1995) and in Holt (2004) who testify to the silence in academia and the acquiescence in the acceptance of the lowering of standards. There is an inference that lecturing staff are expected to manage all 'service encounters' (Athiyaman, 1997) so as to maximise consumer satisfaction.

For these four respondents the central organizing principle (White, 1987) around which they construct their narratives is **Education as a Public Good**. This is the kind of education in which they believe and which they feel is the 'right' education to facilitate in students. They enact their role in the moral drama, the latent purpose of which is to moralise the events they describe by identifying with their social system. Their image of reality bears the imprint of their social system which, consciously or unconsciously, authorises the rankings of the importance of events. They are unhappy with what they see as a trade in third-level qualifications, not in return for developmental education, but in return for, typically, a short-term memory test. All bear testimony to Illich's (1972) complaint that education constitutes massive waste as resources are used to two main effects. First, to teach the answers to predetermined problems in a ritually defined setting and, secondly, to create new educational packages. Kelsey's (2002) criticism of the Finland and Ireland models of education as models which are devoid of any sense of nation, interested only in the knowledge economy, would be likely to find support here. Lecturers are experiencing disorientation from what they see as the toppling of their god and its replacement by another central organizing principle – **Education as Accreditation**.

There is no happy ending in these four narratives although they all achieve a measure of closure, accented by a **tragic heroism**. Despite their belief that the educational system is failing students and that they, by their part in it, are also failing students, they have resolved their cognitive dissonance, in most cases, by claiming that it would be more unfair to students not to give them packaged education since this is what they expect, this is what they need in order to get a qualification and this is what other institutions are doing currently. One adds to this defence her enjoyment of the institution and the company of her colleagues plus, as mentioned earlier, the opportunity her work affords her to keep in touch with her children's business careers. In the face of their difficulties all have sought, heroically (in the Becker sense of attributing meaning to their lives), to accommodate the demands of both students and management by preparing notes which are specifically geared to examinations, by disregarding poor grammar and syntax as elements of education and by maintaining a high pass rate. They have discovered how to survive.

While acknowledging that they see no option but to adapt to the system, the other two respondents appear to have achieved a measure of objectivity in their contemplation of the student cohort, remaining sanguine and, even, upbeat. A significant secondary trope in these two narratives is **comedic detachment**, evidenced by much laughter throughout the interviews. One respondent is female and from the youngest group; the other is male and the oldest. Amusing metaphors are frequently employed – 'the lightbulb going off in their head' ... 'lifebelt ... insurance policy'... 'survival rations' ... 'lifejacket' ... 'mincing machine' ... 'sending the drill bit down on a hit-or-miss basis' ... 'offside flag'. These are in sharp contrast to the 'bloodbath' metaphors of two of their colleagues.

Despite their own very positive and quite classical educational experiences these two respondents recognise that the central organizing principle has shifted and that the purpose of education is now accreditation. The younger experiences tedium in being faced with uninterested students but asserts that her morale is not diminished. She is hopeful that things will improve. The older is fully aware of the differences in the student cohort over his 30-year teaching span and is accepting of their differing objectives and attitudes. He has never experienced a diminishing in his levels of motivation despite the obvious attitude change among students. He questions the right of academics to assume that their own educational values are paramount, especially in the light of students' success in accessing careers after college. Both of these narrations, therefore, have a happy ending. It might be said that the narratives of these two respondents exhibit a **good-humoured heroism**; they accommodate their students also but do so in good faith, in contrast to their colleagues whose heroism is underscored by a tragic motif.

While there is a measure of **irony** in the accounts it is probably diminished by the utter involvement of four of the respondents in their own crises and is absent from the accounts of the two respondents who exhibit an acceptance of their situation. Even the cry 'It's very hard to teach students who are not there' is delivered without a trace of irony. There are some exceptions, however, as when the issue of part-time work is referred to – 'they need to work, they need cars ... they need at least one or two holidays a year ... there's a lot of things like that making demands on them' ... 'They have to be at their part-time job at 10 o'clock on a Thursday and they've got an eleven hour day' ... 'When can they read? When? They have to work'. In a comment on poor writing skills one respondent declares: 'it doesn't really matter if there's a full stop. Does it really matter if there's an initial capital ... let's drop the apostrophe ... sure nobody knows about that anyway ...'

Much **metaphor** is employed as an efficient expression of deeply held feelings. Respondents talk about 'picking up the pieces'; 'capturing' students with Moodle; education as a 'Dutch auction'; 'losing students'; 'curl up in a ball', 'bloodbath'; honours degrees 'two a penny'; 'keeping the lid on teaching'. In addition, reference is made to the student as consumer and to the process of education, for students, as a shopping experience – even internet shopping because of their expectation that they should be able to contact lecturers at all hours.

Lecturers, caught between the demands of management and the demands of students, see developmental education slipping from their grasp. They have, unwillingly, become complicit in the system by providing sets of notes closely geared to examination requirements, by shrinking the course because of students' non-attendance and by ignoring serious literacy issues when marking examinations. They over-teach, over-assess, perceive that students are concrete thinkers and feel real stress at work. In an unusual finding, which is also revealed in the path analysis conducted on the lecturer survey, it seems that the brevity of the semester provides relief to lecturers who feel that they work at high octane level during the teaching weeks of their programme.

Chapter 11

The Testimony of Students

The main actors on the stage of education are the students. In the light of their central position in the system, an examination of their attitudes provides the most accurate prism through which current educational practices can be viewed; all other observers are on the outside looking in. Students have been shaped by 14 to 18 years of education and they internalise attitudes and behaviours as a result of these experiences. Their unique testimony appears below and provides a fascinating insight into the kind of educational world with which previous generations may not be familiar.

The interviews are very loosely structured on the five factors identified in the analysis of the students' survey. They are **Best Educational Practice, Interest in Course, The Limiting Effect of Examinations, Encapsulation** and **Career.**

The overwhelming majority of the students interviewed displayed little evidence of being skilled choosers (Gewirtz et al., 1995). Eighteen chose the college because of its proximity to home. Of these, three had previously had experiences of a large city university but could not cope with being away from family and friends. Others said that, while they enjoyed student life, it would be a different story if they were not living at home.

The predominant reason for choosing third-level education was the belief that one cannot get a job without a third-level qualification. 'Well, you'd get a job, like in Tesco's or something but that wasn't for me, I definitely wanted a qualification'. ... 'without it you have nothing' ... 'that's where the money is' ... 'you'd get a factory job, but ... '. Only three respondents claim that a qualification is not their primary motivator. One of these, an entrepreneur-in-waiting, is in third level to learn as much as possible because he plans to take over the running of the family business in a few years time; he is motivated purely by interest in the subject matter and is learning for himself, not for a degree and not for anyone else. The qualification is irrelevant, he says. He does not intend ever working for anyone else. The other two believe that it is not possible to get a qualification without learning; this is why their predominant objective is to learn. Additional drives for third-level education were family trends, family pressure, and because friends were going.

Twelve chose their course by default. One said it was the only thing in which she has even a vague interest, it is better than working, she does not really care what she studies but college is something to get up for in the morning, it is better than nothing. Another, who initially attended a large city university, simply selected random courses on her third-level application form – 'whatever one the points stuck to was the one you ended up going for'. After 6 months, this student realized that while she really enjoyed her course, particularly the reading, she did not want to work at it for the rest of her life so she left and took a job for 6 months on a night shift from 9 p.m. to 3 a.m. The next time she applied for a college place she eschewed universities because the large classes of 400 to 500 students did not suit her and also because she could not afford to pay university fees. She chose her current (smaller sized) college as she remembers it – 'Ah sure, I'll go to (*names college*), I had done Business Studies in school, I'll try that' – a manifestation of the suggestion by one of the lecturers interviewed that students are not given sufficient assistance to make wise choices. Others offered explanations such as they didn't know why they chose their course; they always loved computers; they did not know what else to do; they did not get the necessary points to do any other course; they would hate to go to a university in a big city; work would be more difficult; they were not ready for the big hard world immediately after leaving second level; they would be working long enough. Five of the respondents want to do teaching (an interesting outcome in view of Singal's admonition on the importance of recruiting brighter candidates into teaching and Colton's warning on the dangers of error) but since there was no course in their college which offered a mix of their favourite subjects they chose a general Business Studies course. One of these five, who initially attended a large university but left it because she hated the city and could not cope with being away from home, chose her current course because it offered a language option, which, in fact, did not run. Her plan now is to finish two years, then

> I think about going to (*names university*) and picking up an arts degree because that's definitely the course I want to do and then that would be for another two years so I will be two years older and wiser and hopefully then, I'll be ready to leave home.

Eight students deliberately chose their course. One, a first year student, considered his options very carefully. One of his brothers had completed an apprenticeship and another had done Computing Studies at the same college. The latter had just bought a house and is employed in the computing industry. Taking a long view, the respondent feels he would prefer to get a qualification now than to take on a trade or get a job and then have to come back after fifteen years when he would be long out of study. Of the eight who made a clear choice, six did so because they enjoyed those subjects best at secondary school and they thought that it offered the best opportunities for career, although one, who would finish fourth year within five weeks, was still not clear what he wanted to do. The remaining two were entrepreneurial in outlook and saw themselves as self-employed in the future.

Wrong-footing Illich, who claims that there is a belief that learning depends on attendance, that the value of learning increases with increased input and that the resultant value can be measured and documented on certificates, five respondents say that they attend fewer than 50 per cent of their classes with two attending as few as 20 per cent. All agree that attendance is amazingly low: 'Monday mornings are non-existent and then Friday mornings just don't happen. After the balls and after any stuff that does be on like, I don't know, I think it could definitely be better'.

Sixteen say that they skip class in order to study for a continuous assessment. This is very common, they say. There are often as few as 4 or 6 students, out of a class of 60, present in lectures on a day when there is an assessment in some other subject. Only one respondent claims to attend all classes and others feel it is unfair, frustrating and annoying that so many students pass without attending.

Nine assert that they enjoy learning and are happy with the content of their course, although closer inspection reveals that enjoyment is often confined to one or two subjects. The learning rarely extends beyond the notes they get from their lecturers. Of the nine who enjoy learning, six do some study on a regular basis. For many of these 'regular study' simply means organizing notes or reading over their notes on the bus in the morning. One claims that he does some work every night, even if it is simply organizing his notes. He practises questions again and again on an ongoing basis with the question at the top of the page and the solution beside him. Because of his study method he is able to keep on top of things, he says, and he begins serious study for the examination about a week or a week and a half in advance.

Just three students out of twenty devote considerable time to study. One studies for up to twenty hours a week on a regular basis and for forty hours a week during the weeks before and during examinations. Despite this effort he finds examinations somewhat of a problem and he has some particular difficulty with one subject; he says that he knows the material but 'not the headings' – a reflection of the encouragement by the system to learn predetermined answers to pre-determined questions. A second is so interested in the subject matter that he spends several hours in the library every day, reading and researching topics while the third studies for up to twenty hours per week because, he says, he cannot afford to fail.

Thirteen students undertake no study at all on a regular basis. Sixteen cram for examinations for between one and three weeks beforehand. One of these crams for each examination in turn the night before; this has always worked for him and he sees no problem with it because he has no interest in the course. One believes that too much study can be counterproductive. He cites examples of some friends who did not do very well last semester. 'They probably did too much study type of thing and confused themselves'.

Fourteen admit that they forget what they have learned because of their method of study. 'You cram, write and forget', says a fourth year. 'That just does you for the exam', says another. Despite this, they say that passing the examination is important because it brings them to the next stage. Only one worries that she will not know enough when she goes out to work. Others claim that the employer will train them on the job and that much of what they study at college may be irrelevant anyway – 'its get my degree, do high, looks good on my CV'. They seem unaware of Chaharbaghi and Newman's (1998) suggestion that if learners have no specific context for application they are neither sensitive nor hungry and are not ready to learn. All but two are confident of passing their examinations although some recognise that they are not remotely prepared at this point, 4 weeks beforehand. There is plenty to be done, they say, but it will get done. There is no suggestion of the 'whole-person involvement' mentioned by Abbott (2002) but, simply, the black box approach he eschews as having little value in educational terms. They seem to have learned how to jump through the required hoops (Brown & Scase, 1994).

Only four students, one first year, two third year and a fourth year, possess all their essential texts. Twelve have between one and four texts while four respondents have no texts whatsoever. One of these, a fourth year, who is going to be a teacher, says:

> I've gotten through without using the book, but I find I have enough notes to learn, if not too much, whenever I just get the class notes and just write around them myself. If I went to go and get the book, it just wouldn't all get learned.

She asserts that she works hard and needs an honours degree; so far she has had a 2:1 all the way through. This year all the notes are on the open directory, so she can download them in her free time but she says she will probably not look at them until examination time. She uses the internet rarely, and only for an assignment. Another fourth year student says he never opened a textbook until this year and even now he consults them only for assessments and examinations. One first year student has four texts but he does not bring them to college because 'the bag would be too heavy'. Instead he tries to consult them when he goes home at weekends if he is not too tired as he works part-time for twenty two hours. For many of these students two essential texts are workbooks which are used in class all the time.

There appears to be a belief that texts are not useful unless they are workbooks, used and referenced in class on an ongoing basis. Some say that texts are a waste of money, pointless, not practical: they get notes in class anyway – the 'lecturer takes all the snippets out of the book and all the important bits . . .' One asserts that different people tell him that textbooks are not really necessary for some subjects. Another says that she does not want to be left with a pile of books which she has not used and will not use; if she finds that she needs a book in the future she will photocopy the relevant pages, she says. She would prefer to search the internet than to search a book but she does not actually do this in practice.

Only seven consult their texts with any degree of regularity; two of these are first year, three are third year and two are fourth year. This consultation is masked, however, because some of the texts are workbooks, used in class, and in other cases the student consults just one text regularly. Only two students read their texts out of interest. One, a fourth year, unusual in that she is an avid reader, says that she becomes very bored reading only notes which are exam-focused; she says she hates texts (usually in quantitative subjects) which are exam-focused – 'point, point, point . . . they actually just hurt your head to read after a while'. She reads in the library every day and perceives that books on the same subject say the same thing, a view which is not shared by other respondents who find different words and different phrases 'confusing and annoying'. Most students consult texts only at exam time, if at all. One, who intends being a second-level teacher, says he enjoys working with another student because, between them, they can cut the workload in half. 'There's no point in learning all the chapters', he says. He finds it discouraging if he is expected to study material which is not going to be on the examination. He finds it equally discouraging that some students get notes at the last minute and do just as well. He would hate a system of independent learning and feels that he would lose heart because he would not know what to study.

Only two of the students interviewed are independent learners and would prefer a system where they had to research information themselves rather than learn or take down notes prepared by the lecturer. One is the entrepreneur in waiting. He reads texts, purely out of interest, on an ongoing basis and spends time in the library twice a day, coming in early even if he has few classes. If he misses class he will research the topic himself and will never photocopy another student's notes. Unlike this respondent the other independent learner, a first year, enjoys some degree of encapsulation and does not read as widely; however, she prefers books to notes and, unaware of the irony, says that she would like it if lecturers would bind their notes in a bound book format. Her independent approach may be related to her unusual history – she had a back operation when she started fifth year and did not sit her Irish Leaving Certificate, undertaking, instead, two separate Post Leaving Certificate courses. She dislikes taking down notes from an overhead which she sees as a waste of time that could be better spent on lecture and discussion. 'I think one hour of listening would be better than three hours of taking down notes . . . and kind of listening'. Although she says that she would like a book for every subject, in fact, she possesses just two essential texts, one of which is a workbook. The other eighteen students are resistant to independent learning. It definitely would not work – except, perhaps, for a highly motivated student, says one, or for 'active students who have absolutely nothing else to do'. 'I'd find it hard to just . . . bother, you know', says another.

Even those who are interested in their course and enjoy learning have little confidence that they would know what to read and learn, revealing their propensity to learn what is useful for the examination rather than to read out of interest. Notes give them reassurance. If they had to read independently they would lose heart, would not trust themselves to get the right information and they would find it confusing. The general view was that students would not do the reading if lecturers did not give comprehensive notes and would therefore not attend lectures if they had not done the reading. They figure that the information the lecturer gives is the information the lecturer wants them to know. They would be too lazy to 'read a big book' and have to cut it down and still be wide of the mark. The mind-set coming out of second-level school is that they like to be 'force-fed', they say. One says he finds texts very long and appears not to find it easy to synthesise information. He is dismissive of what he calls 'complicated language . . . these people who have a million degrees in the subject . . .' He is planning to be a secondary teacher and has no other career in mind. He thinks it is crucial for teachers to be able to reduce everything to very simple language and sees it as a problem if they are 'too qualified', a situation in which he would not like to find himself. He is irritated by lecturers who use 'big, complicated language and you haven't a clue ...' and prefers simple words and phrases. For many students, regular study involves consulting a text which is a workbook used in class while some study just one subject with any regularity. Even the few who acknowledge that learning a set of notes is not educational would prefer that this system remain in place. They like the ease and the convenience. This is the case even for the most diligent of the students, a third year. She wants the package, she needs guidance, she says, and, in turn, is willing to play her part and study hard.

This lack of independence in learning is exemplified in the common theme running through all the narratives – the pointlessness of learning anything that will not come up in the examination. 'No, there's no reason, why would I bother?' asks one, seemingly genuinely astonished. 'No one will learn what they don't have to write down in an examination', says another, 'they are only here for the qualification'.

Commonly, if students miss class, they will get the notes from a fellow student. One has never been in this position because she attends every lecture and three respondents assert that they would not trust notes from other student colleagues. Of these, two say that they would approach the lecturers for help and the other chooses to research the topic independently: 'I'd find out what was done and research it myself. But I don't go photocopying', he says. The remaining sixteen have trust in their friends' notes. One, whose attendance is as low as 20 per cent, as is his friends', has complete faith in notes from others. '... it's grand, between us all we'd enough to go. And people in the class would give you notes anyway if you're lucky'. Another, also with a 20 per cent attendance record, covers for his absence 'very smartly' by getting notes and learning them even if he does not understand them. Some photocopy notes and others transcribe them because they cannot study anything that is not in their own handwriting. This transcription falls into the category of 'study'. Eleven confess to *learning* even if they do not understand the material if they have not been to class – 'but you'd prefer to understand . . . most of the time I'd prefer to understand the stuff', says a fourth year.

All respondents rely on notes as the source of course content and believe that the preparation of packaged notes by lecturers means that they care about their students. In general, students find their lecturers caring and approachable. Students like the ease, the security and the reassurance that notes give them. 'It's aggravating if lecturers won't do it. I am used to good packaged notes and they are all very useful for me'.

'I think it's brilliant', said another respondent who had attended a different college where she failed and took five years out. She acknowledges that learning notes for an examination is not developmental or educational; it is simply a memory test, but, despite this, she 'likes it easy'. With notes, says another, you don't have to be completely motivated and you can still get the notes and learn them. She is not keen on the open directory, believing that there is 'too much stuff up there and you wouldn't need half of it'. Another would like all notes on the open directory while another thinks they should be on the internet because then he could download them without having to come in to the college.

The belief is widespread that students can pass without attending class by simply getting the notes and learning them. According to one fourth year, who admits that he never opened a text until his honours degree year, says that, not alone is there a belief among students that they can get through on the notes, but they can get through on last year's notes or those of the year before. He estimates that only about a quarter of his honours degree class of one hundred and forty students consult texts – an inference he makes from the number of students whom he sees studying in the library; the others manage on notes, often photocopied notes. Another fourth year says: 'I think the notes are good, I think if you just, not delve too much into it, I think it works well'.

One student, exceptionally able academically, claims that she could easily get over 80 per cent in examinations by attending lectures once or twice a week and studying the notes. After a while she got to the stage of wondering what was the point in going to class? If you check your notes from the lecturer, she says, you'll have everything you need to pass the exam. Packaging notes makes students lazy, she believes, but she thinks that students would read independently only if they were marked on it as part of an assessment process. She recognises that it would not be a popular option but students would be better educated, better skilled and more employable.

Eleven respondents read all handouts, others give them a quick glance and others read them only if they are relevant for an examination, never out of interest. Some find it difficult to assimilate information from them but they like to have them for comfort at examination time.

Seventeen feel that the standard of education is high. One believes that it is not high, just medium. Another finds it very worrying that so many pass without attending class and she feels that lecturers work hard at *scraping* students through. The third, the exceptionally able student, has real concerns about applying for jobs with her qualification. Attending a relatively small college, she is aware of the amount of reading that has to be done at more prestigious academic institutions, having attended one herself for six months and from speaking with friends who have to study six or seven books just to 'get by'. These institutions do not give above 60 per cent without a good reason, she says, and she sees how hard her friends in these institutions work to get such a mark. 'They never leave their books. You just think, if the exams were that hard here, I don't think anyone would pass them'. This student is extremely able and is an avid reader. The only reason she came here was a bad reason, she says. Having given up her first university course she could not afford to pay fees. Asked if her student colleagues had the same view about the standard she said, yes, that is the case, but they say, 'ah, we can get a 2.1 here handy'.

Five read a prestigious daily newspaper regularly. Eleven read tabloids, enjoying sport and celebrity gossip while six read no newspaper at all on a daily basis. Two read their local paper at weekends for entertainment notices, sport and death notices. Seven read magazines – the favourite topic being celebrity gossip – and just one reads Newsweek business magazine; he eschews all general magazines and is dismissive of tabloids. Eleven respondents occasionally read books. One respondent who says he is a reader asserts that he gets sore eyes if he reads too much. Interests vary over a wide range – sport, light novels, science fiction, magic, history, crime, biography and classics. The student who reads classics is exceptionally able and is the only one who reads on an ongoing basis.

There is a distinct paucity of **metaphor** in these summaries although there are the hidden metaphors, for the reader, of qualification as education and memory as learning. Expressed metaphors include 'picking up' an arts degree; 'forcing it all into your brain'; 'just want to get through'.

Much of the narrative, therefore, is akin to a report. However, as Hayakawa et al. (1990) observe, while a metaphor expresses deeply held feelings, facts at lower levels of abstraction can also be affective without special literary devices. Statements of fact in the interviews which are very affective include:

you cram, write and forget.
I don't bring them (texts) up here because the bag would be too heavy
I just want to pass, to be honest
it's the only thing I have even a vague interest in.
I never, ever read books.
The Irish Times? – no, never . . . never ever.

There is a total lack of **irony** in the telling of the narratives, although not in the hearing or reading. Students seem utterly unaware of the irony (for traditional educators) of being confident of achieving a 2:1 despite working evenings and weekends, neither possessing nor consulting texts and leaving examination study until a week or two before finals. Shaped by their experience, they are similarly unaware that, for them, a short memory test passes for learning and that a qualification is the same as education. Students who claim to enjoy learning, on closer inspection, are shown to enjoy just one or two subjects. Some who consult texts regularly consult just one or two and, in many cases, these are texts used in class every day. One student who prefers books to notes, nevertheless, possesses just two out of six essential texts and wishes that lecturers would bind their notes in book format. Although many admit that they forget what they have learned, the irony of spending time cramming and forgetting is lost on them. They justify it to themselves on the grounds that it is part of the journey towards a qualification and that an employer will provide training in what is needed at work.

The dominant trope in these narratives is a **feel-good factor**. Students are, for the most part, confident of success. In stark contrast to the lecturers they seem utterly relaxed and appear to have the situation sorted. Winnicott (1947) might have suggested, however, that since they appear to experience no awareness of oppression, their oppression, as they conform to the educational system, must be absolute. Unlike the lecturers, students are familiar with a different central organizing principle – **Qualification is the Goal** – and they experience no dissonance with any possible competing central organizing principle such as the one held by the lecturers – **Education as a Public Good**. The social system with which they identify seems very different from that of the lecturers. They have learned how to achieve success, what hoops they must jump through and how. In contrast to the lecturers there was not one sigh during the ten hours of recorded interviews. There is, therefore, less sign of a tragic motif in their combined consciousness although there is much **pathos** for the reader in the story of the student who keeps his texts at home because his bag would be too heavy if he brought them to his digs and to college. There is pathos too in his struggle to pass one particular subject despite regular study of twenty hours per week and forty hours during examination time. However, apart from this subject he is confident of success. There is more than a hint of **tragedy** for the student who would love to study history but feels that he would never get a job if he had chosen to study it. Instead, he drifted into Business Studies, rarely attends, survives on notes from friends and leaves it to the last minute to study for examinations.

There is a certain **fatalism**, linked to the choice of college for seventeen students because of its proximity to home and to the choice of course, which for twelve students was by default, often strikingly so, as evidenced by the compelling metaphor 'whatever one the points stuck to was the one you ended up going for'. They are compliant with the system and will do whatever is necessary, often the minimum, to get through.

All narratives are underscored by the **heroism** trope. That is, the students have found a way to negotiate the system and they pursue their chosen path with a high degree of equanimity. In the final analysis there is a happy ending to all of these narratives as all respondents have a high degree of confidence that they will succeed.

In summary, these interviews with students reveal that many chose their course by default and chose their college because of its proximity to home. The majority do not study regularly, they tend to cram for examinations and to rely on notes, which they are willing to 'learn' even if they do not understand them and which they feel are sufficient to pass examinations. Their experience of the educational system seems to contribute to synecdochism[1] – almost all of them work part-time, they like the 'capsule' approach and expect success in their examinations. With one or two exceptions, they seem to be adept at negotiating the system.

[1] Contagious magic, something done on a part will affect the whole.

Part 3

Chapter 12

Reflections

'Proud Ireland hurt you into poetry', Auden remarked to Yeats, in respect of the motivation of the latter to write. In the case of this present work the impetus came from the realization on the part of the author that there existed a lacuna between the education she wished to facilitate and that which students wished to receive; she experienced a sense of diminished authenticity in her work.

The initial question was: 'Are students treating higher education as a consumer experience and seeking capsules of knowledge rather than embracing their course?' An intuitive answer to such a question is, in Hayakawa's words, simply intensional. As such, any debate about it is a 'non-sense' argument. It cannot be satisfied by endless discussion. By carrying out research, however, it becomes a 'sense' argument as an appeal can be made to extensional (real-world) data in order to reach a conclusion on the issue.

This book claims validity on all four of Habermas' (1987) criteria. First, it is **meaningful**, addressing as it does a serious issue in education. Secondly, it is **true** as the primary research has been collected and analysed in line with scientific practices and has been couched in theory. Third, as a practising educator, the author has a **right to address** the issue. Fourth, the author is **sincere** as investigation was carried out to achieve understanding and not for any other purpose.

There appears to be overwhelming support for the hypothesis. From the survey results it seems clear that students appear to view education as a consumer experience, receiving 'capsules' of information rather than achieving an integrated understanding.

Having established that there is a significant basis for the hypothesis, there are two very striking outcomes. First, the seminal finding in this work is that, while the student cohort seeks and receives 'capsule'

education, most of the forces which cause encapsulation – and, therefore, the students' approach – come from outside the remit of the
survey (see Chapter 9). The corollary of this finding is that the solution is not to be found within the classroom. Exploring these external
causative issues is a basis for further study. Secondly, the finding that
teaching appears to be a popular career choice among students (see
Chapter 11) presents serious cause for concern, bearing in mind
Singal's (1991) caution that only very able students should be
recruited into teaching and Colton's (1829) warning that error is
more dangerous than ignorance. If the five students in these interviews are in any way representative of the student–teacher population,
education for future students seems likely to be seriously diluted.

Featherstone (1996), borrowing from Feifer (1985) and Urry
(1988), refers to as 'post-tourists' those people who adopt a postmodern approach towards tourism experiences. Such tourists have
no interest in authenticity but enjoy the simulated nature of contemporary tourism which, he says, they know is only a game. The abandonment of a commitment to education and cultural imperatives in
favour of a more populist ethos is evident even in museums. Given
the parallel in education where students have a brief skirmish, rather
than an engagement, with their studies, it may be apposite to wonder
if they might be called 'post-students'. Education, it would appear, is
at the fourth stage of Baudrillard's simulacrum. This is borne out in
the analysis of both the student survey and the lecturer survey and in
the interviews with both groups. The salient findings are summarised
as follows. The greater proportion of students do not have all their
essential texts. The greater proportion of students consult essential
texts *rarely* or *almost never.* In spite of this, most students expect to
pass their examinations. They like to have notes *packaged* for them
by lecturers. They favour a minimalist approach and do not have
an understanding of the 'big picture'. They rank knowledge third
in importance, after a job and qualification, as an outcome of their
course. They do not engage with the education process. Lecturers see
the term 'capsule education' as an appropriate one to describe the
students' approach. Lecturers respond to students' demands by packaging notes closely geared to examination requirements, by shrinking
the course because of non-attendance and by ignoring serious literacy

issues when marking examinations. Lecturers are de-energised and stressed.

The demand for education would appear to be not just a *derived* demand, but a *derived* 'derived demand'. That is, students want education because they want a qualification, because a qualification is seen as necessary for getting a job. The student is therefore at a third remove from education. Economics teaches that demand is underpinned by *felt needs*. The *drive* is the force that makes someone respond to a need. The strength of the drive depends on the width of the gap between the actual state and the desired state. If lecturers, as educators, meet students more than halfway by, for example, packaging notes, ensuring that questions have been covered thoroughly in class before putting them on an examination paper, assessing knowledge of a set of notes rather than a subject, they may, in effect, close that gap which is so essential for student motivation (Bloom, 1987). There is no opportunity for knowing to emerge from the void (Freire, 1974; Habermas, 1987). The drive is an internal force which pushes the individual. This book raises the question as to whether, or to what extent, current approaches to education may have caused this internal force to be neutralised.

The thrust of the research described in this book is to discover if current consumer culture is having an effect in reducing education to a commodity by encapsulating it for easy consumption. The results of the research confirm that this is the case. The commodification and quantification of education distorts the ideal of an education which energises and enthuses the individual. While Einstein's dictum may be accepted – 'not everything that can be counted counts and not everything that counts can be counted' – nevertheless, the market approach to education described in the literature is heavily dependent on quantification. No cognisance is taken of other forms of intelligence such as those described by Gardner (1983, 1997) – spatial, kinaesthetic, musical, interpersonal, intrapersonal, environmental, existential. Quantification is reductionist and confers qualification on memory, not on learning.

The traditional paradigm of the market is a binary one where there is a producer and a customer who engage in a mutually satisfying exchange relationship. No model of publicly funded education can

provide any degree of fit with that model. A publicly funded education system displays competing hexagonal responsibilities and moti-
vations, its stakeholders being students, staff, employers, the public
(including parents), the government, and universities and colleges.
Some of these stakeholders occupy two roles – as a producer and consumer. The metaphors 'student-as-customer', 'student-as-consumer'
are, in the opinion of the author, quite distinct. A customer is one
who pays to engage in some form of exchange to the mutual satisfaction of both parties. In this way, s/he is entitled to sovereignty.
A consumer, who is not also a customer, does not pay a price. How
much sovereignty is s/he entitled to? This is not to suggest that s/he
is not entitled to the highest quality. The query is simply raised as
to where the sovereignty belongs. Given that it is often governments
and parents who influence students to undertake higher education
(Chaharbaghi & Newman, 1998; Illich, 1972; Coren, 2005) there is
a case for arguing that sovereignty does not accrue to the student.
On the other hand, the student at a grind school is certainly a customer, at least through his/her parents or guardians. Grind schools
provide quantifiable inputs in order to achieve quantifiable outputs
in the form of optimum examination points. The popularity of these
schools is attested to by their success in a thriving *market*. The success
of that market suggests that mutually satisfactory exchange relationships are taking place.

While the above might seem an endorsement of a customer-driven
approach, it is important to note that this kind of education represents
market efficiency, not *effectiveness* and certainly not *equity* – although
many would claim that the only positive characteristic of publicly
funded education is that it is equally *unfair* to all; its one-size-fits-all
approach has the effect of thrusting mediocrity onto the talented
(Brubacher & Rudy, 1976). A market in education takes into account
private utility only and takes no cognisance of *externalities*. The pursuit
of private utility in education means that an individual undertakes
the amount and type of education which will satisfy his/her own
private objectives. These objectives are often called *production benefits* because the benefits from education result in the production
of higher salary returns over a lifetime. Externalities, that is, benefits to society in general, will not be taken into account in a private

consumption decision. These social benefits are more diffuse and less precise than private benefits. Nevertheless, this does not diminish the importance attached to them. Le Grand and Robinson (1992) point to the socialisation function of education. That is, education seeks to provide students with a set of values that will enable them to function effectively in the wider society outside the college, with consequent benefits for those with whom they interact. These values may encompass consideration of major moral and ethical issues, the belief in the superiority of reasoned debate over emotional prejudice and the achievement of what Robbins calls a 'common standard of citizenship'. This book refutes the notion, therefore, that the customer driven approach to education is an effective one since individual customer choice may make no contribution to the commonweal, as a student will simply choose subjects/courses which yield the maximum production (private) benefits (Zemsky, 1993) and will not take externalities into account.

In the context of externalities the author notes the whittling away, in recent years, of some behavioural science subjects for students of Business courses and, in one college surveyed in the primary investigation, the total abandonment of the wider Business course in favour of the more vocational Accounting course. The behavioural science subjects are subsumed by vocational subjects. If, however, as is apparent from the surveys, students do not have an understanding of the 'big picture' they may not actually benefit sufficiently from the vocational subjects whereas the discussion generated among students by the behavioural science subjects may go some distance towards their enlightenment and, therefore, towards the creation of social benefits for society in general.

The marketing approach to education is fraught with difficulties: the terms 'consumer' and 'producer' are polar opposites. Education, according to the writers reviewed in this book, is a process which requires that students become co-creators in their own education. This polarisation of student and lecturer occasioned by the 'student-as-customer' metaphor, places the student on the outside as a receiver of a service provided by academic staff. In line with current shopping practices of long opening hours and non-stop service, such consumer creep has made its way into academia. Many students who do not attend lectures nevertheless have expectations that lecturers will be constantly available to them, that they will make special arrangements for them if they skip assessments and will tell them exactly what to study for an impending examination. Such 'shopping' practices are documented in the lecturers' interviews in this research and are a source of stress to lecturers as, in an effort to seek an equilibrium with both students and administrators, they race to keep ahead of the academic realities of diminishing standards. Success is not rooted in the competence of the student (Robotham, 2003) but in the willingness of the lecturer to serve the demands of the student by delivering a qualification. This 'shopping' behaviour places the student/lecturer relationship on a continuum which progressively becomes more adversarial (Cheney et al., 1997). Locked between the twin constraints of student retention, underpinned by the market refrain that the 'customer is always right', and the increasing assessment of lecturers by students – none of whom have been educated on how to critique a situation – the lecturer capitulates, thus missing a real educational opportunity to develop a degree of personal responsibility in the student. Interviews with lecturers reveal an awareness that in meeting student demands they are failing to deliver real education – the kind of moral relativism identified by Bloland (1995). Education continues its repression, failing in its fundamental mission to facilitate maturity in students and making oppressors of lecturers (Freire, 1972; Carroll, 1998).

Another claim implicit in the customer driven approach is that the paying customer (student) is entitled to waste his/her investment by not studying. Again, this suggestion can be refuted. Resources are limited. Therefore, any waste of resources represents an opportunity cost for society in general, although this depends on whether one espouses Durkheim's or Baudrillard's concept of waste.

To view the (non-paying) student as consumer is to look at the student through a very narrow angle lens. There is no question of education being free – someone has to pay. In a publicly funded system it is the taxpayer who foots the bill. In as far as there is a customer in this sector it may be argued strongly that the taxpayer is the customer. Is this customer satisfied with the exchange relationship, with the outcomes resulting from this massive spend? We may postulate that if the taxpayer were consulted s/he would choose a system of education which would maximise *both* production (private) benefits and social benefits. It is unlikely that s/he would be happy with the minimalist approach which this survey reveals, if this minimalist approach reflects what is happening throughout the education system generally. If, however, the taxpayer sees education as a fiscal liability and not an investment, if s/he sees accreditation as more important than education it is, of course, supremely rational to aim at productivity through large class sizes and a content-driven syllabus.

This brings us to the chasm which appears to exist between the anti-reductionist intent of lecturers and the consumer approach of students. Karl Marx first drew attention to the worker alienation which results from capitalism and the consequent rupture between labour and needs. That is, the creativity of the worker is bought by the capitalist. The worker is no longer expressing his 'species being' through his creativity in producing a product. The product is now defined by the capitalist and the worker trades his creativity for wages. The result is, in the words of Lee (1993), 'an impoverished realization of essential species being' (p. 6), the outcome of which is a fossilised product unrecognisable from the energies which were invested in it. Marx's own words express this alienation. 'In tearing away the object of his production from man, estranged labour therefore tears away from him his species life' (in Lee, p. 7). A parallel situation seems to exist in current education provision. The lecturer seeks an educational zymurgy[1]. S/he seeks to ignite in the student a quest for knowledge, where the question is the answer (Chaharbaghi & Newman, 1998), to encourage the student to fashion the richest tapestry possible, shaped and patterned by the many coloured threads of knowledge and experience. The lecturer sees knowledge as resisting compartmentalisation. Yet, according to this book, compartmentalisation, minimalism and quantification are what the lecturer is forced to be complicit in – truly a petrified product.

The adherence of administrators to the market model not only undermines student motivation but also makes the job of lecturing unattractive. Writing on quality in education, Stone (1995), Gibbs and Iacovidou (2004), Knight (2002) and Fielding (1998) attest to

---

[1] Leavening.

the necessity of developing the student. Rather than develop the students' sense of responsibility for outcomes, the concept that *the student/customer is always right* diminishes it. This concept brings to mind the conflict between being a 'good' parent and being a responsible parent and the parallel conflict between being a 'good' (perhaps fearful?) lecturer and being a responsible lecturer. In terms of analysing the power structures in academic institutions, it might appear at first glance that students are the weakest stakeholders. The writings reviewed in this book and the opinions expressed in the lecturers' interviews (Chapter 10) suggest that this may not be the case. Both the literature and the findings in this study support the view that students prefer ease and convenience to difficult and time-consuming effort; they prefer high grades to low grades even if they do not deserve them. Their objectives dovetail neatly with those of management who seek to maximise and maintain growth. According to Stone, in the education market, student dissatisfaction is seen as undesirable irrespective of its cause. Lecturers who elicit student satisfaction are rewarded. Those who elicit dissatisfaction may have to defend themselves. Such ideas are supported by vivid accounts of stress in the interviews in this book as lecturers seek to accommodate the demands of students and management. Any battle between student and academic will most likely see the student emerge as victor, according to the findings in this book. Stressful as this may be for academics, a more thorough examination reveals that students' power is superficial, perhaps the equivalent of childhood pester power. They achieve a Pyrrhic victory; while they may win the battle they, nevertheless, lose the war. It is important to remember Baudrillard's (1998) warning that the consumption of social signifiers – including, in this case, paper qualifications – which creates the illusion of democracy and achievement simply shifts inequality to a hidden field where, functioning more subtly, it becomes all the more irreversible. Such consumption of signs, warns Baudrillard (1988), constitutes the purest and most illegible form of domination. Academics are fighting, not the student, but *for* the student. They seek to provide developmental education rather than the oppression which is a concomitant of capsule education. In this, the academic and the student are both losers.

What of the student's perspective on education? There seems no doubt that students are undertaking a consumer experience and they see education as a commodity. It may be speculated that their attitudes, formed by their experience in education, represent simply the inexorable outcome of the points dominated system which, many would assert, has distorted the real meaning of education at second level. Such a view is evident in interviews with lecturers.

It would appear that the general approach of students is affected by the cultural effects of postmodernism. Postmodernism is described as a worldview which is characterised by a fascination with the ephemeral and the fleeting, by the superiority of image over reality and by the consumption of social signifiers. It seems just a short step to suggest that the appeal of a qualification, *image*, may be more important than the reality, *knowledge*. This is certainly borne out in this book. In the stark words of one student, 'Yea, but a lot of people wouldn't take on board "Oh gosh, I'll need to know this for working". No, it's get my degree, do high, looks good on my CV'. Baudrillard (1998) emphasises the pursuit of signs which emphasise difference. 'All men are equal before objects as use-value, but are by no means equal before objects as signs and differences which are profoundly hierarchical' (p. 91). It would appear that the pursuit of more and more qualifications is caused by a desire for difference. As more and more people pursue qualifications the logical outcome is credential inflation.

In considering the nature of the students' approach to education the author wondered if, basing her query on Bernstein's (1961) work, social class might be an indicator of students' willingness to learn. There appeared to be no clear connection. This is no surprise as, in the age of postmodernism, the defining of social class resists the old taxonomies. As people consume more and more goods and services, including qualifications, the differences between classes, previously expressed in economic hegemony, become blurred. A system of social plutocracy now depends on *cultural capital* where, previously, ownership and possession of material goods were the markers of social prestige. The receipt of cultural capital, according to Lee, is entirely conditional upon a long-term investment of time spent, chiefly, in education. Cultural capital loosely translates as class taste which informs class-specific cultural judgements. He asserts that the working classes lack the cultural and educational capital to classify symbolic goods by any means other than the pragmatic and purely functional. Performativity is what counts. Concepts and metaphor have little meaning for the working classes – a fact that is revealed about the student population in both survey findings and in interviews with both lecturers and students. Lee suggests, for example, that the kind of photograph which appeals to the working class is *content* centred and depicts a clearly recognisable image, a 'pragmatic document of social ceremonies, family occasions, national or traditional events' (p. 37). The middle classes on the other hand are not *content* focused, but have an appreciation of the composition of the photograph and the 'extra-textual knowledge which underpin and inform the aesthetic judgement of the photograph' (p. 37). Lee claims that what produces these different consumption patterns among the middle class is the time spent in, and qualifications gained from, education. He goes on to engage a topic which is germane to this study. That is, he seeks to define education by asserting that it is important to note that education, in this context, is not simply

> a vehicle for the transference of discrete and epistemic facts (of simply knowing about something). On the contrary, educational capital is valued for its capacity to code and contextualise social experience in a way that grants a sense of distinction to those who possess it. In short, educational capital produces a privileged linguistic form.
>
> (p. 37)

Halsey (1995) reminds us that in former times, when society was almost fractured by the polarisation of the ownership of wealth, a safety net was provided in the shape of widening education provision. He suggests that society may now be facing another threat through the polarisation of the distribution of cultural capital.

Given the propensity of current educational systems to provide the student with a set of discrete facts, it might be suggested that such systems have created an educational proletariat instead of a culturally competent citizen. It seems clear from both the surveys and the interviews that, in broad terms, the uptake of education is simply for the achievement of pragmatic aims, i.e. to get a qualification in order to get a job. Class difference is suggested by the evidence in students' interviews that they do not appear to be skilled choosers. In terms of a market in education, classes differ on two counts – in their inclination to engage with it and their ability to exploit it (Gewirtz et al., 1995). Overwhelmingly their choice of educational institution is influenced by proximity to home and by the company of friends. The promise of higher education to deliver equality of opportunity to all is a fuzzy concept as it delivers only a simulacrum which continues to stratify and confine, adding educational to class rigidity (Halsey et al., 1980). The hierarchy and stratification of institutions appear to have a significant impact on graduate opportunities and employment destinations (Ainley & Corbett, 1994; Ainley 2000; *Graduate Survey 2004*). In the 1970s concern centred on why so many working-class children went into working-class jobs; Pugsley (1998) suggests that it may be apposite to enquire now why so many of them get working-class degrees.

Chapter 13

An Alternative View

The students need to be defended. It seems clear that they are disabled by the education they are offered (Freire, 1972; Barglow, 2001) and are then blamed for being *unable*. They did not create the system of education they have encountered but it is the only one they know and it has shaped their response – 'those who are invaded, whatever their level, rarely go beyond the models which the invaders prescribe for them' (Freire, 1972, p. 48). Perceiving what they judge to be a lack of ability, the response of academics is often to redouble their efforts at banking. Fearful of a backlash from disgruntled students or from management who are concerned with student retention (Stone, 1995), instead of encouraging independent learning they deliver more and more capsules of information, thus suppressing opportunities for dialogue. Additionally, the widespread introduction of semesterisation and modularisation has the effect of annihilating any possibility of leisurely reflection and absorption on the part of the student (Armstrong, 2004). When, as revealed in the interviews, management encourages lecturers to avoid examining topics already tested in a continuous assessment, the effect is to further reduce learning to memorising even smaller quantities for shorter periods.

Higher education, a modernist institution is, in fact, showing its *disappearing reversed front* (*Foster*) and is behaving as a postmodern construct. The rhetoric of the promise and opportunity of democratic education is shown to be a fiction (Halsey et al., 1980; Pugsley, 1998; Ainley, 2000). While continuing to promulgate the myth of a high status career through education (Bloland, 1995) it provides not education, but a simulacrum of it, a qualification. Lyotard (1984) asserts that economic performativity is the only criterion that counts in a postmodern environment and, therefore, the sole raison d'etre of higher education is to contribute to the economic system. If there are no legitimate grand narratives there is no need for lecturers to teach them. The lecturer will therefore, in Lyotard's view, be reduced to instructing students in the use of terminals, or, as revealed in this book, to the delivery of pre-packaged capsules of information geared to examinations.

Convenience and social signifiers are the distinguishing leit-motifs of contemporary western consumer culture (Featherstone, 1996; Baudrillard, 1982, 1983, 1988, 1998). Current education provides the convenience of capsules of information, called modules, delivered over a short twelve-week time period and certified before time erases the memory of what has been studied. Students are unlikely to shift to a new learning trajectory (Akbar, 2003) since the memorising of discrete facts condemns them to remain on the second stage of Kember and Gow's (1994) five-level hierarchy of learning. This, according to Ainley (2000), is a feature of Further Education rather than Higher Education. The current headlong rush to finish and file away subjects in as fast a time as possible necessarily excludes real dialogue and means that mistakes and misinterpretations by students are not addressed (Akbar, 2003; Marrington & Rowe, 2004), thus perpetrating the *stubborn error effect* (Marx & Marx, 1980). Colton warns that misinformation has more serious consequences than non-information – error is busier than ignorance. An examination snapshot is the only testament to a student's ability. Assessment criteria are morally barren, no credit is given for effort (Gibbs & Iacovidou, 2004) and ingenuity is subtly but actively discouraged by the preparation of expected answers to examination questions. Students who gain marks as high as 80 per cent due to the proficiency of their short-term memory may not be aware of how little they actually know. However, one may be accused of behaving in a curmudgeonly fashion to suggest such a thing. Given education's unrivalled power in the economic order (Illich, 1972) no 'patriot or man of feeling could oppose it' (Smith, 1776).

No more than a passport attests to the worthiness of its holder, a qualification does not guarantee knowledge, skill or ability. So comprehensive is the power of signs, however, that business and industry seem prepared to accept such qualifications as proof of ability. Higher education is prescribed for all – a higher education qualification is the tick in the first box. In true modernist tradition, however, there is a pecking order in qualifications; degrees from old universities – like Baudrillard's antiques metaphor – being the top brand, with new colleges offering succour, overwhelmingly, to the lower socio-economic groups (Holland, 2007).

The consumer society, of which higher education is a crucial cog, is a superstructure of massive proportions. Any study of this superstructure may leave one with the irresistible notion that it is a game with its own arcane rules and understandings. As with all games, those who can play succeed. Those who accept the situation (the Jefferson compromise) and, possessed of a long spoon, adjust accordingly, may be the happier members of society, although both Whyte (2004) and Ball (1999) warn against the possible loss of soul. The alternative is to be a disgruntled philosopher (Freire would recognise him/her, branded a reactionary, a dreamer) forever on the sidelines, passed over for promotion, ignored, or at best, tolerated by the system (Freire, 1972; Illich, 1972; Stone, 1995), seeking to base his/her understanding of the world in modernist ideals such as truth, integrity and meaningfulness. Modernist nostalgia, however, is no match for economic rationalism. To succeed in the educational institution intellectualism is neither a necessary nor a sufficient characteristic. Understanding the rules of the market is the essential criterion.

The reification of education is rooted in consumption, not production; populist ethos places more value on the symbolic than on the real. Social understandings are supplied by marketing and advertising agencies which steal meanings and re-appropriate them (Jhally, 1989; Hayakawa, 1965; Hayakawa et al., 1990). It may be postulated that, given this postmodern scenario, the real learners are the students who recognise the system, have an intuitive understanding of how it works and adjust their input accordingly (Heffer). Accepting the exchange value of their qualification, they do not question its intrinsic worth. They put in the minimum attendance and spend the minimum amount of time necessary to achieve their chosen qualification (Bloom, 1987; Stone, 1995). These are the ones who can tune into systems and how they function (Gee, 1992) – a necessary armament in the world of institutionalised work.

Aside from poor attendance at lectures, the educational field should perhaps not be astonished if students plagiarise the work of others or get assistance with assignments which are marked for their degree. Where assessment of merit is morally deficient (Gibbs & Iacovidou, 2004) and market imperatives provide the underpinnings for education, it is logical for students to evaluate inputs against outputs. With performativity as the driver (Lyotard, 1984; Ainley, 2000; Chaharbaghi & Newman, 1998), students question the value of non-core subjects, the learning of which is not seen to have a direct effect on job activities (*Graduate Survey 2004*). In the market, everything must have a defined financial worth. If a student recognises at some level that s/he is engaging with an adversarial, rather than a caring, system the main concern of which is its own survival and which delivers a simulacrum instead of an education, it may seem supremely rational to gain such qualifications by any possible means. Attempting to achieve balance on the Aristotelian framework of honesty, a modernist concept, may seem as foolhardy as engaging in high wire antics without a safety net.

Concerns about ethics are, at best, a pretence, if no serious effort is made to establish them as an intrinsic element in higher education. Academic institutions may be in danger of being accused of bad faith if they do not address issues of academic integrity. Any call, therefore, to have students behave in an ethical fashion in connection with the submission of work calls for a commensurate response from the academic institutions. Institutions which provide a qualification as a simulacrum for education may not be in a position to query the ethics of their partners in the market. In any market the currency must be acceptable to, and necessary for, the partners. In a postmodern setting it might appear to be no better than foolish for a student to sacrifice the possibility of gaining, unethically, a good result in the matter of submitted work if higher education institutions do not, themselves, practise in an ethical fashion – honesty being an open door to stupidity (Barthes, 2005). The learner student will unman the opposition by (in the archaic sense) *turning the other cheek*.

Should the above statements astonish or horrify the reader, it might be worth considering the scenario if hegemony in the western world had been achieved by sports people and not by financiers and economists. In such a world those who excelled at (unpaid) sport would achieve the greatest status. Social stratification would be arranged according to how high one could jump or how fast one could run – there would be none of the kind of financial reward received by sports stars in what is essentially the *business* of sport in current times. In this imagined world students would be required to undertake higher education in a sports activity. Many who now sparkle in the academic and business fields might find that they had little light to shine either under or over the bushel of a sports class-room. They might well be the inattentive, the reluctant participants, unwilling to undertake more than the bare minimum, attending as rarely as possible and studying, or practising(!), especially in the wind and rain, at the minimum level. They would greet every direction with the common querulous student complaint 'do we need to know this for the exam?' and, altogether, do as little as possible to gain a qualifi-cation in something in which they have peripheral interest or limited expertise and which they would resent having to study/practise. This seems an apposite reaction to the social straitjacket of the compulsory imposition of an education in which one has no interest. Similarly, if everyone was expected to study music, the Gaussian model would be stretched to screeching point with an unimaginable cacophony of sound. The failure of massification is its 'one size fits all' approach.

In considering the dominance today of the doctrine of higher edu-cation for all, it is important to note that treatises which extol the virtues of education are proposed by people whose stock-in-trade is words – the tools of academic salesmanship. Perhaps we should not be altogether surprised if these words sometimes fall on stony ground. Personal interest would appear to be a crucial but much neglected factor in the debate surrounding engagement with education (Chickering & Claxton, 2003). However, research has not yet suc-ceeded in cracking the nut of human motivation. *Nemo dat quod non habet.* An illustration can be drawn from a 1994 claim by Sir Alan Clark, that any bottle of wine costing less than 45 pounds sterling was not worth drinking. Perhaps Sir Alan possessed sufficient cul-tural competence to distinguish between superlatives or perhaps he was bowing in the direction of the consumption zeitgeist and judging excellence by price/label. Whichever the case, there are many people his admonition will leave cold. They will not be motivated to work harder in order to be able to afford a more expensive libation. Is there a parallel in education, with lecturers seeking to enthuse the student in the pursuit of knowledge while the student remains uninterested, even puzzled perhaps, by the aspirations of lecturers?

In the absence of a comprehensive understanding of human motivation it is impossible to understand problems of student retention, attendance or unwillingness to learn. Indeed, in the absence of a clear answer to the great existential question – what is the purpose of human life on this earth? – it is impossible to know if the direction we have chosen, here in the west, serves anything more than material drives. Given, however, that man has become extremely busy while waiting for his promised salvation – or endeavouring to escape the knowledge that there is none (Becker, 1980) – we might ask how well the current education system works. How well it is judged to work depends on one's master trope or signifier.

If the earning of **money** is one's master trope the achievement of a qualification is the necessary passport to current career offerings. More qualifications mean more money.

If **career status** is what matters most a qualification will provide access to a career ladder and social position. A credential collection facilitates the shifting to a higher trajectory.

If **entrepreneurship** is the master trope the individual may be somewhat hampered by society's demand that everyone should have a qualification but s/he will probably possess the enterprise to negotiate the system in order to achieve the prescribed qualification with the minimum input. The bar is often set obligingly low. Alternately, a gift of enterprise provides a by-pass for those who wish to elude the educational straitjacket altogether. The world of business and industry abounds with stories of entrepreneurial successes without the attendant badge of higher education.

If **organization size** is what counts to the educational institution, the current provision of suites of courses in education is tailor-made to attract even reluctant participants and to ensure a high rate of certification. Should competition from rival suppliers be an issue, then it is functional to follow marketing advice – in consumer markets (for non-elitist products) competition leads to reduced prices. The parallel in the education market is to lower standards in order to attract as many students as possible. The pressure of excess supply from institutions, sometimes located for politically strategic reasons rather than educational needs, makes reduced standards the marketing strategy of choice.

If **international comparisons** matter to governments then the lowering of standards and the increasing of student:lecturer ratios achieve the twin aims of showing national participation rates in a positive light while still increasing the apparent rate of return on investment (Chaharbaghi & Newman, 1998; Coren, 2005; Stone, 1995; OECD, 2004).

If **economic performance** is what counts this system of education provision is society's economic rainmaker, providing jobs which create demand for more goods and services thus creating more jobs in what is usually seen as a *virtuous* circle. Will anyone query the value of producing, say, more and more T-shirts when their production is such an important cog in the wheel of job creation? Similarly is it not just as valid to earn one's living from the provision of capsule education as from the manufacture of T-shirts since both exert positive pressure on the accelerator of the economy? The modernist might assert, however, that both the T-shirt and current education are fashion items – not much use, not needed, but *desired* by, and a passport into, postmodern consumer culture. However, given the rhetoric that what a thriving economy needs is entrepreneurial thinking and that megalithic assessment systems do the opposite by putting people in their boxes as early as possible so that they can take their place in the new factory jobs, it would be wise to bear in mind James' warning of a fast approaching time-horizon – there are always larger hives of more compliant worker bees in developing nations.

If **control** of society is what matters, then the form of education offered is certainly a success – *education for oppression*. If it is the case, as Illich claims, that learning is the human activity which requires the least manipulation, why is it that governments are so keen that more and more students undertake higher education? Could it be that such an education system fulfils the custodial requirement identified by Illich, Freire (1972) and Chaharbaghi and Newman? Capsule education diminishes one's capacity to think and gives unprecedented power to governments who, through media manipulation, preach a tabloid doctrine to massive populations whose ability to read and to synthesise information is in doubt. The economic success of education, (as the world's single biggest employment sector), is a prime mover, and it facilitates the consumption of such an array of consumer products and comforts that it seems ungrateful not to quell the uneasy Pascalian voice which continues to search for contentment. Thinkers are dangerous, as Shakespeare's Julius Caesar well knew. Whatever one may think of Michael Moore's ability as a documentary film maker, it is singularly striking to hear the question he raises at the end of Fahrenheit 9/11 – why is it that there are so many poor, black young men with no choices other than to be the cannon fodder of the twenty-first century. In as far as they have been educated, they have been educated for oppression; the educated man adapts well to the demands of society (Freire, 1972; Illich, 1972; Beer, 1989). It is clearly the case that the socialisation function of education delivers different levels of socialisation to different classes of people (Bourdieu & Passeron, 2000).

Against the above postmodern triumphant claims that capsule education *works* the dissenter's voice is a lone cry from the wilderness. Current systems of education may present a problem only to those who are rooted in *phronesis* (Carr, 1987), that is, those who are guided by modernist principles such as truth, trust, honesty, integrity and meaning. Foucault (1979) would ask: why we are so in thrall to these values rather than to their opposites? White (1987) would probably answer that they underpin the central organizing principles for many sectors of society. Powerful speakers such as Habermas (1987), Illich (1972), Freire (1972) and Whyte (2004) have all attempted to raise the issue of the dehumanising effects of fixed information delivered in digestible packages. Educators who wish to light the fire of interest in their students may find that they are in the wrong market, peddling goods of little relevance in a postmodern world.

So, if the student is floating in a postmodern habitus, what can be said of the locus of the lecturer? It may be postulated that the lecturer, at odds with the student approach to education, is probably firmly bonded to *modernism*. This immediately places him/her in opposition to third-level institutes which have embraced a postmodern approach, despite their continuing outward promulgation of a modernist faith. The educational debates and practices of modernism are characterised by what Lyotard (1984) describes as the grand narratives – the belief that human development and social progress can be achieved through the application of reasoned judgement and scientific knowledge. In modernism, mastery of knowledge is progress. Individual development, social and economic development, enlightenment and liberal democracy are mutually interactive and reinforcing. The pursuit of education/knowledge is the lynchpin of human progression. The postmodern, by contrast, is characterised by a questioning of the old certainties. This clearly shows the chasm between the student located in postmodernism and the lecturer rooted in modernism. It becomes necessary to challenge the old certainties and to establish if postmodernism has a positive contribution to make to education. The way is set for conflict if the objectives of lecturers and those of students are diametrically opposed. But, in fact, the situation of the lecturer and that of the student may be closer than it first appears. They may both be unwitting victims of the system.

The traditional view of the academic is of one who is elitist and controlling. According to Featherstone, academics have an interest in reclaiming the investment they have made in accumulating their own cultural capital. Influenced by the politics of nostalgia and reflecting their own modernist, elitist background, this cognitariat exhibits a taste for high culture and distaste for mass culture, shying away from philistinism and *Readers Digest* simplicity. Fearing the populist creep in the long running conflict between populism and elitism they may be guilty of creating institutional barriers, acting as gatekeepers and deciding who can be a member of their elite squad (Chaharbaghi & Newman, 1998). Most significantly, however, they control the production of knowledge, proclaiming what is and what is not legitimate and they make judgements on the validity of its acquisition. Any knowledge or skill gained outside an academic institution is viewed askance. *Sitting next to Nellie* is only sanctioned as a means of knowledge acquisition if it is supplemented by a certificate validated by an institutionalised education structure.

Perhaps academics were so inwardly focused that they did not see their levees being breached. Subtly the established hierarchy was overturned in favour of a newly constituted symbolic structure. The dynamic of changing power balances shifted academia into an industry (Illich; Chaharbaghi & Newman) and education became a consumer good with academics, unwittingly, the foot soldiers of the new production system. Educational institutions, informed by the logic of budgetary pragmatics, conducted academic raids on other long established symbolic hierarchies – infiltrating diverse fields from the professional to trade, from nursing to plumbing and pottery – the postmodern symptom of a global move towards cultural declassification (Featherstone). The academic, whose own background was in most cases a university, middle class one, found him/herself adrift in a postmodern sea. Seeing education as primarily knowledge creation through research and enquiry s/he inevitably faced a difficulty in the tertiary sector which sees education in terms of applications and uses of knowledge (Skilbeck, 2001; Ainley, 2000; Bloland, 1995; Lyotard, 1984). The binary separation of mental knowledge from manual applications, a feature of the Industrial Revolution and an inheritance from the Greco-Roman disdain for slave labour, was reinforced by the success of medieval Christianity's control of orthodoxy in belief and morals alongside its elevation of the world of spiritual contemplation over action. The superiority of mental knowledge over manual applications is thus deeply embedded in western culture (Ainley, 2000). This difference in perception may well be the kernel of lecturers' dissatisfaction causing the identity crisis indicated by Halsey (1995), Bruner (1957), Tajfel (1981), Tapper and Salter (1992) and Bruner (1993).

Current times see a plethora of time-release courses for plumbers, mechanics, bricklayers, electricians. One may be entitled to ask what specific skill *related to the trade* can be better garnered from a college lecturer than from a practising plumber? If there is a positive answer to this, then the trades are in a sorry state indeed. If as Illich claims, context is important, there is no substitute for learning on the job. It is both cheaper and faster. On the other hand, if attendance at college is to provide an experience of liberal education, it is crucial to ensure the dialogue necessary for such education and to eschew the capsule approach. Anything else represents a waste of resources – and all for the achievement of a simulacrum.

Experts and the culture of expertise create an ever-increasing demand for more and more experts. The accepted pedigree of education discriminates against the self-taught individual in much the same way that fashion dictates the wearing of labels and discriminates against those who wear recycled or home-made clothing. This paradigm of education allows the creation of a monopoly – an industrial process which produces a commodity for mass consumption (Illich; Charabaghi & Newman). It is thus a promoter of reification – learning is a *thing*, not an activity. This *thing* can be accumulated and quantified, providing a measure of the economic and social value of the individual within society. Once learning becomes a commodity it becomes scarce, like any other commodity which is marketed (Illich) – an apparently fuzzy proposition in view of the kaleidoscope of courses on offer. Recent decades have seen the unprecedented growth in the bureaucratic accreditation of learning (Chararbaghi & Newman; Coren). The consumer is unaware of the marketing strategy behind the provision of this extensive range – range creates scarcity masquerading as opportunity. This is marketing at its most efficient, the extending of more and more brands and more and more services for a consumer society which believes that more is better. Like fashion, current educational courses have a short shelf life – ask anyone who struggled with MS DOS before Bill Gates created Windows. However, in view of the economic worth of the superstructure that is institutionalised education, it is functional not to query if its value is undermined by the counterproductive action of the addition of more and more capsule courses even though its underpinnings, literacy and numeracy, remain in doubt (Greer, 1998; OECD, 2004; Singal, 1991; Stone, 1995; Casazza, 1996).

Chapter 14

Exploring the Metaphor

The metaphor used in the subtitle of this book – *capsule education* – describes the introjection of a body of information. A capsule is often understood as a tiny packet which, because of its membrane, can be absorbed by a willing subject without the distress or effort of chewing or tasting. On occasion there is no desire to absorb the constituent at all – the effect of the capsule is to protect the individual from any contamination or unintended reaction. Indeed, the too frequent practice of the swallowing of capsules of drugs by carriers attests to this belief. Carrying this particular metaphor even further it might be hoped that, despite the negative implications of the banking education described by Freire (1972) a large overfilled capsule might burst and *contaminate* the student with the desire to learn more. The findings of this study, however, present a picture of ever diminishing capsules of information delivered to students, portions too insignificant to make any real impact. The term 'introjection' carries even more negative connotations, signifying, as it does, the swallowing whole of patterns of belief, without question and without any realization that one's lifeworld is being colonised by totalitarian managers of information (Habermas, 1987, 1989; Illich). For most people the right to learn has fallen victim to the obligation to attend school (Illich). While attendance at higher education is not a legal obligation it carries a psychological pragmatic which may be just as powerful as legal compliance, the 'enchantment' identified by Lyotard and alluded to by Illich. Featherstone (1996), Baudrillard (1998), Fromm (1979) and others have testified to the power of the market. Fromm talks of the tendency for industrial societies to arrange their lives around 'having a mode', that is, the organizing of themselves around the possession of material objects. Such societies, therefore, see learning as a form of possession. Postmodernism's grip on education is the inexorable unfolding of the logic of capitalism. Instead of becoming a way of *being* in the world, knowledge becomes an acquisition to be exploited and traded, using a qualification as a medium of exchange. The benign acceptance of this state testifies to the success of education. Students do not learn how to think, they therefore do not query the power of consumer culture to hold them in its thrall. Society has won. The educated man is the adapted man (Freire, 1972).

Institutions, including educational institutions, undermine people; they reduce self-confidence, disturb peoples' sense of worth and decrease their faith in their own capacity to solve problems; in short, they dehumanise people (Illich, 1972; Freire, 1972). This charge could probably be levelled against the education examined in this study. Not alone does it present the banking system of education but it presents it in a crippled, encapsulated form. This introjection, not alone diminishes a student's opportunity to flourish, but has the effect of colonising the student's mind at a subconscious level. S/he is fed a worldview, the acceptance of which is predicated on *not* teaching the student how to think. Indeed, capsule education with its reduced content, paucity of context and predetermined answers to predetermined questions (Gibbs & Iacovidou, 2004), obviates the need to think, at least in the quest for a qualification. Would Freire (1972) find as much fault with the banking concept with which he was familiar if he could see the shrunken content that is now capsule education – a brief 12-week contact with students, few of whom read their textbooks? No time for delphic processes, for intellection, for the reflection and 'negative capability' (Armstrong, 2004) so necessary for education or the intellectual auscultation described by Chia , Dilthey and Abbott. While context and process matter enormously in learning, it might be suggested that a more sizeable content would induce at least some readers to develop such interest that they could engage in a form of dialogue with the text and provoke greater reading. Despite Freire's (1972) warning that one cannot liberate by creating another deposit, it may be that, by comparison with capsule education, the banking system, assuming considerable content, might have the characteristics of a bonsai or a stem-cell, representing wholeness and perfection in miniature, and providing the possibility of growing into something beautiful or organic. 'Education', said Yeats, 'is not filling a bucket but lighting a fire'. Desperate academics, having realized long ago that their fire-lighting days are gone, would be, nowadays, very pleased indeed to fill a bucket.

Illich's appeal for deschooling in order to allow people to flourish presents us with a launch pad to generate thinking on how to learn our way out of our current confinement. However Illich is probably right – any useful alternative lies within our conceptual blind spot; we may remain on the launch pad for a long time to come. Abandoning what we have induces fear – we have too much to lose, the task is so great and the pay-off unknown (Becker, 1980). The constellations of the superstructure of our world would be snuffed out; life as we know it would be subverted. Any educational undertaking which might encompass transcultural and pluralistic contexts of knowledge would present a sense of continual dislocation and a need to redefine at all levels (Hannabuss, 2001). By contrast, the systematic order of the rationalists' paradigm of knowledge is comforting, the antithesis of the fuzzy, indeterminate thinking in which one has to engage when contemplating change.

The educational system in every country is the single biggest employer (Illich). If learning were to become context dependent the raison-d'etre of the third-level institution would be unpinned. Tens of thousands of staff, lecturers, administrators and support staff, would become unemployed. Campuses would lie idle, construction firms would see the stream of building projects trickle to a stop. The economic multiplier, accelerating backwards, would decimate the demand for all sorts of consumer goods, especially those with added value brands. We would return to a pre-industrial scenario, reduced employment reducing the demand for goods and services thus diminishing demand for labour in those industries too. There would be little demand for crèches and childcare as unemployment would be rife, thus creating for parents the, for some, dubious privilege of an unlimited opportunity to educate their younger children at home.

And what about the students, displaced from their expected higher education regime? Where would they *be* all day, what would they *do*? There would be an immediate high tide of young people flooding the job market, not alone hampered by the competition of numbers and diminished opportunities but also lacking competency in basic educational attainment such as literacy and mathematics (Greer, 1998; Stone, 1995; OECD, 2004). Reading Illich inspired this author to carry out a quick computation on the financial costs of education. She examined very briefly an educational institution with a combined population of approximately four thousand five hundred staff and students, the running costs of which are around twenty million euro per year. If these people were, instead, in receipt of unemployment benefit, at the single rate only, the costs to the exchequer would be at least forty five million euro annually. What a wonderful idea education is. Five hundred staff have well paid, secure employment, four thousand students have somewhere to go every day, they will get a qualification which enables them to seek white-collar employment, parents and older generations envy them their opportunity to learn and the general population is in some awe of the education process. Viewed through a financial frame, education is an amazing enterprise – mass employment, mass production and mass appeal, the perfect justification of idleness without stigma (Halsey, 1995).

Illich cannot be serious about deschooling, can he? The only cause which could produce a scenario to rival the one above would be a sudden war, but even that would provide opportunities for production and service. Mankind is so unused to simply *being* and not either producing or consuming that the prospect presented by the abandonment of education cannot be contemplated without a feeling of serious disorientation. Like God, if the consumer society did not exist, we would have to invent it. Mass consumption seems to have replaced religion as the opium of the people. We would appear not to be yet ready to have our citadel besieged by the enemy of deschooling (Rilke, 2004).

For at least the last two decades policy analysts and observers have been warning that enrolment-driven funding was responsible for incentivising institutional growth at the expense of academic standards and the public interest (Stone). This two-decade education warning has been largely ignored. Pressure to survive and grow particularly affects those institutions in areas of excess supply; enrolment-driven funding makes grade inflation bureaucratically profitable.

There is a strong incentive for diluted criteria and no financially sound basis for following rigorous grading standards. Volume and not utility is what matters (Chaharbaghi & Newman). The drive to increase enrolment necessarily means accepting more poorly prepared students. Whether it is viniculture, agriculture or education, it is axiomatic that increased quantity comes at the expense of reduced quality. Stone notes that some universities in the state of Tennessee attempt to ameliorate this situation by providing non-credit remedial courses for such students. However, such an intervention would play havoc with the OECD's model of education as an investment, the rates of return of which vary from 6.5 per cent in Italy to 17.3 per cent in Britain. The calculation computes the costs of study, including earnings foregone, as the investment, and the higher earnings (post tax) compared with school leavers, as the pay-off. Shorter university courses are one reason why rates of return are so high in Britain, a situation which pertains to Ireland, too, particularly in the wake of the implementation of the Bologna Agreement. Large class sizes and reduced student contact hours also increase the rate of return.

In order to artificially support retention rates a policy is often pursued which allows a student to repeat a failed assessment (O'Grady, 2007). Such a policy is sold to lecturers as assistance for a weaker student. A more academically authentic support might be to ensure that students be better prepared before they enter higher education. Stone's (1995) reminder that institutions are effectively governed by those who exercise budgetary control underlines the reality that the lecturer is constrained in his/her efforts to improve standards. As has been the well-documented case in America, there is a clear incentive for administrators to manage lecturing staff as administrative instrumentalities in areas such as enrolment, student recruitment, programme development and externally funded research. Savings rather than value are the drivers for administrators (Handy) who encourage and support non-teaching activities which bring in extra funding. Yet teaching is what educators have a vocation to do (Stone).

In the business world the promotion and achievement of quality underpins market success. Quality is a seductive concept and only the foolhardy would say that it does not belong in education. The importation of marketing principles into the education field is, therefore, broadly welcomed. However, at this juncture, it becomes necessary, in Lacanian terms, to *unpack the signifier*. Quality is just a word. In Hayakawa's terms it has no extensional meaning. You cannot touch it, taste it or measure its depth. It means different things to different stakeholders. Gibbs and Iacovidou, Stone, Lomas, Shanahan and Gerber, Athiyaman, and Yorke and Longden are just some of the writers who attest to the different, and often opposite, interpretations of the word. The OECD business model, Tayloristic and mechanistic, is the one embraced by governments and administrators in the institutes of higher education. It assesses quality in terms of measurable outcomes – numbers of students qualified, retention rates and size of the market captured. The administrators' understanding of quality, therefore, derives its authority purely from the convenience of its measurability.

It is quite extraordinary that a market model should be accepted as an indicator of what is good in education. Fatuous statements about marketing's desire to please the customer, or the superlative, to delight the customer, belie the fact that the critical motivation underpinning marketing effort is to part us from something, usually from our money, but *always* from our ideas and from our ability to be critical thinkers (Williams, 1976). The market, actually, requires us to be gullible. Shanahan and Gerber (2004) have testified to the power of advertising in education where judgements of quality are often founded on the colour and glossiness of the promotional material. Such is the power of advertising that the author of this book, despite empirical and secondary evidence, often wonders if she has imagined low standards in education when confronted with media images of higher education promotion.

Lecturers possess a different understanding of quality from that of administrators. They feel a responsibility to discharge their duties in a manner which is consistent with their understanding of academic and intellectual ideals. Administrators employ an understanding of quality which is amenable to measurement. That is, quality depends on immediate and visible elements such as numbers of students, size of organization and the breadth of the suite of programmes. While it is acknowledged (Shanahan & Gerber, 2004) that the value-for-money objective espoused by administrators is often anathema to some academic staff, there is no suggestion that financial matters are of no concern to academics and that academic integrity does not matter to administrators. It is important to note, however, that there inevitably exists a different emphasis in their concerns. Lumby and Tomlinson (2000) claim that managerialism and professionalism are polarised cultures. Gibbs and Iacovidou (2004) remind us that the concept of quality espoused by administrators has nothing to do with 'good'. In the same way that justice is apparently open to all, academic staff, according to Stone, can pursue any actions they choose but it is administrators who control the consequences which will stamp these actions as attractive, unattractive or, indeed, viable.

The notion of educational integrity in the maintenance of academic standards has become illusory, claims Stone, as academics and administrators have had to adjust their values and habits to a bureaucratically governed social and intellectual climate. Lecturers who are faced with large numbers of poorly prepared students must reduce their expectations or face an insurmountable pedagogical task. If expectations are not lowered, says Stone, many students fail, enrolment goes down, student dissatisfaction increases and therefore student rating of the lecturer suffers a fall – all unrewarding outcomes. Interviews with lecturers show that they find it less stressful to accept lower standards than to cope with unenviable consequences if they insist on holding the line. If, as Abbott says, learning is about adjusting to one's environment, it may be that it is those lecturers who lower their expectations who are the learners. He reminds us of Heffer's dictum that in changing times it is the learners who inherit the earth while the learned are wonderfully prepared for a world that no longer exists. Discretion may be the better part of valour, but at what cost? The questions 'is it true?', 'is it moral?', 'is it just?' have been replaced by the criteria 'is it efficient?', 'is it marketable?', 'does it work?'

Can higher education accommodate the increasing collection of incommensurate values, ethics and standards or should it try to seek to better understand these values in an effort to agree new ones which will support its mission? In a world of simulacra higher education may have to seek a new kind of authenticity of information and knowledge (Bloland, 1995). Gibbs and Iacovidou (2004) challenge lecturing staff to stay rooted in *phronesis* and to continue to engage, and encourage students to engage, in dialogue, as witnesses to decency without falling into the trap of puritanical modernism.

There appears, from the literature, something of a schism between lecturers and administrators based on their apparently opposing objectives. There is a tendency for hierarchies to become systems of blame allocation (Marrington & Rowe, 2004). It may be possible, however, to achieve a reconciliation of polarised views. Lecturers may be perceived as resistant to the market model of efficiency in education, preferring their own traditional imperative – the highest possible level of education without regard to costs. Despite the ethical appeal of this intent, however, it is of scant use as a policy guide. Resources which are used in education are needed also for housing, health, crime prevention and infrastructural development. Any concern of the lecturer about the quality of education must be rooted in the realization of competing demands in a scarce resource environment. On the other hand, it must be recognised by administrators that their criteria of achieving outcomes such as increased enrolment, student retention and organizational growth may come at the expense of the kind of education which could facilitate independent learning in the student.

The primary research in this book reveals that students are receiving anorexic education, discrete facts which do not form a coherent picture – the kind of 'spotty' approach eschewed by Singal and Bloom. The study attests, too, that (in the opinion of lecturers) students, in general, are unable to understand concepts and metaphor. In such a situation it seems an extraordinary conceit to attempt to teach concepts, such as those represented by diagrams, to students who do not understand their provenance and who simply learn to copy them as a piece of drawing. Greer's study also indicates the preference of students for thinking at the concrete operational level. It would appear that the education budget could be better spent especially when literacy, the foundation for academic learning, is a problem.

Chapter 15

A Compromise Proposal

In view of Joy's injunction that it is the duty of the lecturer to teach from the level where the student is, rather than from the level from where the student might be expected to have reached, the following solutions might be usefully applied.

- Achieve recognition by the student of the limiting nature of the capsule approach, which is the only form of education they know, and develop in them an awareness of the concept of independent learning.
- Provide information literacy education as an integral part of teaching.
- Impose the standard recommended by Joy that no more than a grade 'D' be awarded to any examination candidate, irrespective of the content of the paper, if grammar and syntax are not at a high level.
- Develop practical courses in how to think and promote engagement within written and spoken discourse at higher level.

It is crucial to start from the level of the student (Singal, 1991; Foy, 1994). In this case the fundamental problem is low literacy levels. Illich's concern, that any effort to carry out remedial action at higher education level is like attempting to achieve slum clearance from the twelfth storey up, should not permit us to be laissez-faire about the neglect of those who are currently participating in education at levels beyond the primary. To do so would be the equivalent of agreeing to the (perhaps apocryphal) suggestion that the Euro should not have been adopted until all the older people, confused by its arrival, were dead! The old adage that the longest journey begins with a single step has as its corollary the assertion that, if we wait until all obstacles are removed, no project would ever be commenced.

If a student develops a high standard of literacy s/he has, subject to personal motivation, the necessary tools to become an independent learner. If a student chooses not to study further there is no need for concern that s/he will not learn subjects such as economics or marketing or personnel management or organizational behaviour. All we have to lose is the illusion. What is clear from the primary research is that students are not learning these subjects anyway – they are simply memorising a set of disconnected, crippled facts, and then forgetting them, the bulimic effect described in the interviews (see Chapters 10 and 11). With raised literacy levels, the current intensive teaching could be reduced as students would be capable of independent reading. Immense cost savings could be achieved, thus contributing to the attainment of one of the prime objectives of administrators. There is a parallel in third world development with aid agencies pleading for the provision of a fishing rod rather than a fish: 'give a man a fish and you give him a meal. Give him a fishing rod and you feed him for life'.

The advent of the virtual university provides possibilities for ongoing education for those with the launch pad of motivation and literacy skills. Many academics are fazed by such a prospect, emphasising the importance of engagement and dialogue. However, if students are not engaged with their subject and are not attending lectures they cannot develop dialogue and are simply exercising short-term memory at examination time. The self-help approach of e-learning, based on personal responsibility, presents opportunities which are accessible, location loose and cost effective (Ball, 1996; Ives & Jarvenpaa, 1996; Sambataro, 2000; Wood et al., 2005; Bartlett, 1997; Kerr, 2002) where the student can engage with the author of the text. The downside of such a scenario, it will become apparent to the reader, will be the trimming of a massive industry with consequences for the economic multiplier.

Implementing the suggestions outlined above faces a serious hurdle at both micro and macro level. At micro level the stumbling block may be the competition from other third-level providers. Because the potential for oversupply of third-level places (especially in a dwindling market) renders the strategy of competitive devaluation more and more likely – as evidenced in interviews with lecturers – it would be necessary for all institutions of education to agree on a protocol. At macro level is it likely that governments really want all their citizens to be competent thinkers, interested in exercising democracy and querying the activities of those in power? It may be time to reflect on Freire's (1972) claim that methodological failings can always be traced to ideological errors.

Only a supreme optimist would believe that the problem of wasteful capsule education will be addressed. Unlike Durkheim's perspective on waste which sees it as a burning of reserves thus compromising survival, the postmodern interpretation sees waste as consumption which fosters more wasteful consumption (Baudrillard, 1998). Expenditure on capsule education is therefore useful to the economy even if it does not achieve the promised modernist aim of the opportunity for freedom from narrow thinking. Systems are concerned primarily with their own survival and depend for that survival on the promotion of those individuals who most quickly and comprehensively allow their lifeworld to be colonised by the ideas and values of the organization. Third-level education, with its current postmodern outlook, seeks the agreement of most while tolerating some disagreement (Rorty, 1989). Indeed, a trawl through history reveals that pragmatic hegemony has always tolerated disagreement. This convinces the onlooker that the ruler is genuinely democratic. The ruler, on the other hand knows the reality – that the dissenter is not important enough to present a real problem. His/her ideas will appear to be out of line, they will not have career success – which surely proves that their ideas are wrong! In short, the conscientious objector will be considered a minor furuncle on the body politic. Those who have been unafraid to *bell the cat* with studies on low literacy, falling standards and education for oppression seize the imagination of educators but not of administrators or governments. The archaic understanding of the word 'furuncle' – little thief – may explain the attitude towards those whose research unmasks the illusion of academic opportunities and excellence for all. Apart from occasional blitzkriegs, usually from the media – and mainly from the English media – about falling standards, the other stakeholders show little dissonance about the situation in which the education world finds itself. The emperor is beautifully clothed.

Many stakeholders are content with the outcomes of education. *Students* wear the badge of qualification which provides them with a passport to the world of work. For them it may be important not to be different from their peers (Fromm, 1966). This book reveals that it is possible to gain an honours degree without buying textbooks, or consulting texts, or attending fulltime. 'We can get a 2:1 here handy' reports a student in interview. This is also supported by the findings of the Nuffield Review (2006). Students can gain accreditation for very little input and thus satisfy the primary drive of consumers, to get as much as possible for as low a price as possible.

Employers may enjoy the imagined security of thinking that a reputable institution has rubber-stamped the student as an able candidate. In many circumstances the employer sees this as the first tick in the box and proceeds to give the new candidate training specific to the job. Interestingly, students are aware of this and suggest that their peers, in general, are not concerned about knowing their course for the purposes of applying it at work; they simply want the 'look of a good CV'. Additionally, the high proportion of people who do not practise according to their qualification, a matter of which the students are also aware, minimises the possibility of being found out by employers. In line with the performativity criterion of the modern workplace (Ainley, 2000; Lyotard, 1984; Bloland, 1995), workers will not be called upon during their workday to exhibit their knowledge of subjects such as management, economics, marketing, personnel management or production – most of their work will be carried out at a computer terminal.

The *public*, including *parents*, to borrow a phrase from Lyotard, are in thrall to an 'enchanted' world, wanting what society wants for them, little understanding the structural violence (Habermas, 1989; Bourdieu, 1986) which underpins it. With recent memories of an education system where opportunities existed only for the privileged, they may be convinced that a panoptic system of education prevails and may be heartily grateful for increased accessibility. In Illich's view, poor parents, aware that poverty is understood as the gap between one's current position and some advertised ideal of consumption, are less concerned with learning than with earning. Steeped in semi-urgy – the total domination by the code of sign exchange

(Baudrillard 1998) – they may not see or, indeed, wish to see, that the job opportunities open to the vast number of graduates are the kind which were performed by school leavers thirty years ago (Ainley, 2000) or by those who had the minimum two-year vocational training. The fact that their offspring go to work in a suit rather than in overalls may obscure the fact that some jobs, such as those in call centres, are the new factory jobs. Such a situation suggests two possibilities – either that an enormous number of people are overqualified for their jobs or that their qualifications lack real weight. The findings of this book would support the latter argument. However, economic success may be sufficient to convince parents and public, unaware of O'Leary's comments, that students are benefiting enormously from what they learn rather than from the simulacrum. Qualifications *work*. The performativity criterion has replaced truth as a measure of knowledge (Lyotard, 1984). Access to higher education for all appears at first glance to have provided a level playing field, democratic in principle, although its merit may be questionable (Bloland, 1995; Halsey, 1995). Finding fault with the system would traduce the rights of individuals to believe in progress through education. Confused by semiology, they may not wish to see that this apparent democracy shifts inequity to a more arcane field where, functioning more subtly, it is all the more oppressive (Baudrillard, 1998). Symbolic violence is everywhere inscribed in signs – the purest and most illegible form of domination (Baudrillard, 1988).

From the point of view of *governments*, there is political capital to be mined in the widespread beliefs held by students and the public. In addition, the high uptake of higher education allows governments to hold a respectable position in OECD league tables – participation in Ireland, for instance, encompasses 55 per cent of school leavers (Report by the Expert Group on Future Skills Needs, 2007) and is expected to reach 72 per cent by 2020. Education has morphed from Masefield to massification, enabling governments to maintain control, even in the face of rising participation rates. Until the advent of free education for all, access was confined to the children of the elite and a few scholarship candidates, too few in number to destabilise the prevailing plutocracy. The provision of capsule education for all presents no threat to the established order. The function of education is no longer to train an elite to guide the nation but to provide the players capable of fulfilling their roles at the pragmatic posts of institutions (Lyotard, 1984).

Universities and *colleges* see greater access as the key to expanded growth. Despite pedagogical and financial constraints, increased enrolment is the mechanism by which they can improve their profile and build their empires in a market where share is an indicator of success. Like a church which insists on spirituality instead of accepting the sporadic pragmatic engagement by many of its followers at major life events such as births, marriages and deaths, an institution which is more concerned with the purity of its message than with meeting the demands of its clients may find itself with few customers in a buyers' market. Higher education can no longer argue that what it does is *true*, only that it is useful (Bloland, 1995).

There is an irony in the articulation of a market solution for education as a new master narrative in the postmodern context in which education currently finds itself. This master narrative is, says Ball (1999), a deeply fissured but primary discourse. It would appear that the market principle embedded in massification has been accompanied by a serious diminution of standards as students achieve what is merely a simulacrum of education. But this is not a zero sum exercise. The triumph of massification is its apparent democratic intent. Elite education, on the other hand, despite its much vaunted higher standards, is reminiscent of what was worst in ancient Greece – the division of society into slaves and citizens. This work raises questions, not about the provision of higher education for all, but about the vocational nature and low standards of much higher education which sees students undertaking a course of study which does not interest them in order to get a job. It is questionable how much the almost universal provision of higher education has really contributed either to education or to class mobility (Halsey, 1995). It is clear from Chapters 9, 10 and 11 that, in general, students are receiving a simulacrum and that the basic 3 R's – in past times a feature of primary education – are seriously compromised. The question might certainly be raised about the value-for-money outcome from this massive expenditure if transformational education should be the aim. There is a case for wondering if anything has changed apart from the illusion. This is not to deny or underestimate the competency, hard work, dedication and intellectual excellence of many in the population but it may well be wondered if the excellent (in academic terms) make up any greater proportion of the population, now, than they did in former generations. What is clear is that skills and knowledge, formerly aimed at small children, need now to be delivered at third level although that is not, in fact, happening.

The author puts forward another, perhaps heretical, proposal. That is, that all students attending third-level institutions be awarded a pass degree. Such is their addiction to signs, including the signs of education, that giving them a pass degree would satisfy this need/want and satisfy the need of administrators for high levels of enrolment. Lest the reader be shocked by such an idea it is important to remember that the current model of education provision – *education as a consumer experience* – rewards the memorising of discrete capsules of information geared to facilitate students to pass examinations with the minimum engagement. In the interest of justice and fairness, it should be possible for more able, engaged students, to achieve a higher award through the medium of reading, research and serious application.

Conclusion

The new techno-economic paradigm, by which all matters are viewed through a financial frame, may have the appearance of achieving efficiencies, but as this book suggests, this is a smokescreen with educational pintoism[1] the result. What is efficient about a system which sees vast numbers of students qualified with what can only be described as bulimic education – they cram, write and forget? Their minds are not stretched as they reproduce prepared answers to flagged questions. Like McDonalds, there are no surprises. What is efficient about paying highly qualified staff large salaries to teach a simulacrum to

---

[1] From the decision by Ford to continue manufacturing the Ford Pinto despite the knowledge that the fuel tank was faulty, and likely to cause deaths.

a shifting audience of students? In world terms, is expenditure on education efficient when the cost of education for the average student is at least five times the median life earnings of over half of the world's population (Illich, 1972)? What is really affective about this study of higher education, however, is to see the waste of time, energy, service, altruism and motivation among both staff and students which was uncovered in the interviews carried out in this work. It is interesting to see all players make a prison out of freedom (Becker, 1980). Such waste cannot be excused even by an appeal to Baudrillard's definition. Whyte (2004) and Ball (1999) would raise concerns about the loss of soul among educators and students alike, although Whyte (2004) also warns us not to get caught in paralysis, self-indulgence and self-preoccupation. There will be many who will strenuously deny that there are serious problems in education – *the sick animal in the herd* syndrome. This is understandable, according to Whyte (2002). To face reality, he says 'is to cease to exist in the very way you have taken so much time, effort and will to make yourself' (p. 260).

Reality is sometimes forced on a country by Commissions of Inquiry or Tribunals. Perhaps Education might be a subject for such an inquiry – but probably not, since, as Freire might have said, those who are suffering from it are not able to see it as a problem. If Higher Education were a trading organization it might find itself liable under the Trade Descriptions Act with its modernist promises and postmodern delivery. Bearing in mind President Bill Clinton's claim that what preoccupies the public at large is the economy, we may be lulled into a false sense of security because unemployment is so low in current times. However, even if we consider nothing but the economy, we have to heed the warning that countries like China and India are not just able to match us in skills but also to beat us on costs and numbers of workers (James, 2004). In this context, it might not be too dramatic to see Capsule Education as a Trojan horse. We have welcomed it in, but it may torpedo the very economy it is meant to serve. It is time to reflect on the aphorism – *if you think education is expensive, you should try ignorance.* Higher Education appears to be carrying out such an experiment.

There are significant man-made problems facing the world at this time, problems resulting from lifestyle choices and/or genuine ignorance, among them dangers to the environment, damage to fish stocks, a dependence on fast food and an addiction to qualifications which bear no resemblance to competency. Newman (1943) reminds us that it is the lot of children and slaves to be ignorant. Free adults can claim no such absolution. In the case of all these problems we are eating the seed-corn; ignorance and error perpetuate a negative multiplier. Greater and greater levels of ignorance in respect of food, environment and education are being thrust on subsequent generations. Rumplestilskin philosophy reminds us that the fundamental requirement is to name the problem. Only then does it cease to have power over us.

References

Abbott, J. (2002) Learning as a community-wide activity: the nursery for civil society. *International Conference: Richness in Diversity, Fairways Conference Centre, Dundalk, Ireland*, 27–29 May. Speakers' Notes, 39–40.

Ainley, P. (1993) *Class and Skill: Changing Divisions of Knowledge and Labour*. London, Cassells.

Ainley, P. (2000) Teaching in a learning society: the acquisition of professional skills. Paper for the ESRC Teaching and Learning First Programme Conference, University of Leicester, November.

Ainley, P. and Corbett, J. (1994) From vocationalism to enterprise: social and life skills become personal and transferable. *The British Journal of Sociology of Education*, 15, 3, 79–95.

Akbar, H. (2003) Knowledge levels and their transformation: towards the integration of knowledge creation and individual learning. *Journal of Management Studies*, 40, 8, 1997–2021.

Amnesty International. (2004) Death penalty: Amnesty International's Human Rights Concerns. www.amnestyusa.org

Anderson, W.T. (ed.) (1996a, abridged) *The Fontana Postmodernism Reader*. London, Fontana.

Anderson, W.T. (1996b) *Four Different Ways to be Absolutely Right*. In Anderson (1996a).

Appignanesi, R., Garratt, C., Sarder, Z. and Curry P. (1995) *Introducing Postmodernism*, UK, Icon Books.

Archimedes (287–212 BC) *Maths History*. http://mathforum.org/geometry/wwweuclid/bio.htm

Armstrong, K. (2004) Creativity cannot be hurried. *Guardian*, 24 April, 12.

Athiyaman, A. (1997) Linking student satisfaction and service quality perceptions. *European Journal of Marketing*, 31 July–Aug, 7/8, 528–536.

Ball, C. (1996) More means different – revisited. *The Thirtieth Anniversary Seminars: presented by the vice-presidents*. London, SRHE.

Ball, S.J. (1995) Intellectuals or technicians? The urgent role of theory in educational studies. *British Journal of Education Studies*, 43, 3, 255–271.

Ball, S.J. (1999) Global trends in educational reform and the struggle for the soul of the teacher. Paper presented to the British Educational Research Association Annual Conference, University of Sussex at Brighton. http://www.leeds.ac.uk/educol/documents/00001212.htm

Banning, J.H. (1985) Clients, customers or designers? *Campus Ecologist*, 3, 1. http://isu.indstate.edu/wbarratt/dragon/ce/v3n1.htm.

Barglow, R. (2001) Silently the wolves are watching: an essay on the Lacanian Gaze. http://www.lacan.org/gaze/paint_gaze_fast.htm.

Barthes, R. (2005) *The Neutral*, translated by Rosalind E. Krauss and Denis Hollier. New York, Columbia University Press.

Bartlett, T. (1997) The hottest campus on the internet. *Business Week*, 3549, 10, 77–79.

Barzun, J. (1989) The culture we deserve. In Cheney et al. (1997).

Baudrillard, J. (1982) The Beauborg effect. Implosion and deterrence. In Featherstone (1996).

Baudrillard, J. (1983) *Simulations*. New York, Semiotext.

Baudrillard, J. (1988) Simulacra and Simulations. In Poster M., ed., *Jean Baudrillard, Selected Writings*. Stanford, Stanford University Press, pp. 166–184.

Baudrillard, J. (1998) *The Consumer Society, Myths and Structures*. London, Sage.

Bauman, Z. (1992) *Mortality, Immortality and Other Life Strategies*. Stanford, Stanford University Press.

Becker, E. (1980) *The Birth and Death of Meaning. An Interdisciplinary Perspective on the Problem of Man*, 2nd edition. Harmondsworth, Pelican Books Ltd.

Beer, S. (1989) Chronicles of wizard prang. In Marrington and Rowe (2004).

Beloff, L. (1990) Universities and the public purse: an update. *Higher Education Quarterly*, 44, 1, 3–19.

Benjamin, W. In Hollier, D. *Mimesis and Castration*. In Barglow (2001).

Benson, P. (1993) *Anthropology and Literature*. Chicago, IL, University of Illinois Press.

Bergson, H. (1913) Introduction to metaphysics. In Marrington and Rowe (2004).

Bernstein, B.B. (1961) Social class and linguistic development: a theory of social learning. Economy education and society. *Education Research*, 3, 163–176.

Blake, N. (2000) *Education in an Age of Nihilism*. New York, Routledge.

Bloland, H.G. (1995) Postmodernism and higher education. *Journal of Higher Education*, 66, 5, 521–545.

Bloom, A. (1987) *The Closing of the American Mind*. New York, Simon & Schuster.

Bologna Declaration. (1999) Joint declaration of the European ministers of education. www.bologna-berlin2003.de/pdf/bologna_declaration.pdf

Bottery, M. (1992) *The Ethics of Educational Management*. London, Cassells.

Bourdieu, P. (1986) *Distinction: A Social Critique of the Judgement of Taste*. London, Routledge.

Bourdieu, P. and Boltanski, L. (1978) Changes in social structure and changes in the demand for education. In Giner, S., & Archer, M. (eds.). *Contemporary Europe: Social Structure and Cultural Change*. London, Routledge and Kegan Paul.

Bourdieu, P. and Passeron, J.-C. (2000) *Reproduction in Education, Society and Culture*, 2nd edition. London, Sage.

Bowles, S. and Gintis, H. (1976) *Schooling in Capitalist America*. London, Routledge and Kegan Paul.

Braverman, H. (1974) *Labour and Monopoly Capital: the Degradation of Work in the Twentieth Century*. New York, Monthly Review Press.

Bridgman, P.W. (1927) *The Logic of Modern Physics*. New York, Macmillan.

Brint, S. (ed.) (2000) *The Future of the City of Intellect: The Changing American University*. Stanford, Stanford University Press.

Brown, P. and Scase, R. (1994) *Higher Education and Corporate Realities: Class Culture and the Decline of Graduate Careers.* London, University College London Press.

Brown, T. (1999) Challenging globalisation as discourse and phenomenon. *International Journal of Lifelong Education*, 18, 1, 1–35.

Brubacher, J.S. and Rudy, W. (1976) *Higher Education in Transition: A History of American Colleges and Universities, 1636–1976.* New York, Harper & Row.

Bruner, E.M. (1993) Introduction: the ethnographic self and the personal self. In Benson. P. (ed.). *Anthropology and Literature.* Chicago, IL, University of Illinois Press.

Bruner, J.S. (1957) On perceptual readiness. *Psychological Review*, 64, 123–152

Buckingham, D. (1998), Introduction: fantasies of empowerment? Radical pedagogy and popular culture. In Buckingham, D. (ed.). *Teaching Popular Culture: Beyond Radical Pedagogy.* London, UCL, pp. 1–17.

Burbules, N. (1993) *Dialogue in Teaching: Theory and Practice.* New York, Teachers' College.

Caillois, R. (1960) *Meduse et Cie.* In Barglow (2001).

Caraman, P. (ed.) (1958) The Holy Bible (New Testament Section). London, Caxton Publishing Company.

Carnegie Council (1980) *Three Thousand Futures: The Next Twenty Years for Higher Education.* San Francisco, Jossey-Bass.

Carr, W. (1987) What is educational practice? *Journal of Philosophy of Education*, 21, 2, 163–175.

Carroll, D. (1998) What's your problem? Giving more than lip-service for learning support. *Quality Assurance in Education*, 6, 2. MCB University Press, 112–128.

Casazza, M. (1996) Evolution of learning assistance in higher education. *Learning Assistance and Developmental Education: A Guide for Effective Practice.* San Franscisco, Jossey-Bass, Higher and Adult Education Series, pp. 3–34.

Caulkin, S. (2007) Tying a firm up in a budget straitjacket is madness. *Observer Business*, 7 January, 40.

Chaharbaghi, K. and Newman, V. (1998) When production management takes over education: the rise & fall of organised education. *Management Decision,* 36, 8. MCB University Press, 509–516.

Chang, J. (1991) *Wild Swans: Three Daughters of China.* London, Hammersmith.

Cheney, G., McMillan, J. and Schwartzman, R. (1997) Student-as-Consumer. *Communication Education.* http://www.google.com/search?q=cache:ZFDLON4

Cheng, Y. and Van de Ven, A.H. (1996) Learning the innovation journey: order out of chaos. *Organisation Science,* 7, 6, 573–614.

Cheng, Y.C. (1999) A CMI-triplisation paradigm for reforming education in the new millennium. www.emeraldinsight.com

Chia, R. (1999) A 'rhizomic' model of organisational change & transformation: perspectives from a metaphysics of change. *British Journal of Management,* 10, 209–227.

Chickering, A. & Claxton, C., (1981) *What is competence?* In Nickse, R. (ed.). *Competency-Based Education: Beyond Minimum Competency Testing.* New York, Teachers College Press.

Clinton, J.P. (1975) The Extension of Third-Level Non-University Education. *Masters Thesis,* Trinity College, Dublin, unpublished.

Clinton, W.J. (2005) *My Life.* London, Arrow Books, Random House.

Collins, R. (1979) *The Credential Society: an Historical Sociology of Education and Stratification.* New York, Academic.

Collins, T. (2005) Promoting active citizenship and social inclusion in civil society. *The Learning Age: Towards a Europe of Knowledge.* http://www.lifelonglearning.co.uk/conference/sp14-tc.htm

Collins.T. (2006) Second-level change should start with the Junior Cert. *Irish Times,* 3 October, 12.

Colton. (1829) The Lacon. In G. Seldes (ed.). (1985) *The Great Thoughts.* New York, Ballantine Books.

Coombs, P.H. (1968) *The World Educational Crisis. A Systems Analysis.* London, Oxford University Press.

Cooper, D.R. and Schindler, P.S. (1998) *Business Research Methods,* 6th edition. Boston, MA, Irwin McGraw-Hill.

Coren, V. (2005) A real-life Hogwarts? Hogwash. *Observer,* 14 August, 10.

Corry, M. (2005) Don't blame the children, blame the school system. *Irish Times, Health Supplement*, 1 March, 6.

Cross K.P. (1983) The state of the art in needs assessment. *Community/Junior College Quarterly of Research and Practice*, 7, 195–206.

Daniel, J. (1993) The challenge of mass higher education. *Studies in Higher Education*, 18, 2, 197–202.

Dearing, R. (1997) *Higher Education in the Learning Society. The National Committee of Inquiry into Higher Education.* London, HMSO.

Delors, J. (1996) Learning the treasure within. *Report to UNESCO of the International Commission on Education for the Twenty-First Century.* Paris, UNESCO.

Derrida, J. (1976) *Of Grammatology.* Baltimore, MD, John Hopkins University Press.

Dewey, J. (1966) *Democracy and Education.* New York, Free Press.

Dewey, J. (1993) The ethics of democracy. In Morris, D., & Shapiro, I. (eds.). *The Political Writings.* Indianapolis, Hackett Publishing Company, pp. 59–65.

Dill, D. (1997) Higher education, markets and public policy. *Higher Education Policy*, 10, 3/4, 167–185.

Dilthey, W. In Moncayo (2003).

Donnelly, R. (2004) Critical evaluation of the impact of global educational reform: an Irish perspective. *International Journal of Education Management*, 18, 6, 351–359.

Dundalk Institute of Technology Careers Service. (2005) *Graduate Survey 2004*, July, www.careers@dkit.ie

Dunne, J. (1993) *Back to the Rough Ground: Phronesis and Techne in Modern Philosophy and in Aristotle.* South Bend, IN, University of Notre Dame Press.

Dunne, J. (1995) What's the good of education? In Hogan, P. (ed.). *Partnership and the Benefits of Learning.* Dublin, Educational Studies Association of Ireland, pp. 60–82.

Durkheim, E. (1893) *The Division of Labor in Society.* In Halsey (1995).

Edmundson, M. (1997) *On the uses of a liberal education. Harpers Magazine*, 295, 1768.

Edwards, R. (1993) The inevitable future? Post-Fordism in work and learning. In Edwards, R., Sieminski, S., & Zeldin, D. (eds.).

Adult Learners, Education and Training. London and Buckingham, Routledge and Open University Press.

European Commission. (2001) *Making a European Area of Lifelong Learning a Reality.* Brussels, European Commission, COM (2001) 678 final.

Expert Group on Future Skills Needs. (2007) *Tomorrow's Skills – Towards a National Skills Strategy.* 5th Report, Dublin, Forfas.

Featherstone, M. (1996) *Consumer Culture and Postmodernism.* London, Sage.

Feifer, M. (1985) *Going Places.* In Featherstone (1996).

Fielding, M. (1998) Philosophy, education policy and the nature of community: why effective policies won't work. Paper presented at the BERA Conference, Belfast, Queen's University, 27–30 August, pp. 12–15.

Fitzgerald. G. (2005) Huge improvement in education levels in recent years. *Irish Times,* 26 November, 16.

Flexner.A. (1930) *Universities: American, English, German.* In Halsey (1995).

Flynn, S. (2005) DCU president warns of 'yellow pack' universities. *Irish Times,* 19 October, 3.

Flynn, S. (2006) Honours maths pupils fail to grasp basics. *Irish Times,* 5 April, 11.

Foster, H. (1985) *Postmodern Culture.* London, Pluto Press.

Foucault, M. (1979) *Discipline & Punish: The Birth of the Prison.* New York, Vintage Books.

Foucault, M. (1988) Truth, power, self: an interview with Michel Foucault. *Technologies of the Self.* Amherst, The University of Massachusetts Press.

Foucault, M. (1996) *Strategies of Power.* In Anderson (1996a).

Foy,J.G. (1994) Academic standards & basic skills in higher education, empowerment of the student & the teacher. *College Student Journal,* 28, 275–280.

Franzblau, (1934) In Moncayo (2003).

Freire, P. (1972) *Pedagogy of the Oppressed.* Harmondsworth, UK, Penguin.

Freire, P. (1974) *Education for Critical Consciousness.* London, Sheed & Ward.

Freire, P. (1995) *Pedagogy of Hope: Reliving Pedagogy of the Oppressed.* London, Continuum International Publishing Group.

Freire, P. (1998) *Pedagogy of Freedom: Ethics, Democracy and Civic Courage.* Lanham, MD, Rowan and Littlefield.

Fromm, E. (1966) *Heart of Man.* In Freire (1972).

Fromm, E. (1979) *To Have or To Be.* London, Abacus.

Fulton.O. (1991) Slouching towards a mass system: society, government and institutions in the United Kingdom. *Higher Education*, 21, 589–605.

Gadamer, H.-G. (1975) *Truth and Method.* New York, Seabury Press.

Garavan, T., Costine, P. and Heraty. N. (1995) *Training and Development in Ireland: Context, Policy and Practice.* Dublin, Oak Tree Press.

Gardner, H. (1983) *Frames of Mind: The Theory of Multiple Intelligences.* New York, Basic Books.

Gardner, H. (1997) Multiple Intelligences/New Directions MI/ND. Summer Symposium, Milton, Harvard University, July.

Garrison, J. (1997) *Dewey and Eros: Wisdom and Desire in the Art of Teaching.* New York, Teachers' College Press.

Gee, J. (1992) *The Social Mind, Language, Ideology & Social Practice.* New York, Bergin & Garvey.

Gewirtz, S., Ball, S. J., and Bowe, R. (1995) *Markets, Choice and Equity in Education.* Buckingham, UK, Open University Press.

Gibb, G. (1997) *Times Higher Education Supplement*, 24 October. In Carroll 1998 (*no title*).

Gibbs, P. and Iacovidou, M. (2004) Quality as pedagogy of confinement: is there an alternative? *Quality Assurance in Education*, 12, 3, 113–119.

Giroux, H. A. (1992) *Border Crossings.* New York, Routledge.

Gleazer, E.J. (1970) *High Stakes, High Performance.* In Casazza (1996), p. 23.

Goad, T. W. (2002) *Information Literacy and Workplace Performance.* Westport, CT, Quorum Books.

Gorsuch and Alashire (1974) In Moncayo (2003).

Grace, G. (1989) Education: commodity or public good? *British Journal of Education Studies*, 37, 3, 207–221.

Greer, P. (1998) An evaluation of the cognitive demands of written scientific discourse on students in their training as biology technicians. *PhD Thesis*, National University of Ireland, Maynooth, unpublished.

Haas, H.A. (2004) Teaching and the butterfly effect. *Chronicle of Higher Education*, 50, 27, 12–14.

HM Government, London. (1963) 'The Robbins Report' Higher Education. Report of the Committee Appointed by the Prime Minister under the Chairmanship of Lord Robbins (1961–1963), London, HM Government.

Habermas, J. (1987) *The Theory of Communicative Action, vol. 2: Life World and System: A Critique of Functionalist Reason*. Boston, Beacon Press.

Habermas, J. (1989) *The Structural Transformation of the Public Sphere*. Cambridge, MA, MIT Press.

Halsey, A. (1995) *Decline of Donnish Dominion: The British Academic Professions in the Twentieth Century*. Oxford, Clarendon Press.

Halsey, A.H., Heath, A.F. and Ridge, J.M. (1980) *Origins and Destinations. Family, Class and Education in Modern Britain*. Oxford, Clarendon Press.

Hammersley, M. (2002) *Educational Research, Policymaking and Practice*. London, Sage.

Handy, C. (1996) *Beyond Certainty*. London, Arrow Business Books.

Hannabuss, S. (2001) A wider view of knowledge. *Library Management*. MCB University Press, 22, 8–9, 357–363.

Harman, G. (2002) Academic leaders or corporate managers: deans and heads in Australian higher education, 1977 to 1997. *Higher Education Management and Policy*, 14, 2, 53–70.

Harris, C. C. (1989) The state and the market. In Brown, P., & Sparkes, R. (eds.). *Beyond Thatcherism: Social Policy, Politics and Society*. Buckingham, UK, Open University Press.

Hartley, D. (1997) The new managerialism in education: a mission impossible? *Cambridge Journal of Education*, 27, 1, 47–57.

Harvey, L. (2002) The end of quality? *Quality in Higher Education*, 8, 1, 6–22.

Harvey, L. and Green, D. (1993) Defining quality. *Assessment and Evaluation in Higher Education*, 18, 1, 10–21.

Haskell, R. (1997) Academic freedom, tenure and student evaluation of faculty. *Education Policy Archives*, http://olam.ed.asu.edu/epaa/v3n11.html.

Hayakawa, S.I. (1965) *Language in Thought and Action*, 2nd edition. London, Allen & Unwin.

Hayakawa, S.I. and Hayakawa, A.R. (1990) *Language in Thought and Action*, 5th edition. London, Harcourt Inc.

Heffer, E. In Abbott (2002).

Hegel, G.W.F. (1956) *The Philosophy of History.* In White (1987).

Hermann, N. (2004) Habermas and philosophy of education. www.vusst.hr/ENCYCLOPAEDIA/habermasenglish.htm

Hill, F. (1995) Managing Service Quality in Higher Education: the role of the student as primary consumer. *Quality Assurance in Education*, 3, 10–21.

Holden, L. (2005) There's no point in knowing about stuff that's not going to come up in exams. *Irish Times*, 20 September, 13.

Holland, K. (2007) Universities rely on institute intake to keep "elite" status. *Irish Times*, 16 January, 5.

Holt, E. (2004) Consuming Academia. *Irish Times Weekend Review*, 18 Dec, 2.

Hunt, D.P. (2003) The concept of knowledge and how to measure it. *Journal of Intellectual Capital*, MCB University Press, 4, 1, 100–113.

Hutton, W. (2007) Ancient Rome is where our heart is. *Observer*, 7 January, 23.

Huyssen, A. (1990) Mapping the postmodern. In Alexander, J. C., & Heidman, S. (eds.). *Culture & Society, Cultural Debates.* Cambridge, Cambridge University Press, pp. 355–375.

Illich, I. (1972) *Deschooling Society.* Harmondsworth, Middx., UK, Penguin.

Inkpen, A. C. and Crossan, M.M. (1995) *Believing is Seeing: Joint Ventures & Organisational Learning.* In Akbar (2003).

Ives, B. and Jarvenpaa, S. (1996) Will the internet revolutionise business education and research? *Sloan Management Review*, Spring, 33–41.

James. O. (2004) Sting in the tale. *Observer Magazine*, 29 November, 77.

Jarratt Report (1985) *Report of the Steering Committee for Efficiency Studies in Univeristies.* London, CVCP.

Jhally, S. (1989) Advertising as religion: the dialectic of technology and magic. In Angus, I., & Jhally, S. (eds.). *Cultural Politics in Contemporary America.* New York, Routledge.

John, L.G. (1977) Student consumer protection in post secondary education. *NASPA Journal*, 15, 1, 39–50.

John, L.G. (1989) *Advertising as Religion*. In Lee (1993), p. 17.

Kaku, M. (2005) *Parallel Worlds*. London, Allen Lane.

Kalantzis, M. (1998) *Designing Futures: Challenges for Leaders in Education*. VASSP, Aug. www.infotrac.london.galegroup. com

Kay, A.C. (1991) *Computers, Networks and Education*. Scientific American, Sept. http://scholar.google. com/scholar?hl=en&lr=&q= cache:v-

Kelsey, J. (2000) Education as nation building. Address to Quality Public Education Conference, Palmerstown North, New Zealand, 21 July. www.infotrac.london.galegroup. com

Kember, D. & Gow, L. (1994) Orientations to teaching and their effect on the quality of student learning. *Journal of Higher Education*, 65, 1, 58–72.

Kerr, C. (1963) *The Uses of the University*, 4th edition. Cambridge, MA, Harvard University Press, 1995.

Kerr, C. (2002) Shock wave 11: an introduction to the twenty-first century. In Brint, Steven (ed.). *The Future of the City of Intellect: The Changing American University*. Stanford, CA, Stanford University Press.

Kistan, C. (1999) Quality assurance in South Africa. *Quality Assurance in Education*, MCB University Press. 7, 3, 125–134.

Knight, P.T. (2002) Summative assessments in higher education: practices in disarray. *Studies in Higher Education*, 27, 3, 275–286.

Lacan, J. (1966) *Kant avec Sade*. In Barglow (2001).

Lander, D. (2000) A provocation: quality is service. *Quality in Higher Education*, 6, 2, 135–141.

Lanham, R. (2002) The audit of virtuality. In Brint, Steven (ed.). *The Future of the City of Intellect: The Changing American University*. Stanford, CA, Stanford University Press.

Laskey, K.B. (1998) Are students our customers in the education marketplace? *Mason Gazette/Education News*, Nov. http://www. gmu.edu?news/gazette/9811/studcus.html

Lawson, T. (1997) *Economics & Reality*. London, Routledge.

Lea, R. (2005) *Education and Training: A Business Blueprint for Reform*. London, Institute of Directors. www.epolitix. com/EN/Forum

Lee, M.J. (1993) *Consumer Culture Reborn*. London, Routledge.

Lefrancois, G.R. (1972) *Theories of Human Learning*. CA, Brooks/Cole.

Le Grand, J. and Bartlett, W. (1993) *Quasi Markets and Social Policy*. Basingstoke, UK, Macmillan.

Le Grand, J. and Robinson, R. (1992) *The Economics of Social Problems*. London, Macmillan.

Levin, B. (1998) An epidemic of education policy: what can we learn from each other. *Comparative Education*, 34, 2, 131–141.

Lindsay, V. *The Leaden Eyed*. In Whyte (2004).

Lomas, L. (2004) Embedding quality: the challenges for higher education. *Quality Assurance in Higher Education*, 12, 4, 157–165.

Lumby, J. and Tomlinson, H. (2000) Principals speaking: managerialism and leadership in further education. *Research in Post-compulsory Education*, 5, 2, 139–151.

Lyotard, J.F. (1984) *The Postmodern Condition – A Report on Knowledge*. Minneapolis, MN, University Press.

Lyotard, J.F. (1988) *Interview: Theory, Culture & Society*. www.infotrac.london.galegroup. com

Mace, M. (1974) Gibson's strategy for perceiving: ask not what's inside your head but what your head's inside of. In Shaw, R., & Bransford, J. (eds.). *Perceiving, Acting and Knowing*. In Ainley (2000).

MacIsaac, D. (1996) *The Critical Theory of Jurgen Habermas*. http://www.physic.nau.edu/danmac.

Maguire, M., Macrae, S. and Ball, S.J. (1996) Open days and brochures: marketing tactics in the post-16 sector. Paper presented at the BERA Conference, Lancaster.

Manhire, B. (2004) *Grade Inflation, Ethics and Engineering Education*. In O'Grady and Guilfoyle (2007).

Marcuse, H. (1986) *One-Dimensional Man*. London, Ark.

Marrington, P. and Rowe, J. (2004) The usefulness of management education. What has the university done for us? *Management Decision*, 42, 3–4, Emerald Group Publishing Ltd, 454–463.

Marris, R. (1984) *THES*, 6 April.

Marshall, A. (1872) *The Future of the Working Classes*. In Halsey (1995).

Marshall, T. H. (1963) *Sociology at the Crossroads and Other Essays*. London, Heinemann.

Marx, M.H. and Marx, K. (1980) Confirmation of the stubborn error effect in human multiple choice verbal learning. *Bulletin of Psychonomics Society*, 16, 477–479.

Masefield, J. (1946) in Chaharbaghi and Newman (1998).

McArdle, D. (2007) Capsule education: cultural influences in higher education. *PhD Thesis*, Education Department, Maynooth College, National University of Ireland.

McDonald, L.C. (1968) *Western Political Theory, Part 3*. New York, Harcourt Brace Jovanovich.

McGregor, D. (1960) *The Human side of Enterprise*. New York, McGraw-Hill.

Mejia, A. (2004) The problem of knowledge imposition: Paulo Freire and critical systems thinking. *Systems Research and Behavioural Science*, 21, 1, 63–83.

Miller, T. (1974) Column in THES, 25 Jan. In Halsey (1995).

Moberly, W. (1949) *The Crisis of the University*. London, SCM Press.

Moncayo, R. (2003) *Psychoanalysis & Postmodern Spirituality*. http://www.lacan.org/Moncayo.htm

Moodie, G. C. and Eustace, R. (1974) *Power and Authority in British Universities*. London, Unwin.

Morgan, G. (1986) *Images of Organisation*. London, Sage.

Murray, M. (2004) Buying toys that work. *Irish Times Health Supplement*, 1 Dec., 2.

Murray, M. (2005) Finding out who we are. *Irish Times, Health Supplement*, 1 Feb., 4.

National Adult Literacy Survey. (1993) *A First Look at the Findings of the National Adult Literacy Survey*. U.S. Department of Education, Office of Educational Research and Improvement.

Neave, G. (2002) The future of the city of intellect: a brave new world – European style. *European Education*, 34, 3, 20–41.

Newby, H. (2003) The management of change in higher education. *Higher Education Management and Policy, OECD*, 15, 1, 9–22.

Newman, J. (1943) *On the Scope and Nature of University Education*. London, Everyman.

Newman, J.H. (1959) *The Idea of a University*. Garden City, Image Books.

Nietzsche, F.W. *Beyond Good and Evil*. Translated by Marion Faber (1998). Oxford, Oxford University Press.

Nisbet, R. (1971) *The Degradation of the Academic Dogma: The University in America 1945–1970*. London, Heinemann.

Nuffield Review (2006) *Third Annual Report.* http://www.nuffield 14-19review.org.uk/index.shtml

O'Donoghue, J. and Maguire, T. (2005) The individual learner, employability and the workplace. *Journal of European Industrial Training*, 29, 6, 436–446.

O'Donohoe, S. (1997) Raiding the postmodern pantry: advertising intertextuality and the young adult audience. *European Journal of Marketing*, 31, 3/4, 234–252.

O'Grady, M. (2007) *Regulation Changes Contributing to Grade Inflation: The NCEA/HETAC Case Study.* www.stopgradeinflation.ie

O'Grady, M. and Guilfoyle, B. (2007) *Evidence of Grade Inflation (1994–2004) in the Institute of Technology Sector in Ireland.* www.stopgradeinflation.ie

O'Grady, M. and Guilfoyle, B. (2007) *Grade Inflation in Irish Universities (1994–2004).* www.stopgradeinflation.ie

O'Grady, M. and Quinn, S. (2007) *The Causes of Grade Inflation: An exploration of Social and Institutional Pressures and Policy Choices.* www.stopgradeinflation.ie

O'Leary, J. (2005) Education system not a cause for celebration. *Irish Times*, 4 Feb., 5.

O'Toole, F. (2007) Universities are becoming places of restricted learning. *Irish Times Weekend Review*, 14 April, 6.

OECD. (1989) *Education and the Economy in a Changing Society.* Paris, Organisation for Economic Co-operation and Development.

OECD. (2004) *Education at a Glance: OECD Indicators.* www.oecd.org/document

Pattison, M. (1868) *Suggestions on academic organisation.* In Halsey (1995).

Pears, D. (1971) *What is Knowledge?* New York, Harper and Row.

Pieterse, J.N. (1995) *Globalisation as hybridization.* In Featherstone (1996).

Polanyi, M. (1958) *Personal Knowledge: Towards a Post-critical Philosophy.* In Ainley (2000).

Polanyi, M. (1962) *Personal Knowledge: Towards a Post-critical Philosophy,* corrected edition. Chicago, IL, The University of Chicago Press.

Polanyi, M. (1966) The logic of tacit inference. *Philosophy*, 41, 1–18.

Pollitt, C. (1990) *Managerialism & the Public Services: Cuts or Cultural Changes in the 1990s?* 2nd edition. Oxford, Blackwell.

Postman, N. (1988) *Conscientious objections.* In Cheney et al. (1997).

Postman, N. and Weingartner, C. (1969) *Teaching as a Subversive Activity.* New York, Dell Publishing Company.

Pritchard, R.M.O. (1994) Government power in British higher education. *Studies in Higher Education,* 19, 3, 253–265.

Pugsley, L. A. (1998) Class of 97 higher education, market and choice. *PhD Thesis,* University of Wales, Cardiff, unpublished.

Raelin, J.A. (1985) *The Clash of Cultures: Managers Managing Professionals.* Boston, MA, Harvard Business School Press.

Rakoczy, K.L. (2002) *Academy Report reveals grade inflation nationwide.* Harvard University, USA. http://www.uwire. com/content/ topnews.

Randle, K. and Brady, N. (1997) Managerialism & professionalism in the 'Cinderella Service'. *Journal of Vocational Education & Training,* 49, 1, 121–139.

Rhys, S.M. (1994) Dilemmas? Focus on some potentially contending forces underlying the process of improving the quality of Student Learning. In Gibbs, G. (ed.). *Improving Student Learning Theory and Practice.* Oxford, UK, Oxford Centre for Staff Development.

Richter, E.M. and Buttery, E.A. (2004) Economic rationalism: serving tertiary business education needs? The Australian case. *Quality Assurance in Education,* 12, 3, 120–127.

Riesman, D. (1961) *The Lonely Crowd.* New Haven, CT, Yale University Press.

Rilke, R.M. In Whyte (2004).

Robbins Report. See HM Government (1963).

Robinson, D. (2005) *GATS and Globalisation of Higher Education: The Change Agenda in Higher Education,* Address to TUI Conference, Dublin, Sept.

Robotham, D. (2003) Learning and Training: developing the competent learner. *Journal of European Industrial Training,* 27, 9, 473–480.

Rockman, I. (2004) *Integrating Information Literacy into the Higher Educational Curriculum: Practical Models for Transformation.* New York, Wiley.

Rorty, R. (1989) *Contingency, Irony and Solidarity.* New York, Cambridge University Press.

Rosovsky, H. and Hartley, M. (2002) *Evaluation and the Academy: Are We Doing the Right Thing?* Cambridge, MA, American Academy of Arts and Sciences.

Saito, N. (2002) Pragmatism and the tragic sense: Deweyan growth in an age of Nihilism. *Journal of the Philosophy of Education,* 36, 2, 247–263.

Salisbury, M.W. (2003) Putting Theory into Practice to build knowledge management systems. *Journal of Knowledge Management,* 7, 2, 128–141.

Sambataro, M. (2000) Just in time learning. *Computer World,* April, 50.

Sardar, Z. and Curry, P. (1995) *Introducing Postmodernism.* UK, Icon Books.

Schmoker, M. and Wilson, R.B. (1993) Adapting total quality doesn't mean turning education into a business. *Education Leadership,* 51, 1, 62–64. http://www.infotrac.london.galegroup.com

Schumacher, E.F. (1974) *Small is Beautiful. A Study of Economics as if People Mattered.* London, Abacus.

Scott, P. (1984) *The Crisis of the University.* In Halsey (1995).

Scott, P. (1989) Accountability, responsiveness & responsibility. In Glatter, R. (ed.). *Educational Institutions & Their Environments: Managing the Boundaries.* Buckingham, UK, Open University Press.

Seligman, D. (2002) The grade inflation swindle. *Forbes,* 18 Mar., 94. http://www.infotrac.london.galegroup.com

Shanahan, P. and Gerber, R. (2004) Quality in university student administration: Stakeholder conceptions. *Quality Assurance in Education,* 12, 4, 166–174.

Shils, E. (1955). In Halsey (1995).

Shweder, R. (1996) *Santa Claus on the Cross.* In Anderson (1996 a).

Singal, D.J. (1991) The other crisis in American education. *The Atlantic Monthly,* 268, 5, 59–74.

Skilbeck, M. (2001) *The University Challenged: A Review of International Trends and Issues with Particular Reference to Ireland.* Dublin, Higher Education Authority.

Smith, A. (1776) *An Inquiry into the Nature and Causes of the Wealth of Nations*. A selected edition by Kathryn Sutherland (1993). Oxford, Oxford University Press.

Spender, J.C. (1996) Organisational Knowledge, Learning and Memory: three concepts in search of a theory. *Journal of Organisational Change Management*, MCB University Press, 9, 1, 63–78.

Spivak, G.C. (1985) *Can the Subaltern Speak?* University of Phoenix. www.uopxonline.com

Spivak, G.C. (2005) Interview. Fusion of the edgy and the orthodox. *Irish Times*, 1 Aug, 13.

Srikanthan, G. and Dalrymple, J.F. (2002) Developing a holistic model in higher education. *Quality in Higher Education*, 8, 3, 215–224.

Stephens, M. (1994) *Jurgen Habermas, The Theologian of Talk*. www.nyu.edu/classes/stephens/Habermas%20page.htm

Stone, J.E. (1995) Inflated grades, inflated enrolment, and inflated budgets: an analysis and call for review at the state level. *Education Policy Analysis Archives*, 3, 11. http://olam.ed.asu.edu/epaa/v3n11.html

Tajfel, H. (1981) *Human Groups and Social Categories*. Cambridge, University Press.

Tapper, T. and Salter, B. (1992) *Oxford, Cambridge and the Changing Idea of University: The Challenge to Donnish Domination*. Buckingham, UK, Open University Press and SRHE.

Taylor, P. (1993) *The Texts of Paulo Freire*. In Mejia (2004).

Telford, R. and Masson, R. (2005) The congruence of quality values in higher education. *Quality Assurance in Education*, Emerald Publishing Group Ltd. 13, 2, 107–119.

Thornhill, D. (2003) Education and the economy: what can business do? Address to IBEC, Cork, 14 March.

Tomlinson, P., Edwards, A., Finn, G., Smith, L. and Wilkinson, E. (1992) Psychological aspects of beginning teacher competence. A Submission to CATE, London, BPS.

Tomlinson-Keasey, C. (2002) Becoming digital. In Brint, Steven (ed.). *The Future of the City of Intellect: The Changing American University*. Stanford, CA, Stanford University Press.

Trow, M. (1974) *Problems in the Transition from Elite to Mass Higher Education*. Berkley, CA, Carnegie Commission on Higher Education.

Trow, M. (1998) The Dearing report: a transatlantic view. *Higher Education Quarterly.* 52, 1, 93–117.

Urry, J. (1988) *Cultural Change and Contemporary Holiday-making.* In Featherstone (1996).

Veblen, T. (1918) *The Higher Learning in America.* In Halsey (1995).

Vetter (1958) In Moncayo (2003).

Vidich, A. J., Bensman, J. and Stein, M.R. (eds.). (1964) *Reflection on Community Studies.* New York, Wiley.

Wagner, A. (1998) Redefining tertiary education. *The OECD Observer,* No. 214.

Wallace, J. (1999) The case for student as customer. *Quality Progress,* 32, 47–52.

Walsch, D. (1998) The student as customer: other points of view. *Mason Gazette/Education News,* Nov. http://www.gmu.edu/news/gazette/9811/studcus2

Warmington, P., Murphy, R. and McCaig, C. (2005) Real and imagined crises: the construction of political and media panics over education. BERA Conference, Research Intelligence, British Educational Association, pp. 12–15.

Warner, D. and Palfreyman, D. (eds.). (1996) *Higher Education Management: The Key Elements.* Buckingham, UK, SRHE and Open University Press.

Waters, M. (1995) *Globalisation.* London, Routledge.

Weber, M. (1918) *The Protestant and the Spirit of Capitalism.* Translated T. Parsons (1958), New York, Charles Scribner & Sons.

White, H. (1978) *Tropics of Discourse. Essays in Cultural Criticism.* Baltimore, MD, The John Hopkins University Press.

White, H. (1987) *The Content of the Form.* Baltimore, MD, The John Hopkins University Press.

Whyte, D. (2002) *The Heart Aroused: Poetry and the Preservation of Soul in Corporate America.* New York, Doubleday Currency.

Whyte, D. (2004) Life at the frontier: leadership through courageous conversation. Seminar presented by Cathedral Books, IMI Conference Centre, Dublin, June.

Williams, R. (1976) *Keywords.* London, Fontana.

Williamson, B. (1981), Class Bias. In Warren-Piper, D. (ed.). *Is Higher Education Fair?.* Guildford, SRHE.

Williamson, J. (1978) *Decoding Advertisements*. London, Marion Boyars.

Willis, P. (1977) *Learning to Labour*. Farnborough, Saxon House.

Wingspread Group on Higher Education. (1993) *An American Imperative: Higher Expectations for Higher Education*. Racine, WI, The Johnson Foundation, Inc.

Winnicott, D.W. (1947) *Paediatrics & Society*. In Marrington and Rowe (2004).

Wood, B.J.G, Tapsall, S.M. and Soutar, G. (2005) Borderless education: some implications for management. *International Journal of Education Management*, 19, 5, 428–436.

World Bank and UNESCO. (2000) *Report of the Taskforce on Higher Education and Society*. www1.worldbank.org/education/

Yeats, W.B. (1865–1939) Irish prose writer, dramatist and poet. Nobel prize for literature in 1923.

Yorke, M. and Longden, B. (2004) *Retention & Student Success in Higher Education*. Buckingham, UK, Open University Press.

Young, I.M. (1990) *The Ideal of Community and the Politics of Difference*. In Bloland (1995).

Zemsky, R. (1993) Consumer markets and higher education. *Liberal Education*, 79, 3, 14–18.

Zimbardo, P.G. (1972) The Stanford prison experiment. In Myers, D.G. (ed.). *Social Psychology*, New York, McGraw-Hill, 1996 6th edition, 132ff.

Zuboff, S. (1988) *In the Age of the Smart Machine; The Future of Work and Power*. Heinemann, London.

Author Index

Subject Index

Academia
  silence in 45, 96, 175, 227
Academics
  as affected by postmodern
    world 215
  and financial matters 121, 223
  adjustment of values 223
  their standards in higher
    education breached 27,
    89 ff
  traditional view of 214 f
Accountability
  moral 45
  market 81, 101, 103
  political 101
  professional 101
Administrators
  adherence to market model 65,
    201, 221–224, 231
  values 90, 222–227
Advertising (in education field) 6,
  26, 48, 69, 70–80, 130, 208,
  222
Aims of students 5, Ch. 9, Ch. 10,
  Ch. 11
'Anorexic' education 224

Best educational practice
  basis for structure of student
    interviews 179

component in students' survey
  146 ff
Bologna Declaration (1999) 84,
  120, 221
Budget *and* Budgeting 84, 90,
  104, 117, 215, 221, 224
'Bulimic' education 226, 231
'Butterfly effect' 52

Capsule education
  appropriateness of term 137,
    143, 196
  as 'Trojan Horse' 232
  as oppression 202, 206, 207,
    212, 217, 218, 229
  'bite sized semesters' 166
  concept, origin of 3
  current education provision 26,
    135, 145, 195, 207, 215,
    217, 231
  explanation of term 4, 217
  exploring the metaphor
    Ch. 14
  lecturers' perspective on 196
  students' attitude to 147, 149,
    156, 191
  usefulness to economy 212,
    227
  wastefulness not likely to be
    addressed 216, 227

Lightning Source UK Ltd.
Milton Keynes UK
UKOW042225140612

194444UK00002B/17/P

9 781441 179197